MARY GAUNT

Independent Colonial Woman

Published by Melbourne Books
Level 9, 100 Collins Street,
Melbourne, VIC 3000
Australia
www.melbournebooks.com.au
info@melbournebooks.com.au

Copyright © Bronwen Hickman 2014
All rights reserved. No part of this publication may be reproduced, stored in a retrieval system, or transmitted in any form or any means electronic, mechanical, photocopying, recording or otherwise without the prior permission of the publishers.

National Library of Australia
Cataloguing-in-Publication entry
Author: Hickman, Bronwen
Title: Mary Gaunt : independent colonial woman
ISBN: 9781922129369 (paperback)
Notes: Includes bibliographical references and index.
Subjects: Gaunt, Mary, 1861-1942.
Women--Australia--Biography--20th century.
Women novelists, Australian--20th century--Biography.
Women travelers--Australia--Biography.
Dewey Number: A823.2

MARY GAUNT

INDEPENDENT COLONIAL WOMAN

Bronwen Hickman

M
MELBOURNE BOOKS

Contents

Introduction 7
1 The Letter 9
2 Life on the Goldfields 14
3 Colonial Childhood 20
4 Student Life 31
5 What is a Girl to Do? 39
6 Rescue 45
7 Building a Writing Career 53
8 A Voyage 'Home' 57
9 Consolidating 64
10 Warrnambool and Dr Miller 68
11 Publishing and Praise 78
12 Disaster 87
13 Days of Turmoil 96
14 A 'Dull and Stony Street' 102
15 The End of the Bleak Years 113
16 Collaboration 119
17 The Adventure Begins 127
18 Writing about Africa 139
19 London 1909–10 146

20 The Storm Breaks 153

21 Back to Africa 158

22 After Africa 173

23 'Why Not a Book about China?' 182

24 China of the Ages 187

25 Peking and the Summer Palace 194

26 'A Sunday Walk in Hyde Park' 201

27 'You Say "Go", Mus' Go!' 211

28 The War Years 219

29 The Other End of the Trade 229

30 To Italy 237

31 At Work in the Villa Camilla 244

32 The Darkening Skies 253

33 'I Trust I Shall Be Able to Live On Here' 265

34 The Darkness Closes In 275

35 Finale 279

Acknowledgements 283

Endnotes 286

List of Publications 292

Index 396

Introduction

I have relied on evidence from a most unreliable source — Mary herself. No diaries or journals of hers have survived (or have been found), and she did not keep letters. The few people still alive who knew her have only limited recollections, so I have had very few 'witness statements'. It was fortunate that I found her unpublished autobiography when I had almost finished the book, and was therefore better able to evaluate what she had to say.

Long before her autobiography appeared, I plundered her fiction for biographical evidence. This is a dangerous practice. Apart from the obvious — she might be making it up, as fiction writers tend to do — it does not allow for shifts and changes in cultural context, for the inevitable shaping of life to fit the text, for poor memory, or for 'glamorising' of the less attractive aspects of life. While we might be scrupulously honest in what we tell our family and friends, we can lie to readers with impunity.

Mary Gaunt, by modern standards, was racist; she genuinely believed in the superiority of the British over the coloured people she met in Africa, China and Jamaica. It seems pointless to judge and condemn her because of it, but more useful to evaluate how well or badly she behaved towards Africans, Jamaicans and Chinese. She was a writer; she was interested in everyone and everything. She looked at people all over the world with curiosity, occasionally exasperation, but almost always with tolerance and acceptance. (It has to be said, though, that she was less accepting and tolerant when she felt that the subjects of her interest did not treat her with the respect that was due her as British!)

I have not been concerned with Mary's literary achievements, nor made comparisons with other writers of the time; rather I wanted to write about a person of remarkable ability and determination who was also a successful writer. She lived at a time when neither ability nor determination was considered desirable or 'nice' for a young lady. She broke down barriers and championed the right — the desirability — of women to earn their own living, and provided great role models by ensuring that many of her heroines did just that.

Quotations of Mary's own words come from her unpublished autobiography, *Strange Roads*, written over several years and revised when she was in her seventies in Bordighera. The manuscript is owned by her family in England; there is a photocopy in the State Library of Victoria.

All Chinese place names are written in the Wade-Giles Romanisation, which Mary used in her books. For example, 'Peking' is used rather than 'Beijing'.

All titles of books with no author name are by Mary Gaunt. There is a list of her novels, articles and short stories at the end of this book.

Bronwen Hickman,
Melbourne, 2014.

Chapter 1

The Letter

My daughter Miss M. E. B. Gaunt, having some time since passed the Matriculation and Civil Service Exams, is desirous of attending the Arts Course at the Melbourne University. Will you be kind enough to let me know what steps it will be necessary for her to take, the fees payable and the date it will be necessary for her to take up residence in Melbourne. Would you also be pleased to say if any other ladies are attending the University. Yours obediently, William Gaunt.[1]

It is the letter that brings Mary Gaunt to life — a fleeting glimpse of her in historical records as a flesh-and-blood person. The letter, dated 5 February 1881, is to A'Beckett, the registrar of The University of Melbourne. It is written by Mary's father. 'My daughter is desirous of attending the Arts Course at the Melbourne University.' So simple a statement, so much weight to it then.

It was a raw, young university, set up in the muddle and bustle of goldrush Melbourne less than thirty years before, and still only a quadrangle in a park. There were less than four hundred students when William Gaunt wrote his letter — all male, of course. Nowhere in any of the Australian colonies had a young woman attended a university before.

The letter from Mary's father was not the first document in the University Archives about Mary. There was another one — her application, five years before, to sit the Matriculation Exam. She applied to do nine subjects: Greek, Latin, English, French, arithmetic, algebra, Euclid, history and geography. These were all of the subjects on offer, except that a candidate could take German instead of French. The application form was filled in by her father, who gave his profession as 'Barrister at Law' and his address as 20 Camp Street, Ballarat, his business address. Beside 'religion' he wrote 'Church of England', and filled in Grenville College, Ballarat as Mary's last place of education. Whatever the status of the finishing school her mother chose for her after Grenville College, William clearly did not consider it a place of education.

At the bottom of the application form Mary added her signature: 'Mary E. B. Gaunt'. Mary for her father's sister and her mother's mother, Eliza for her mother's mother, Bakewell for her father's mother. The signature — neat, well-formed letters, no-nonsense squarish shapes, 'shockingly strong-minded' her mother called it — spoke of education and discipline. It looked very like her father's.

The application was dated 25 October 1876; the fee of two pounds fifteen shillings was paid, and Mary was assigned the examination number 569. She was fifteen years old and had stepped out of the shadows. After the registering of her birth as required by law, her matriculation record was her second appearance in the historical records of the colony.

Now, having waited five years for the rules to change, she was twenty, a young woman confident of her place in the world. She had fine, light curly hair and regular, even features; not a beauty, perhaps, because of a certain firmness about her mouth and that square, determined chin, and at that time feminine beauty was bound up with the idea of fragility. The eyes that gazed steadily and seriously at her new surroundings sparkled easily into laughter. On the surface were the polite diffidence and restrained manners instilled by her mother and by governesses and private academies; underneath was the exuberance and tomboyish freedom of a goldfields childhood.

She had fought battles to get to this point, overcoming her mother's misgivings, the sarcasm of her younger brothers, and the social and financial hurdle of leaving home to study in Melbourne. And the battles were not only at home. While the university had officially, if somewhat grudgingly, made ready to receive them, much of Melbourne was not yet ready for the idea of ladies at the university.

The first young woman who asked to sit the Matriculation Exam in 1871 was turned away. Then she and two others were somewhat reluctantly accepted. The gates were open, and the number of young women applicants for matriculation grew rapidly year by year. By the time Mary sat in 1876 many girls' schools were preparing their students to take the examination. But there was another battle, all through the 1870s, to gain women the right to sign the university's Matriculation Roll. This was a huge step; it opened the door to studying at the university.

The opposition was strong: the studies were too difficult, women did not have the strength needed, they would have to be taught separately and there weren't enough classrooms, society would be thrown into chaos by women being out of their proper sphere. Why let women matriculate when graduating from university and taking up a profession was unthinkable?

While the learned gentlemen of The University of Melbourne adjusted to the idea of women students, the press had to do the same. *The Australasian Sketcher* reacted to the prospect of female university students with mock horror. When the first woman signed the Matriculation Register, there were cartoon sketches of young women with dainty books in their hands, in gathered and embroidered dresses better suited to a ballroom than a lecture room, with their academic gowns flowing behind them like fancy capes. There is another sketch of a thin, haggard-looking woman with a monocle studying late into the night, and another of stern, glaring figures in mortar boards and glasses with the caption: 'Are there to be Lady Professors?' Jokes about 'professoresses' and the Alma Mater joined those about degrees for Spinsters and Mistresses of Arts.[2]

Ladies were now finally allowed to attend the university. But did it mean they *would*? Would Mary's father have allowed her to go if she were to be the only woman there? And Mary herself — would she have gone alone?

Mary didn't have to make that decision. Lydia Harris, from Dunolly, joined Mary Gaunt, of *The Willows*, Ballarat — two young women from the country, long skirts under their black undergraduate gowns, trencher cap above, button-up boots below. In March 1881, they arrived with their chaperones to attend lectures in the new sandstone university beside the lake.

When she started her studies in 1881, Mary knew at least one of the students already. George Ernest Morrison (later to become famous as 'Chinese' Morrison) was studying medicine there. Mary was in an Arts course and Morrison was in his second year of medicine, but with 346 students the campus was only the size of a modest high school, and the Gaunt and Morrison families had social links.

Mary was in Melbourne on Friday 18 March when Ormond College was officially opened by the Governor. She had moved into her lodgings in St Kilda. She signed the university's Matriculation Register the next day — Saturday — and started lectures the next week.

...oOo...

Mary's early education had been a rather haphazard business; her mother had difficulty choosing suitable governesses, either because of a lack of judgement on her part or of a shortage of good governesses in the colony. But her father had chosen to send Mary and her sister Lucy, who was fifteen months younger, to Grenville College in Ballarat.

The boys were not going to Grenville College; a few years later Cecil and Ernest would go down to Melbourne to the Church of England Grammar School, but for now they were doing their schooling close to home.

A picture taken of Grenville College a few years after Mary and Lucy's time shows the pupils standing and sitting in three rows outside the school building, with the girls wearing white pinafores and boots.[3] It was a small school; about forty pupils, twelve of them girls, all studying in one big room. Mary wrote of it:

> That was a wicked school room at Grenville College. The windows were high above our heads. Facing south, not a ray of sunlight ever entered. The desks were high, so were the narrow backless forms that

we sat on for so many hours a day. If it had been planned to round our shoulders, cramp our legs and generally destroy our health, things could hardly have been better arranged.[4]

While Lucy claimed to have learnt nothing at Grenville College, or so Mary reported, Mary blossomed under the tutelage of John Victor, a graduate of Trinity College, Dublin, and the school's first principal. He had a fine mind, and an enlightened educational policy: he felt that girls should be taught as well as, and along with, boys. The girls learned Greek, Latin and geometry — the same subjects the boys did. And over and above the curriculum, Victor offered something Mary valued a great deal, and got little of at home — encouragement and praise. She worked hard over her weekly compositions, and John Victor saw promise in them. One of his comments stayed with her for life: 'My girl, one day we'll see you a novelist!'[5]

Chapter 2

Life on the Goldfields

To the Honorable the Colonial Secretary, 9 August 1853: Sir, I do myself the honour to request that you will be pleased to obtain the sanction of His Excellency the Lieutenant-Governor for the appointment of the gentleman named in the margin [William Henry Gaunt] as clerk in this office, with salary at the rate of £300 per annum, from 6th July last. I have the honour to be, Sir, your most obedient servant — W. H. Wright, Chief Commissioner of Goldfields.[1]

Mary was born on the Indigo diggings in northern Victoria on 20 February 1861. February was the hottest month. On the goldfields in summer, Black Dog Creek often ran dry and water for sluicing had to be used and reused. The skies were clear blue and merciless day after day, and the dry grass crackled underfoot. When tempers flared, and Warden William Gaunt had to intervene, the disputes were nearly always about water.

When Mary was a child, the Indigo diggings were growing into a large goldfield. The township of Chiltern was rough and new, but offered many of life's necessities to its growing number of citizens. Residents in houses, tents or rough huts could read books bought in Conness Street or borrowed from the circulating libraries; they got *Cassell's* Magazine or the *Illustrated London News* by subscription, and Bibles from travelling colporteurs of The British and Foreign Bible Society. They enjoyed lectures and travelling musical and theatre groups at the Star Theatre. The women shopped for laces, fabrics and hats at Horsfall's Bazaar, bought supplies of cheese, bacon, lobster and ham at Rhodes' Store, and got lamps and wallpaper at the Ovens Hardware Co. People could buy a horse or rent a buggy, send messages by telegraph to Sydney or Melbourne, and send or receive money to or from anywhere in the world without leaving the town. There were banks, insurance companies and provident societies, solicitors, estate agents and auctioneers. The men bought wines, spirits or beer to take home, or gathered in hotels to drink beer on tap and discuss the separation of the planned Murray Colony from Sydney, the need for a railway, or the progress of the American Civil War.[2] The universal held true — those with the money could live in comfort.

Elizabeth Palmer, Mary's mother, was no stranger to life in the bush. Her father Frederick, a former purser with the East India Company, had brought his wife and their ten children, and his wife's father, over from England. They settled in Van Diemen's Land — now Tasmania — in 1838, when Elizabeth was two years old. Having tried several ventures with limited success, Palmer later returned to England, where his death in 1849 was possibly hastened by heavy drinking. His enterprising family spread out across the colonies, and two — Thomas and Octavius, who was not quite sixteen — joined the goldrush to California. By 1860, widow Mary Eliza Palmer was living at Dederang, near Yackandandah in north-east Victoria, with her daughters Mary Eliza (known as Polly) and Elizabeth on a pastoral run taken up by two of her sons. With their mother widowed and their brothers coming and going in a remarkable range of ventures, the girls grew to be capable managers of the property.

Elizabeth's brothers and sisters were a lively, somewhat erratic, but extraordinarily energetic family. They formed partnerships, bought and sold land, owned slaughter yards, worked in banks, became tea merchants, sat on mining company boards and hospital boards, and generally contributed much to the expanding colony. One brother is believed to have committed suicide, one was accidentally drowned at twenty-four years old. The husband of one of the daughters, Eliza, built a mansion in Tasmania over his private coach road — a kind of nineteenth century drive-in home.

Thomas employed Afghan labourers on his dairy property, and was accused of murdering one of them. Edward married an opera singer who came to Yackandandah and gave concerts. In a colony creating its own identity as it went along, the Palmers were quite at home.

William Gaunt had been working for the North Staffordshire Railway Company as superintendant of a branch line and canal before he left England at twenty-three years old, to try his fortune in Victoria. The private bank of Fowler, Gaunt & Co. had closed in 1847, when William was seventeen, and although the family still owned property there was none for William to inherit. His administrative skills and impressive testimonials, however, made him an attractive candidate for a government position, and he began work in the rapidly-expanding Goldfields Department soon after his arrival.[3]

Dederang was part of the area for which the young Woolshed warden, William Gaunt, had responsibility. After breaking his ankle in a buggy accident, William seems to have spent convalescent time with the Palmers. He and Elizabeth were married in 1860, though there is no record of their courtship.

For all Elizabeth's years in the colonies, she had an aristocratic image of a woman's role which was quite different from the reality of her life. She liked to paint; she played the piano and she arranged flowers beautifully; she did her best to create for herself the image of a lady of the leisured and servanted class. She was a skilled horsewoman, riding side-saddle in a long flowing skirt. She was an active and energetic woman and her years on country properties had made her a capable manager. She developed a garden, orchard and small farm around the family home in Chiltern. They called it *Woodlands*, after Elizabeth's home in Tasmania. The list of contents of the house, advertised by the auctioneers when the family left Chiltern and the house was sold, suggests comfort, refinement and good taste:

> Magnificent toned rosewood cottage piano, by Broadwood and Sons
> Half Cabinet Wheeler and Wilson's Sewing Machine, quite new
> Mahogany drawing room suite, in Morocco, with patent brass joints

Engravings, chromo-lithographs
Patent washing machine, patent mangle[4]

This was certainly not the rough world that Mary drew on for her stories.

William was employed at a salary which allowed him to live well. He was a reader — he had books of travel and adventure on his shelves, and Rolfe Boldrewood's *Robbery under Arms* was among the books he read with enthusiasm to his children. He valued education and wanted all his children to do well at school. During his time on the goldfields he began to study law; his uncle Matthew Gaunt was a barrister back in Staffordshire, and William's position as a magistrate made him aware of the advantage of being trained in the law. At an early stage, long before he qualified, people who had their claims dealt with by him on Mining Boards or in the Magistrates Courts noticed William's careful legal approach to the matters before him.

The love of conversation and the absence of many of the city's distractions meant that there was story-telling in the evening at *Woodlands*. Many of William's colleagues were cultivated men — sons of clergymen and the nobility, people who valued learning as William did — and the Gaunt children grew up in a world of ideas and stories. There was Virginius Murray, grandson of the Earl of Dunmore and ex-army captain; John W. Jacomb Hood, Assistant Commissioner at Beechworth and later judge of the Supreme Court; Edward Barnard, son of Canon Henry Barnard, Etonian, ex-Royal Scots Fusiliers; Charles Shuter, doctor's son and later president of the Melbourne Club; Matthew Price, a former captain in the Madras Army of the East India Company; Captain Standish, opera lover, gambler and bon vivant who became Victorian Police Commissioner in 1858; former army officer, Jacobite and disciplinarian William Henry Drummond; and John Cogdon, who later studied law with William. Among William's friends was 'an old gentleman who had been a gay young dog in Paris in the [eighteen] fifties' who later told Mary a moving story about a young French nobleman and the beautiful girl he had left behind, and urged her to write the story. Years later, she changed the setting from a

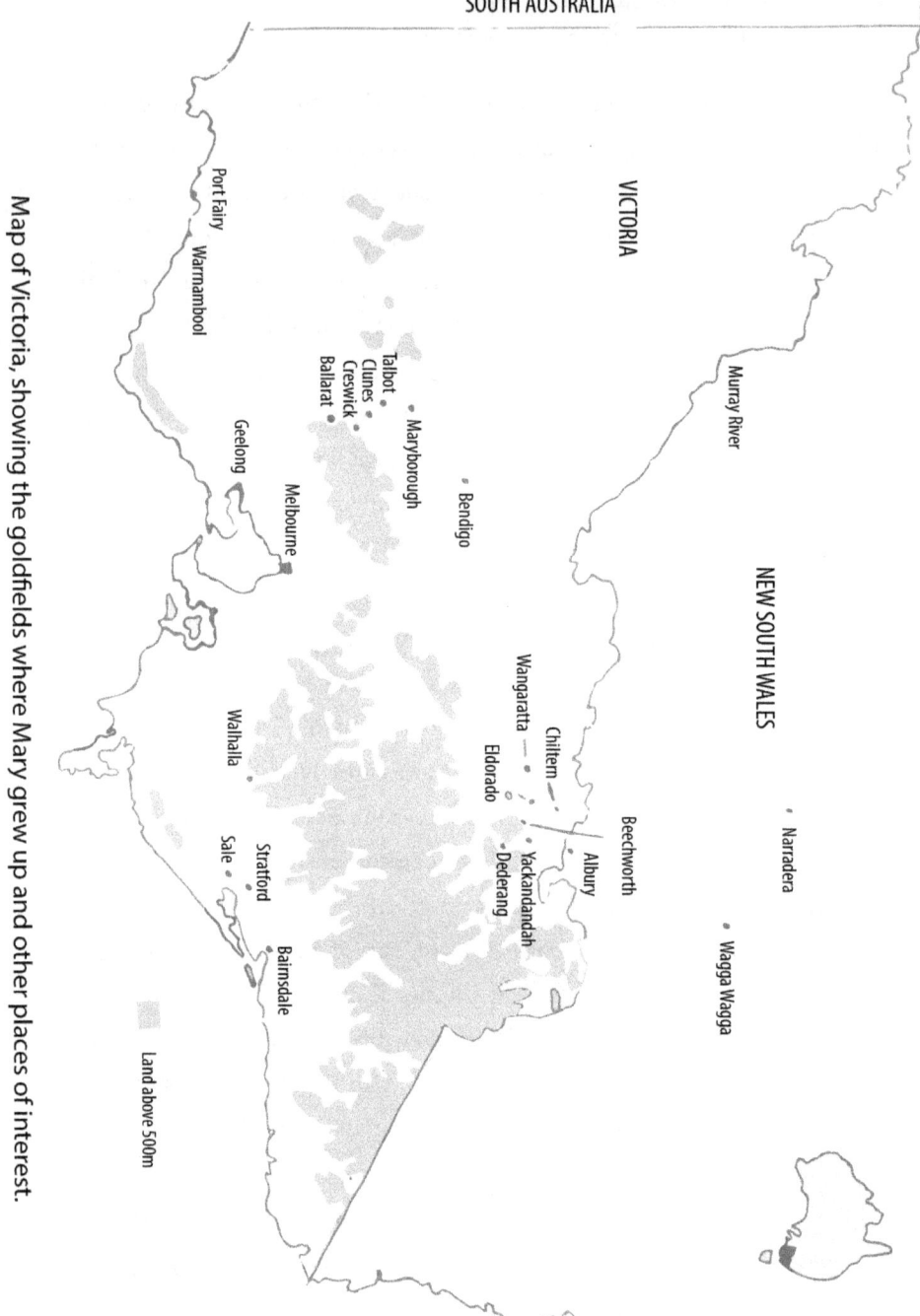

Map of Victoria, showing the goldfields where Mary grew up and other places of interest.

French chateau to a mining camp in Victoria, and turned it into a novel — *Dave's Sweetheart* — which was published in 1894.

In 1865, William was promoted to Beechworth. After the happy, productive years in Chiltern, the township whose institutions he had helped establish, William left abruptly.[5] He moved the family to Beechworth — Elizabeth was eight months pregnant at the time — and sold the house, the orchard and the farm. He sold the pictures and lithographs off the walls. He sold Elizabeth's sewing machine and her rosewood piano, he sold her horse, her prize-winning poultry, the milking cows and their calves. He was shaking the dust from off his feet.

…oOo…

Mary used a real-life incident — the murder of a German vegetable seller on the diggings — in her section on gold for Cassell's *Picturesque Australasia*, which was published in 1887. She used it again later in her fiction. This was the world of S. T. Gill's watercolours — those vivid depictions of men with picks and shovels on their way to the diggings, and of hard-drinking diggers in shanty pubs. It was a world Mary was never allowed to wander in as a child: the world of family lore and legend, the stories and recollections of her parents and their friends soaked up by eager children.

Mary was taken from Chiltern to Beechworth at the age of four, and left the north-eastern goldfields at eight. She published the story of the German vegetable seller when she was twenty-seven and living in Ballarat. By then, the world of the Indigo goldfields and 'Deadman's' — the fictional name she used for her goldfields world, the setting for two of her novels and many of her short stories, the raw, rough world of the vegetable seller's murder — was long ago and far away. But in the Gaunt family it lived on; it was a world for which Mary had a great affection, and it never left her.

Chapter 3

Colonial Childhood

We children always felt that the trooper police belonged in a measure to us, and we always rushed out to see the gold and its escort arrive at Sale — the escort, not the precious metal, being the attraction. They wore dark blue uniform jackets, corded breeches, high boots, and square cloth caps with a straight peak in front, and each man carried a carbine in a bucket. There were probably half a dozen with every mail, but then I thought of them as a large party.[1]

William Gaunt was promoted to Beechworth in 1865. It was a promotion he had angled for; he had had a very public argument with the editor of the *Federal Standard* in Chiltern, and there was considerable ill feeling. The Beechworth paper, in its column about Chiltern affairs, reported the regret of the local people that William was leaving: 'Our public buildings and institutions owe almost everything to him,' it said.[2] The Chiltern *Federal Standard* said nothing.

William had begun his goldfields career at Beechworth when he first arrived in the colony in 1853, and now he was back at 'head office'. Beechworth was now a solid township and the regional centre of the goldfields of north-east Victoria. There was a row of impressive stone buildings along Ford Street: the gaol, the Telegraph Office, the Court House and the Sub-Treasury building. Christ Church had just been completed, the huge benevolent asylum on the hill was under construction, and there were streets of houses and shops. Bullock wagons arrived regularly from

Melbourne, straining through heat and dust, or bogged to the axles in winter mud, hauling foodstuffs and fabrics, glassware and china, bookcases and pianos for the township and the diggings.

There were over 6,000 Chinese miners living in the Beechworth area when the Gaunts arrived, and a well-established Chinese quarter. William's work as Chinese Protector meant that the Gaunt children were brought into contact early with people who were regarded with suspicion and fear by most of the population and resented by the miners. There was a policy of segregating the Chinese diggers in separate camps to reduce friction with Europeans. Even so, Mary remembered Chinese miners coming to the door to claim her father's protection after acts of vandalism and violence.

Neither Mary nor the family thought of these men as individuals, as people with a name and a family and a separate identity. 'John Chinaman' was a common expression; the man who brought the vegetables to the Gaunt house was 'Vegetable John'. When the children did not take care of their baby brother properly, their parents would threaten to give the baby to Vegetable John.

Mary's imagination about the strange and faraway world of China was stirred by her grandmother. Her grandfather, Frederick Palmer, had served with the East India Company and had brought back curios from his travels in the East. Mary never knew him — he died in London before she was born — but Grandmother Palmer, who had a house in Beechworth, told the children stories about the Great Wall and other wonders their grandfather had seen.

…oOo…

Beechworth was the first of several postings for William. Then came a temporary posting to Talbot, halfway between Clunes and Maryborough, then to Sale on the east Victorian coast. The family moved there when Mary was six.

Elizabeth would ride out with her husband when he went to investigate discoveries of gold in the area — Walhalla, Stratford and Grant — leaving the children in the care of a nursemaid. Mary was an inquisitive child and one day, when the nursemaid was busy with her little brother, Mary and Lucy went off into the bush and came to an Aboriginal camp. It was the first time Mary could remember seeing Aboriginal people, and recognising them as different from herself.

> [The Aboriginal people] jumped up to see the white children, and a tall black man paraded proudly in a white collar and tall grey hat that my father had given him. I am sorry to say he had very little else on him. He might have been comely stark, but the tall hat and collar made him indecent. He leaned on a stick, limping a little in imitation of my father...[3]

In Sale they still told the story of the *Britannia* wrecked on Ninety Mile Beach nearly thirty years before, and of the white woman believed to have survived and to have been taken by the Aboriginal people. There were sightings of her belongings, it was said, and carvings on a tree that might have been her initials. Search parties went looking for her, but she was never found. Her story lived on, though, and became part of the Gaunt family lore.

After Sale William was posted to Sandhurst as Police Magistrate and Warden, then in January 1869 he was appointed Returning Officer for the mining district of Ballarat and Visiting Justice of the gaol there, and the family moved again. Ballarat was a large mining centre with gracious homes at its centre and an attractive social life. The frontier settlement days were over.

William and Elizabeth settled their growing family in a house on the edge of the swamp that was later to be known as Lake Wendouree. Reeds and wild marsh grasses grew along the edges. While much of it was dry and sandy in summer, it was deep enough in winter to be dangerous for children.

> Besides the danger of being drowned there was the mysterious bunyip which was supposed to haunt waterholes and would probably eat little children. My father said the bunyip was all nonsense.

> I thought very likely he was right. But on the other hand I knew all the blacks feared greatly the bunyip. And they were very learned in all bush lore. Even my father admitted that.
>
> I must have, privately, believed in the mythical beast, whatever I may have said to him on the subject, for I, who was ever ready to investigate anything, never headed an expedition to the Swamp.[4]

The place was wild and fascinating, a place of danger and unknown threat, although the children later built rafts and sailed them on the lake. The children collected insects, chased animals, learned to ride, played at being Zulus and American Indians, and regularly got into trouble. Many years later Mary, remembering its wildness, set a story of lost children there.

Mary was eight years old when the family settled in Ballarat. She was slight of build and fairly short, with fine curly hair. She was strong-willed and intelligent, and had a well-developed sense of fun, and was the leading troublemaker when there was mischief about. Since she had an inventive imagination and an adventurous streak, she had an enthusiastic following in her young siblings: Lucy was seven years old, Cecil was five and Ernest was four. Their newest brother Guy was born later that year, in 1869.

The children were educated at home by a number of governesses. Perhaps Elizabeth chose women who would provide the least temptation possible to her husband, or perhaps there were very few to choose from, but Mary's recollections were of plain, ill-equipped older women. The children remembered in particular Miss Sadler, of the long, horsey face and lank, colourless hair, who belonged to a strict religious sect and who used to speak of being tempted by the Devil and the risks of eternal damnation. Miss Sadler left abruptly after a schoolroom incident when Ernest threw the inkpot at her.

When Mary was not yet ten, Elizabeth decided on school. A Mrs Abbott and her two daughters ran a small school in a cottage with a garden around it, and the Gaunt children were duly enrolled there.

> [Mother] gave strict instructions we were on no account to play with the daughters of the grocer or the baker…These instructions made

> things very difficult for Lucy and me, who were friendly little souls. The boys had a freer time. It seems it did not matter whom they knew.
>
> I shall always remember how we went home and told how we had met some nice little girls…who were not the grocer's daughters, nor the baker's, nor the draper's. Their papa was an undertaker.
>
> A shout of laughter from my father…

Before long, William and Elizabeth moved their family closer to the town centre. It would be easier for education and bring the family nearer to the social activities of the growing town. They settled in a three-storey house with a basement room whose window faced the stairs up to the street, a room with subdued lighting and no view. This was to be the room for the children's use when they were not at school. It was a room Mary hated. In later years she blamed her mother and the gloomy room for her eyesight problems.

Elizabeth's sister Eliza had married the enterprising and remarkable John Kinder Archer some years before, and they now had ten children. When Mary was about twelve, she and Lucy went to stay with their Archer cousins again, this time at Mannerim near Geelong. The house was built of slabs, with a bark roof and beaten earth floor. Elizabeth thought of her sister as poor. Mary and Lucy, enjoying more freedom than at home, including being able to read without censure, revelled in riding on horseback to collect the mail, carrying in water from the dam, and eating homemade butter on homemade bread and scones, as Eliza was an excellent housekeeper.

Mary was engrossed in a storybook about West Africa when word came that a bushfire threatened the far paddock. All those who could went out to fight the fire; Eliza stayed at the house, and Mary and Lucy carried billy tea and chunks of bread and meat to the firefighters. At last the wind changed direction and there was rain. The threat was over, and the girls returned with the weary firefighters, tired, and wet and dirty without guilt. Mary's one regret was that she never finished the book about West Africa.

…oOo…

From an early age, Mary loved reading. Her father had books, but they were kept in the drawing room and she was not allowed in there except for her daily piano practice after school. But when the opportunity arose, Mary would sneak books from the small bookcase.

> My mother considered music far more important than all my other lessons put together. She deplored the fact that I showed so little aptitude for it, but thought something might be accomplished by diligent practice…I knew that all the practice in the world would never make even a passable musician of me.
>
> There was another book…that really had a very deep and useful influence on my future life. It helped me in a way that no teaching I can ever remember helped me. It was, too, my first introduction to the world of travel, to other countries besides my own! It told at great length how Captain Speke and Captain Grant discovered the sources of the Nile.
>
> I used to play C scale, which I reckoned I could do mechanically, and prop up a book before me on the music-rack…But as much as I loved that book, it got me into trouble many a time. It was heavy, and required a hand to keep it on the music rack. Even C scale requires two hands to play it properly. When I was far away with Captain Speke in Uganda or Unyoro, I am afraid often it did not get one.
>
> Presently a voice would call up the stairs:
>
> 'Darling, what are you doing? Wasting your time reading, I suppose. Do pay attention to your music.'[5]

Elizabeth felt that reading was a waste of time and that many novels were unsuitable for young girls. It was an opinion shared by Dr Kellogg, whose *Ladies Guide* was in many Colonial homes:

> The reading of works of fiction is one of the most pernicious habits to which a young lady can become devoted…[It] destroys the taste for sober, wholesome reading and imparts an unhealthy stimulus to the mind the effect of which is in the highest degree damaging.
>
> When we add to this the fact that a large share of the popular novels of the day contain more or less matter of a directly depraving character, presented in such gilded form and specious guise that the work of contamination may be completed before suspicion is aroused, it should become apparent to every careful mother that

her daughters should be vigilantly guarded against this dangerous source of injury and possible ruin.[6]

Mary's concern was more that the heroines in most of the novels of the day were so helpless and silly; how could men love such foolish women?

One heroine who inspired Mary, and would have met with any mother's approval, was in Charlotte Yonge's *Dove in the Eagle's Nest*. Yonge's novels had a strong moral message. This one was the story of a shy 15-year-old girl who is carried away by a robber baron. He lives in a mountain-top eyrie called Adlerstein — the eagle's nest. The devout young heroine marries his heir in secret and, at only sixteen, has twin boys. Her young husband and his father are killed in battle, and her son becomes heir. Through the firmness and gentleness of her teaching, her son brings an end to the feuding which has plagued the district for generations. Mary was inspired, and longed to have twins at sixteen, just like her heroine.

When a friend of the family left a box of books with them for storage, Mary would sneak into the spare room and get one and read it under the bed; she read *Hiawatha* and *Evangeline* and *Ivanhoe* this way. In spite of the dim light and discomfort, she found a world of magic in them.

Then one day she was given a library subscription. She could go to the library and choose whatever books she liked — except novels, of course. This rule was later relaxed; she could read novels if her mother read them first and judged them to be safe. Since her mother read very little, the arrangement was unworkable and gradually broke down.

Mary would go off to the Library in Ballarat and carry home adventure stories to share with the others — books by William Kingston, Frederick Marryat and James Fenimore Cooper. Like the boys, she identified with the heroes of the stories, not realising that identifying with the heroes of adventure stories was something for boys, not girls. Far from going out in search of adventure, girls must be content to wait at home.

After her return from Miss Gregory's school when she was sixteen, Mary was considered 'grown up' enough to go into the drawing room whenever she liked — without having to play the piano.

...oOo...

Towards the end of 1876, the family moved away from the centre of Ballarat, on the assumption that the growing family could be brought up more economically in the country. They bought a property called *The Willows* at Bungaree, thirteen kilometres out of Ballarat. There was a cottage on the property, not nearly big enough for them all. But William and Elizabeth had learned useful lessons in their goldfields years. From the Woolshed diggings almost twenty years before, where the gold was beginning to peter out, William had made fortnightly inspection visits to the Buckland Valley, where miners were crowding into the new field. The enterprising publican, Reilly, took the shell of the old *Miner's Right* from the Woolshed and carted it up the Buckland Valley and set it up as a pub. Now William and Elizabeth followed Reilly's example. They bought a weatherboard tavern from a disused goldfield, cut it into four and hauled it twenty-four kilometres to Bungaree, reassembling it to stand beside the cottage.

The family was growing. Mary and Lucy, fifteen months her junior, now had five brothers. Cecil, like Mary and Lucy, was born while they were still at *Woodlands* in Chiltern; Ernest was born just as the family moved to Beechworth. Guy was born soon after the family settled in Ballarat. In 1871, when Guy was two, another brother, Vere Arnold, was born; he died five months later. Then came Clive, born in 1872, and Lance a few years later. Alice Maud Victoria was born in 1876.

Once again, moving house coincided with pregnancy for Elizabeth. In Chiltern, she had packed up their clothes and personal belongings and got the house ready for auction when she was eight months pregnant. William's appointment to Ballarat had come in January of 1869, and she gave birth to Guy in May of that year. And in Ballarat baby Alice Maud Victoria was born in the year they moved to *The Willows*. Before long, the house was touched with sadness by the death of little Alice, and by that of Elizabeth's mother, Mary Eliza Palmer, in St Kilda.

As time went on, Elizabeth entered into their life in the country with enthusiasm. After living in a house in the heart of Ballarat, the family now had 9.5 hectares (23.5 acres). Now she could build up a stock of animals again. Unfortunately, it was mostly William who did the buying, even though Elizabeth had grown up with stock and had by far the better eye for a good animal, as her prizes at the Chiltern Show attested.[7]

Nevertheless, Elizabeth raised pigs, chickens and cows; with the fruit trees and shrubs already on the property she developed a fine orchard and garden, growing plums, pears, apples, quinces, apricots, greengages, gooseberries, raspberries and strawberries. Mary did not consider her mother a good housekeeper (she was impractical in many ways), but she was a capable manager of their small farm.

The children now had a huge area to play in, and outside of the ring of fruit trees and berry bushes it was virgin bush. They could wander a vast space, enjoying a freedom they had not had before. Their mother became increasingly occupied as each new child came along, and for the older children there was increasing freedom and independence.

Mary, Guy and Lance all wrote in later years about their childhood, and through each account comes a picture of healthy children running free, running wild sometimes, collecting insects, chasing the farm pigs. Guy told a story of one escapade, in the days when Ballarat had no stock exchange building, and the men used to simply close off a section of the street on Saturday mornings to conduct their business.

> My brother Clive and I strongly resented this interference with the liberty of the subject [the closing off of the street]. One glorious morning we charged down the street on our twelve-hand ponies yelling like Red Indians and scattering the elderly gentlemen in all directions. Hats and papers flew around us, the owners rushed for sidewalks, while one old man, Sir Henry Cuthbert, on all fours crawled into Fawn's Hotel fully convinced no doubt that bushrangers were on the job.[8]

Regardless of their irreverence for authority, the children grew up aware of their place in the British Empire, and of its place in the universal scheme of things. Winston Churchill, growing up in the same Empire at the same time (he was the same age as Lance), expressed the feeling of security and superiority of the position they shared in the Empire:

> I was a child of the Victorian era, when the structures of our country seemed firmly set, when its position in trade and on the seas was unrivalled, and when the realisation of the greatness of our Empire and of our duty to preserve it was ever growing stronger. In those days the dominant forces in Great Britain were very sure of themselves and of their doctrines. They thought they could teach the world the art of government, and the science of economics. They were sure they were supreme at sea and consequently safe at home. They rested therefore sedately under the convictions of power and security.[9]

There was a sense of justice and the natural order about British superiority. It pervaded colonial attitudes to the Aboriginal and Chinese peoples; Mary took it with her to Africa and China and it pervaded her writing about them. It involved the obligation of service which led the boys into the armed forces; they — and Mary — left Australia with a strong sense of their place in the Empire.

Inextricably linked to their sense of being part of the Empire was their sense of being part of God's creation, and of His expression on Earth: the Church of England. William was a churchwarden and took an active part in church affairs, and in the services, and the family worshipped together at the lovely little bluestone church in Bungaree. William was a stern man, and the children were expected to behave reverently in church. Most of the time they did as required, but Mary still remembered in her seventies how triumphant they all felt when they succeeded in sneaking the family dog into church one Sunday.

In later years, Mary carried a Bible with her when she travelled; she loved the beauty of its language and the drama of its stories, particularly those of the Old Testament. It shaped the way she saw the world and reminded her of home. She also loved the sonorous beauty of the Church of England prayer book service, and into old age could go to a service and say the words by heart.

...oOo...

One hot January night in 1882, a fire began in the kitchen area of the house and spread rapidly through the weatherboard building. There was little warning, and the rainwater supply from the tanks made little impression once the fire took hold. In a very short time, *The Willows* had burnt down, and most of their possessions were gone. Lucy's daughter, Miss Ellinor Archer, recorded her mother's recollection many years later:

> The family escaped in coats over their night attire, and clutching a few possessions they had saved, they drove to the township to seek shelter from friends. It was Sunday morning and they drove down the main street just as the Anglican congregation was leaving church. 'Mother [Lucy] told me,' said Miss Archer, 'that there on the front seat of the buggy sat my grandmother [Elizabeth] in her dressing gown; in one hand she held a priceless Chinese vase and in the other a decanter of whisky. All the children were huddled on the back seat, my mother carrying the baby.'[10]

The family moved back into town, renting *Bishopscourt* from the Bishop of Ballarat. It was a pleasant spot overlooking the erstwhile swamp of their childhood years, now Lake Wendouree. They were starting again, with all the emptiness of the loss of their personal possessions. For them all, and for Mary in particular, it was the end of an era.

Chapter 4

Student Life

To tell the truth, I believe this provision [the Bill to allow the admission of women] is not likely to be taken much advantage of, and I don't know that it is very desirable that it should. Nevertheless, it is right to give an opportunity to any lady who chooses to go through so heavy a course to do so. Hitherto ladies have stopped at matriculation, and no doubt they will continue to remain at that point.[1]

From her lodgings in a fashionable seaside residence in St Kilda, Mary travelled an hour by horse-drawn omnibus into Melbourne. What her father encountered in 1853 as a rough colonial settlement was now building itself anew into a gold-rich Colonial capital, with a fine new Treasury and Customs building, and a lovely garden-set house for the Governor. The new, young university was well out of the town. Other ladies rode the Carlton bus to the big International Exhibition in the Carlton Gardens. Mary was the only lady to get off the omnibus at the university.

Mary and another young woman from the country, Lydia Harris, began regular lectures at the university in March 1881. They stood out among the male students. They wore caps and academic gowns over their dresses, which Mary felt was 'very becoming', and had a Lady Students' Room assigned to them upstairs in the quadrangle.

Mary enjoyed considerably more freedom than in her boarding school days. Board and lodging here had been arranged for her with two middle-aged English women whose role in life was to 'cultivate' young women of the colonies. She had an admirer; a young man from Bendigo who came to visit her. They went for walks, had tea and went to church together. In her easy-going childhood this had been normal for Mary, but the women were shocked, and wrote to tell William about it. He wrote back to Mary:

> These schoolmarms of yours seem to be funny old girls. If I were you I should change my quarters![2]

Mary took his advice with fateful results. She knew that what she should have done was to find a quiet place to stay in Carlton near the university, but

> Though I could go to Carlton to work, I knew very well I could not possibly [go] three times a week to St. Kilda for pleasure.[3]

She moved into the household of an acquaintance in St Kilda, a woman who entertained a great deal. After goldfields towns, the bush and Ballarat, she was in a city of 250,000 people. As a female university student, she attracted attention at parties and enjoyed social success. But she was not spending enough time on her studies; she was clever but not brilliant, and she needed to work.

Around the university, though, she enjoyed the novelty of the effect she created. The male students made the new female students very welcome:

> My schoolboy brothers declared, with one voice, that 'awful female' was the least opprobrious term the undergraduates would bestow upon me; but, on the contrary, they were very good to me, and I never lacked some nice young man to carry my books and papers to the 'bus for me.'[4]

The university's Arts curriculum was firmly grounded on the classics, and which meant Greek was a compulsory subject. There were no science or modern language courses, and no literature except for the literature in Latin and Greek. It was not the ideal course for Mary.

Redmond Barry, the first chancellor, wanted students to be the intellectual equals of their counterparts in Britain, and wanted to refine not only their intellects but their taste and manners too. There were already protests at the limitations of the course even for male students, and some thought the course far too onerous, the Latin and Greek texts far too earthy, for women students. Interestingly, during 1881 chemistry, English and modern languages were added to the curriculum, but the changes took effect in 1882 after Barry's death — a year too late for Mary.

Mary had a quick mind and learned things easily if she enjoyed them, but she had no patience for what did not interest her. She shone at history and enjoyed geography. She mastered Latin and mathematics to pass at matriculation level. But she could not get enthusiastic about French and Greek. When the end-of-year results came out, Mary had failed Greek again, along with mathematics and logic. Effectively, she had failed her first year.

Failed! The young woman who passed eight subjects at matriculation level with honours in history, one of the youngest to do so. The young woman regarded as so promising by her teachers, who was first through the barrier to attend lectures at the university. She had failed! She would have to go back home to Bungaree, back to the life she had been living. She would have to explain it to her parents, and face the question of whether they would let her go back to try again. She would have to face her young brothers as well.

She packed up her belongings, checked out of the house in St Kilda, and went home.

> Before the next term our house…was burnt to the ground; books and cap and gown, and everything else that I possessed, were destroyed. I escaped in my nightgown. There were plenty of other expenses for my father then. Whatever happened to me in the future, I saw I could not possibly go back to the University.[5]

…oOo…

Mary never recorded her parents' response to the news. She had persuaded them to let her enrol at the university because it offered a way out of an empty social life. They had allowed, rather than encouraged, her to go. No dream of theirs for her future could have involved a university education until just before she began it. Her mother saw her future leading, via French, needlework and playing the piano, to a suitable marriage. Her father had broader and more varied pathways in mind — the pleasures of reading and learning, the cultivation of intelligence and skill — but these led, too, inexorably, to a suitable marriage. And the only likely career that a university education offered — that of a teacher — was not what Mary herself wanted at all. Her failure was not a disappointment to anyone's plans. To her father it may have seemed a waste of his money; for her mother it was a relief.

Some years later Mary created a heroine, Phoebe, whose younger brother scoffs at her education. In real life, Mary's brothers were in no position to do this. Cecil was having trouble passing matriculation, Ernest had left school early to join the Navy, and Guy wanted to do the same. The boys could rely on the accepted social disapproval of educating women, but not on their own superiority.

The character Phoebe did, however, give her opinion on a situation remarkably like Mary's own. Phoebe is growing restless and resentful at the prospect of waiting patiently for a man to propose. Her younger brother interrupts her conversation to assure her that she's in no danger of marrying. He describes his idea of how a girl should be:

> Well, a girl ought to stick at home. She oughtn't to bother her head about Latin and Greek. Who wants his wife to know anything about mathematics? My wife's going to dance beautifully, and she must play and sing, she might paint a bit — just enough to decorate the drawing room. And then, if she can cook a bit and sew a little, that's all I want…She'll have to be pretty, of course — ugly women ought to be shut up or smothered or something. Blest if I see what use they are.[6]

Mary's mother was convinced that a woman might be practical and capable, but she must give the impression of being fragile, ornamental. At *The Willows*, Elizabeth had a live-in cook and housemaid, and men to do the farm work, so she could be free to oversee the house, garden and farm, or ride out with William on his rounds on the goldfields. There were still practical jobs to be done, but a lady should not admit to doing them, and certainly not enthuse about them, as Mary discovered when the visiting archdeacon's wife asked her if she had learned how to milk a cow:

> 'Oh, yes!' said I innocently. There had been some domestic catastrophe and my aid had been valuable. 'I milked two this morning.'
> My mother hastily interposed. 'She likes to think she is helping.'
> I had helped — materially. I said so in no uncertain voice.
> The parson's wife laughed.
> When she was gone my mother's wrath descended upon me. How could I shame her so?
> Again I voiced my astonishment. Then the truth came out.
> 'No lady ever milks a cow!'[7]

When their schooling was finished, Mary and Lucy were expected to emulate their mother — to cultivate the appearance of leisure and wealth, and to develop drawing room accomplishments while helping out where needed. Many years later, when she and Lucy were making their own way in the world, she wrote an article for the London *Times* about the value of girls being trained for useful work, and she looked back on their life at *The Willows*. She wrote with some delicacy, as if describing someone else's family, but clearly she was writing about the Gaunts, with William in the law practice he had begun in Ballarat and the boys starting their careers.

> I remember in my youth a professional man — a well-to-do man whose quiver was full. The home was in the country, and he, who was an excellent lawyer, was a shocking bad farmer in his spare time. His wife, who really was a good judge of stock, used to bemoan the fact. 'Such a pity I couldn't buy the cows and the pigs. He is so imposed upon.' And there was absolutely no reason, save convention, why she should not have run that farm at a profit. But in those days it would not have been the 'thing' for a 'lady', so she put in a couple of hours every afternoon sleeping peacefully.
> The two eldest daughters were discontented. It was dull — so dull — and they did not see why they should do housework to save

money in order that their brothers might be trained for comfortable positions. Their discontent was aggravated by a parent who remarked to their mother whenever the cares of life pressed heavily upon him — 'Your girls will never marry!' And yet comfort, if not wealth, was within that man's grasp. If his wife and daughters had worked, and learned to manage that farm, he might have pursued his own profession with a quiet mind, and there would have been money in plenty. As it was, in after years those girls had to find some means of livelihood without any training whatever.[8]

When Mary had passed matriculation, she was sent to Melbourne to finishing school. Her mother was concerned about her tomboyish adventures, the misdemeanours with her brothers in which she was often the ringleader. Elizabeth wanted Mary to become more ladylike. The 'school' chosen for her 'finishing' was run by a Miss Gregory and had only six pupils. They learned composition from Miss Gregory, and French, and had music and drawing lessons from visiting teachers, for an extra fee. The girls walked in the streets only when accompanied by their governess, and not in any purposeful way, just for the walk, which Mary found annoying. She disliked the school and gained very little from it.[9] When the expensive music master at Miss Gregory's failed to perform the required miracle of turning Mary into an accomplished pianist, Mary was allowed to quietly drop music lessons.

Ballarat was a growing provincial city made prosperous by gold. There were wide, shady avenues of elegant houses; there were galleries, theatres, shops and all the amusements and diversions young women were supposed to crave. Mary and Lucy were invited to picnic parties, boating excursions and balls. It was a life to be enjoyed — the life for which the French lessons and the piano practice had been intended to prepare her. Mary had a well-developed sense of fun and a healthy enjoyment of life, but during that time before university she began to grow restless and resentful at the prospect of waiting patiently for a man to come along and propose marriage to her.

As daughters of a professional man, she and Lucy had a comfortable home and a modest allowance. Their father was Resident Warden of the Goldfields, as well as Police Magistrate and Coroner, which gave them a certain social position. Her time at university had widened her horizons. She wrote in later years:

> Though I never took my degree, the money expended was not wasted. The University took me out of the narrow up-country town life that hitherto had been mine and introduced me to a new world.

But after her failure at university, she was back at home and back to the old life again.

…oOo…

Her mother Elizabeth, now 46, went to stay with her sister Eliza in Queenscliff for the birth of another child. The baby, named William Henry for his father, died soon afterwards. Elizabeth and William had lost three children as infants: Vere Arnold in 1871, Alice Maud Victoria in 1876, and now little William, born in 1881. This would be Elizabeth's last child.

Cecil, the eldest of the boys, was studying with a tutor for the Matriculation Exam. He had been at the Grammar School and sat twice for matriculation without getting even the five subjects that would get him a job in government service. Now, back at home, he was having lessons with a tutor and trying again. Ernest had finished his training on HMS *Britannia* and was serving as a sub-lieutenant 'on the Australia Station' (in Australian waters) on HMS *Nelson*. Guy was at the Grammar School in Melbourne, preparing — his parents fondly hoped — for a legal career and daydreaming, with Mary's encouragement, of a life at sea. Clive and Lance were nine and seven years old, and were still at home. So now were Mary and Lucy.

Mary now faced an uncertain future; for several years there had been the possibility of university studies, but now that brief bright year was over. Her father pointed out the family prospects for the future. He had seven children to feed, clothe, educate and launch into the world. There would be the expense of setting the boys up in their professions; the commissions in the armed services and the cost of studying Law in Melbourne. There would have to be marriage settlements for his two daughters. These could not be generous, he warned them. In the meantime, the girls would have only a very small allowance each.

Mary felt the unfairness of it. She wanted what the boys could have. They could travel and have a profession while she, academically the most successful in the family, had to stay at home. She wanted more out of life. She wanted her own place in the world.

Chapter 5

What is a Girl to Do?

I want to earn my own living — to be quite independent. I don't care how little I earn at first, if I can go on improving, like a man. I want to earn enough to be sure of being comfortably off in my old age. To be decently dressed, you know, and be able to travel about a little, and buy books, and have money to give away…If I didn't marry then, it wouldn't matter a bit. I'd be a great deal better off than half the women who marry because they must.[1]

Mary began life as an ex-university student feeling restless and unsatisfied. She was now almost twenty-one and it was time to think seriously about marriage. She was still fond of Edward Cordner, her Bendigo admirer from her university days. Her father had no objection, but Cordner had no prospects and her mother disapproved.

Elizabeth arranged for Mary to go on a trip to Adelaide to visit her father's Bakewell cousins. A trip by coastal steamer to another colony was an inviting opportunity, and, fond as she was of Cordner, Mary could not resist it. After all, Bendigo was not so far away — they could meet again. It was agreed that she should go.

The Bakewells lived high on Mount Lofty. They could look out over the growing capital and the plains to the Gulf of St Vincent and, on clear days, to the dim coastline beyond, a vista to set a would-be traveller dreaming. They grew olives and oranges, kept fowls, ducks and turkeys. Mrs Bakewell had a married son called Jack who had studied in Cambridge and had acquired an air of sophistication along with his Cambridge accent;

a colonial himself, he liked to tease his 'little Australian' cousin.

Mary enjoyed the company of the Bakewells and her holiday with them. Mrs Bakewell did not succeed in finding her a better marriage prospect, but Elizabeth's plan had been moderately successful, and Cordner faded without trace from Mary's life.

Mary and Lucy went on occasion to visit friends at Deniliquin and Hay in the Riverina of the New South Wales Colony. Visitors converged in Deniliquin for the races and the Show, and there were parties, picnics and balls. The girls made the journey by train: the first stage was from Ballarat to Bendigo, then to Echuca on the Murray, where they changed to a standard gauge train, then on to Deniliquin in New South Wales. Away from the inhibiting gaze of her mother Mary enjoyed the social life immensely, especially as there were more men than women at country town balls. Sometimes they went on by Cobb & Co. coach across the plains to Hay and the Lavenders, other friends of the family, who welcomed them with open arms. The house had bedrooms like shacks dotted around the garden, and on warm evenings couples would wander away from the music and the crowds of parties to stroll in the garden under the trees. Away from home Mary danced, talked and felt at home, and met many pleasant men but none, to her mother's great disappointment, that she wanted to spend her life with. Lucy, on the other hand, regularly returned having become engaged to someone, and just as regularly changed her mind.

Mary had no power to make a life for herself, as the boys were doing. She chafed at her father's reminders that all the family — and this seemed to apply particularly to Elizabeth and the girls — needed to be careful with money, because the boys had to be assured a secure future. Mary was required to work at home without recognition or reward and wait — which she was not good at — for a stake in a system she despised: 'The very thought that I had to please a man to have any place in the world at all disgusted me.' She thought of her mother's sister Polly Palmer — poor Polly, who was dependent on her brothers and sisters. She pictured herself single and alone like Aunt Polly, growing old in her father's house, tolerated by everyone, needed by no-one.

Life in Ballarat for young women of good family was, nevertheless, very pleasant in appearance. There were plenty of social occasions that brought young people together — picnics, walks, race meetings and dances — and a certain lack of restriction compared with the social life of young women in England at that time.

Mary hated her mother's choice of clothes for her. Already plump at sixteen, she was learning that some styles did not look good on her. Her mother insisted on what *she* considered suitable which, strangely, included black satin. Mary would arrive at a function already self-conscious about her clothes, and was further inhibited by the strictures of what to say and not say. She must not talk too much; she must not appear too enthusiastic, or too clever. She had a lively curiosity that made her a pleasant companion who enjoyed good conversation but, hampered by her mother's strictures, she often said very little to dance partners, and felt dull. She returned home from many a social occasion feeling that she was a failure.

Luckily, among the visitors to the Gaunt household around this time was one who would change the outlook for Mary completely. His name was Edward Morris.

…oOo…

Edward Ellis Morris was head of Melbourne's Church of England Grammar School when the Gaunt boys were there. He resigned in 1882 in the face of dwindling enrolments, and began as Professor of Modern Languages and Literatures at The University of Melbourne in January 1884, two years after Mary's studies had come to their ignominious end.

Morris was a keen scholar and an active, outgoing man. He was also an interested and sympathetic listener, shrewd and sensitive enough to pick up Mary's frustration and desire for independence. On a visit to the family, Morris had a suggestion for her. 'Why don't you write?' he asked.

It was a great idea. She had loved writing at school and had done well at it. And she had not forgotten John Victor's words of encouragement, with their hint of future success. On the other hand, the prospect was a daunting one. Many women wrote, and enjoyed it, but few had their work published, and even fewer wrote professionally. She hesitated. Morris said, 'You can write, if you try.'

He suggested that she read an article called 'The Literary Calling and its Future' by James Payn.[2] Payn's view was that writing was a disciplined business, that to succeed one must set about it in a workmanlike way, and that it had little to do with inspiration and the Muse. Mary read the article and was impressed by the philosophy. It was to guide her throughout her writing career.

Morris sent her a book to review. She disagreed with it — and said so plainly in her review. Morris was impressed with her writing style and encouraged her to try for publication. She sent her piece to *The Argus*, but *The Argus* returned it. She then sent it to *The Age*; they accepted and paid her for it.

Elated, Mary wanted to try again. Her brothers were away, seeing interesting unknown places, and it was to their experiences she turned for a subject. At just the right time, her brother Ernest came home from New Guinea. The Australian colonies were interested in New Guinea and so, they knew, was Germany. The colonies urged the British Government to move in and occupy territory there. Britain somewhat reluctantly agreed, on condition that when a British Protectorate was proclaimed, it would be the job of the colonies to administer it.

The newspaper readers of the colonies had more than a political interest in the matter. Vast areas of wilderness were gradually being conquered in Australia and elsewhere in the world. In neighbouring New Guinea — huge, exotic and unknown — one of the last great wildernesses of the world lay waiting.

In 1883, while interest was high, the Melbourne *Age* and the *Sydney*

Morning Herald sent the young George Morrison to explore New Guinea and write about it. Morrison, until recently Mary's fellow student at the university, failing Medicine there while Mary was failing Arts, was famous for his lone walk down the east of Australia from north to south, covering a distance of 3,220 kilometres in 123 days — 'one of the most remarkable of pedestrian achievements', *The Times* called it — and for his observation at first hand of 'blackbirding', the trade in Kanaka labour in North Queensland. He had reported on both of these for *The Age* in the previous year.

Morrison and his party set off from Port Moresby in July 1883. They pushed through the jungle to the peak of the ranges, but in the highlands Morrison and a companion, Lyons, were attacked by natives and Morrison was badly wounded. With extraordinary tenacity — Morrison had lost a lot of blood, Lyons was already suffering with fever, and they had no food for eight days — they limped back to Port Moresby and home, Morrison still carrying part of a spearhead in an abdominal wound. His reports on the trip made headline news around the world.

In 1884, both Germany and Britain moved into New Guinea. Germany proclaimed a protectorate over the north-eastern section and Britain claimed the south-east. As a sub-lieutenant in the British Navy, Ernest Gaunt raised the British flag on New Guinea soil when the official proclamation was made. There were several proclamation ceremonies, but that did not diminish Mary's pride or interest.

Mary set to work to turn Ernest's account of his experiences into a newspaper article and sent it to *The Argus*. It was refused; the paper did not want to consider material from someone they didn't know, whose reliability could be doubtful. She tried *The Age*, and the article was accepted. She was paid five guineas for it, more money than she had ever had at once before.

There is a studio photograph of Mary that commemorates her new status. It appears in the part of her autobiography called 'My Victorian Youth' that was published in *Woman's Magazine Annual* in England in

1938. Mary is wearing a modest, no-nonsense white dress with a dark bow tied under her chin. Above the bow is a frilled collar, like a humbler version of Sir Francis Drake's. The sash around her waist matches her dark bow. Her hair has been carefully done, in short tight curls and piled up high. She is sideways on to the camera, looking to her left, her head cocked a little on one side, a photographer's ploy to reduce the confronting effect of that determined chin. Beside her is a straw boater and in her lap an open book. This is the new Mary, the self-assured Mary — Mary Gaunt the writer. There is a note of triumph in the caption: 'Mary Gaunt after her first article had been taken by *The Age*, February 15th, 1885'.[3]

Chapter 6

Rescue

> As soon as a woman marries…she resigns the pomps and vanities of this wicked world, takes off most of her savage adornments, shaves her head, and ever after, when not quite bald, presents about the upper regions the appearance of a very much worn-down blacking-brush.[1]

Edward Morris was pleased with Mary's success. He had more writing work for her. He had been approached by the publisher Cassell's to prepare a large descriptive work about Australia and New Zealand to commemorate a hundred years since the British flag had been raised at Botany Bay — at the beginning of white settlement. Morris invited Mary to write a piece for it, and liked what she presented him with. By the time *Picturesque Australasia* was published — the four volumes came out between 1887 and 1889 — Mary had contributed nine articles to it, an impressive twelve percent of the text.

The volumes were beautifully produced, bound in red with gilt edgings. Artists were commissioned to provide illustrations for chapter headings and articles; some were created from existing photographs, most were new. There were several full-page, copper-engraved plates in each volume.

In her article 'Gold' — the longest of her contributions — Mary documented dates and discoveries in a business-like way, told of the murder of the German vegetable seller and the Golden Horseshoes legend of Beechworth, and gave a businesslike, if somewhat flattering, account of the anti-Chinese rioting at the Buckland, without naming her father as the hero of the piece. This was writing about a world she knew and understood well, and it was lively, informative and workmanlike. She had all the racial bias of the times: the Chinese miners were low class, inclined towards dirtiness and dishonesty, addicted to opium and likely to introduce leprosy and other Eastern diseases. But she was also aware of injustices; she noted that it was illegal to impose the poll tax of £10 on miners who came from Hong Kong and who were therefore British subjects.

She contributed a ten-page piece called 'Proclaiming a Protectorate' based on Ernest Gaunt's experiences in New Guinea, which appeared in the third volume. In this her tone was sometimes superficial, playful.

In her section on Ballarat, she wrote of Lake Wendouree:

> …thirty years ago the bright little lake was a dismal swamp overgrown with reeds and rushes, and looked on askance by the blacks as the reputed home of the mysterious 'bunyip', and a place where the digger from the canvas township down by the creek might be sure of bagging a black swan or a wild duck for his evening's meal.

This was familiar territory. So, too, was the country around Hay and Deniliquin, which she wrote about in 'Riverina' — the scene of night-time coach trips with Lucy, of happy social occasions, the setting of her short story about the ghostly rider on the lonely road. She also wrote pieces on the Eureka Stockade, Explorers by Sea and two pieces on Explorers by Land, the heroes of her childhood who had risked unknown dangers to open up the continent to further settlement.

In *Picturesque Australasia* she was a young and unknown writer in distinguished company. There was Richard Twopeny, editor of the *Otago Daily Times* and author of *Town Life in Australia*, published four years earlier. There was Hume Nisbet, a Scot who had travelled extensively in Australia in earlier years and was back on a visit in 1886. And there was Joshua Lake, Cambridge-educated art scholar and lexicographer, who had taught with Morris at the Grammar School.

For the Cassell's project, Mary signed herself 'M. Gaunt' — a cautious identification she used for several years that allowed her to claim the stories without disclosing her gender. Also, since Elizabeth begged Mary not to put her name on things she wrote, it avoided upsetting her mother.

…oOo…

For Cassell's, she had guidelines and a topic. It was like doing a piece of writing at university — she assembled the facts and wrote imaginatively about them. But Mary was not one to keep to safe pathways. Writing freelance articles was like setting out with no path, no map, no compass; anything and everything might be possible, any direction might be good — or not. She was determined to try.

Early in 1888, Guy came home with stories about his experiences on the *Worcester*, the Merchant Navy training ship. Guy was a natural storyteller and Mary took in everything he told her. With his help she drafted her next article — about life on a training ship. She took care with its construction, touching on a subject of wide appeal to readers in her opening paragraph:

> Here in the colonies…it seems rather a difficult matter to send a lad to sea. Either he must go as apprentice when he is little better than a ship's boy, or, which is far preferable, he must be sent to one of the training ships in England, in which case he is completely lost to his own colony…[2]

Having got her readers involved, she went on to describe life on the *Worcester* — not as a journalist, but as one of the trainees. Doubtful of the acceptance of such an article with a woman's name on it, she wrote it in the first person and signed it 'The Captain of the Maintop Starboard'.

The article was careful and thorough, written in a lively and entertaining style. A week after its publication, *The Argus* printed a letter from an old sea captain who had been a trainee on the *Worcester* and who had been 'most interested in the graphic account given of her'. He heartily endorsed the need for a training ship for the colony.

After such a success, Mary wrote two more articles based on Guy's stories, and *The Argus* published these also. She called the final one 'Shakings'. Shakings were odds and ends of rope and canvas that were stored on deck, an appropriate name for the bits and pieces of information and anecdote that she included in her piece. She related the story of the first mate on a clipper whose captain refused to change course even when the mate reported breakers ahead. A few warnings, growing more desperate, did nothing but annoy the captain, who sent the mate back for'ard growling:

> 'Mr. Jones, you look after your end of the ship and I'll take charge of mine.'
> A moment later the skipper heard the anchors being let rip, and the ship was brought to with such force as to shake the life out of her. Up came the skipper, mad with rage.
> 'What the _____ do you mean by this, Mr. Jones?'
> 'Well, Sir,' said the mate calmly, 'I don't know what you intend to do about your end of the ship, but mine's anchored!'[3]

So far Mary had been writing factual accounts, researched articles about events and experiences. Now she turned her hand to fiction.

…oOo…

Many colonial newspapers in the 1880s carried serial stories in a pattern modelled on English newspapers of the time — a chapter per issue, often with a cliffhanger at the end of each. With the newspapers in mind, Mary sat down to write her longest story so far — 47,000 words. It was a novella set in the Kiewa valley of north-eastern Victoria, based on the Palmer family station at Dederang.

In the novella, the gold escort from nearby Devil's Elbow is riding south to Melbourne, with the young Commissioner Elliot in charge, when it is waylaid by bushrangers. Attractive Polly Ingram (modelled on Elizabeth Gaunt) lives at Gnarkeet (Dederang) with her two brothers and is in love with the commissioner (modelled on William Gaunt). She nurses him back to health after a near-fatal shooting by the bushrangers.

The commissioner is rewarded for bravery by the government and — of course — marries Polly. The details of the weighing, guarding and carrying of the gold, and the organising of the escort, are precise and thorough. The description of the bush and the birds is that of one who has lived there and loved them:

> Fresh and cool it was up here among the hills with the freshness of early morning, and, as the sun rose up over the ranges, flooding the earth with a golden glory, the whole country side awoke to life. The magpie poured out his melodious hymn of praise, a number of vivid green parakeets flew screaming across the valley into a clump of tall gum trees, a flock of milk-white cockatoos settled with many discordant cries on a small patch of yellow corn…

The story was published as 'Bingley's Gap' in *The Leader*, a weekly published by *The Age*, and appeared from 8 September to 3 November 1888. The story belonged to the sure territory of the Gaunt family stories; the tales of courtship and marriage, gold escorts and diggings camps, of living on the goldfields.

In the next newspaper story — another novella — she relied even more on Gaunt family identity and events. There are two sisters: the elder one, called Mary, is the narrator, and the younger one is the pretty one. It is set in Ballarat and has as its dramatic finale a shooting incident, similar to an incident that occurred in Mary's mother's family. Interestingly, a large section of the plot concerns a buggy accident after a picnic. A young man from England and a young woman companion drive home from a picnic in a buggy. The buggy overturns and the man's ankle is pinned beneath it, and injured so badly that he afterwards walks with a limp. The young woman helps nurse him back to health, and they fall in love.

The story may well be based on William and Elizabeth's courtship. William did in fact have a buggy accident on the way home from a New Year picnic in January of 1858.[4] He was on sick leave from the Goldfields Department for some time and was in Yackandandah for some of that period. His leg never healed completely and he walked with a limp in later life. Elizabeth was living with her mother, sister and two brothers at Dederang, out of Yackandandah; she and William married two years after the accident, in February 1860.

Mary titled her novella *A Man's Sacrifice*, which appeared in the Christmas supplement to *The Illustrated Australian News* in 1888.

Mary followed it with another story of similar length, set on the goldfields of the north-east. It was to see life later as a complete novel, but one section of it — which told a romantic version of the events in history known as the Buckland riots — made a satisfying novella. Commissioner Ruthven, based on William Gaunt again, has had the area of the Packhorse (the Buckland) attached to his area of Deadman's (the Woolshed) and has to travel up there to inspect it once a fortnight. He deals firmly and not a little heroically with the miners who cause trouble, and protects the harmless Chinese, and all is well. He is capable and fearless. 'The Riot at the Packhorse' appeared in serial form in *The Australasian* starting in January 1890.

'A Dilemma', which was published in *The Bulletin* about this time, is also firmly placed in William Gaunt's world. William was intrigued by the egalitarian spirit of the goldfields, and the difference between goldfields society and the formally structured world he had known in England. In the colonies, a rich man might end up a beggar and a man with nothing might rise to the top. It was a theme that was to appear a number of times in Mary's stories, but none more directly than in 'A Dilemma'. It is a story about the meeting of two old friends — one a goldfields commissioner and the other a fugitive with a price on his head. They have a shared past, they come from well-to-do families, and although the old social order is under threat, the old values of loyalty and friendship remain strong. With its themes of enduring mateship and egalitarianism, and its tough bush setting, the story has her father's influence in every line of it.

William arrived in Victoria as gold fever was gripping the colony. It was a young man's world, a world where talent and energy and ability found employment. William was twenty-three when he arrived; the auditor-general of the colony, H. C. E. Childers, was only a year older. His days as goldfields commissioner at the Woolshed, Reid's Creek, Yackandandah and the Buckland, were golden days for William Gaunt. The diggers, the troopers, the population at large trusted him. He did well and met the challenges — and looked back on his time there the way an old man looks back on the best days of his youth.

Long after the Gaunts had left the north-eastern goldfields, and were settled comfortably in Ballarat, it was the stories of the north-east that William told and Mary remembered. Mary the child, Mary the collector of stories, sat in the evenings listening to her father and his friends. He was a stern father, a father to be respected — the boys called him 'sir' — but Mary loved his stories. From the day when Commissioner Ruthven stepped out of his green-baize-lined tent at Deadman's, William's career provided the central character for her fiction for years.

The physical settings for the stories came easily, as Mary loved the Australian landscape. It was not the land of her ancestors, not the landscape of inheritance — she saw it as hers by right of discovery. She loved trees and she loved the bush in its natural state. She had none of the immigrant's urge to change it, tidy it up, that her parents had. It was far more than a convenient backdrop in what she wrote — it was a living presence, and although she lived the second half of her life overseas, her love of it never left her.

She knew the country around north-eastern Victoria particularly well. She had relatives still living there after her parents moved, and she went back and saw it with adult eyes. In her novel *Deadman's*, published 1898, she writes:

> He [Jocelyn Ruthven] looked out of the long French window gloomily. It was July — midwinter — and a dense white fog wrapped the hills that rose up all round them, shutting them in on every side. Through it he saw dimly the outlines of the tall gum trees and the wattles, with just here and there a faint suspicion of golden-yellow breaking the gloom. It was midwinter, but the spring was close at hand; another fortnight, and the wattles would be all in bloom, and the country would be singing to the returning spring…[5]

With every setback in the bush — the petering out of the gold, the Depression in the nineties, drought, bushfires — outback people moved to the coast, and the population in the big cities grew. The colonies were changing fast, and the outback hero was becoming an endangered species. Mary was preserving images of her father's world that were — in the 1880s — alive in the memory of his generation. Her goldfields heroes and villains would live on in her stories and novels.

She was as fiercely proud of her colonial home as any and she saw, more clearly than most, that it was a very male-dominated society. She wrote the women back into the outback, not as shadowy figures in the background, but as central characters — rescuing a husband, defying the bushrangers, hoodwinking a police sergeant. She celebrated their strength and resourcefulness, and their capacity for loyalty, even sometimes in the face of reason and common sense.

Chapter 7

Building a Writing Career

> I want you to be civil to Mr. Davidson, not turn your back on him and leave the room like you did yesterday. It would be such a comfort to me, such a load off my mind, if I knew you were comfortably settled in life…For an unmarried woman, twenty-five is old, and her life is practically over. She can't pick and choose after five-and-twenty, and you'll be that very soon.[1]

Mary kept a detailed diary, recording emotions as well as facts and events, and drew on it sometimes several times over for her stories. It was a useful technique. A few years after the novella 'Miles Dunlop's Mistake' appeared, she incorporated the same gripping detail of a shipwreck in a storm — the bonfire on the beach, the shooting out of a line to the stricken ship, the rescue of the sailors by breeches-buoy — into another story half the length, called 'The Loss of the Vanity'.

Around 1890, Mary went on a memorable three-day trip with Lucy and Guy, who was home on leave, to visit their uncle Tom, Elizabeth's brother. Thomas Palmer had a dairy farm and cheese-making plant at his property, called *Tooram*, just outside Warrnambool. As was the custom, the young people stayed overnight at stations along the way, where they enjoyed the hospitality of strangers. Mary looked back on a curious visit with interest many years later:

> We were three days on the journey making our first break at a station owned by some very pious folk. They were very kindly too and put us

up apparently with pleasure. They would have put us up if they had not been pleased, for it was the custom of the country. I often think now, how surprised I should be if three people drove up in a buggy and asked hospitality for themselves and their horses. But then, nearly fifty years ago, host and guests took it as a matter of course.[2]

The family they stayed with had an amazing house:

It remains in my mind as the untidiest place I have ever seen. There was a wide mantelpiece simply crowded with things that, it seemed to me, should have been anywhere but on a mantelpiece. Papers, bibles, hymnbooks by no means in their first youth, discarded hair ribbons, old slippers, a derelict plate of butter, half a loaf, the handle of a stock whip, an ancient straw hat and a rusty spur were just a few of the things I noticed. Some of them had been there for some time and were likely to remain there but I think the butter and the bread would probably have been cleared away in the course of a day or two.[3]

The family belonged to a strict, fundamentalist religious group. They had adopted five orphans and taken in two widows who would otherwise have been homeless, and they were generous and warm in their hospitality to strangers. At the close of the day, they went down on their knees, and their guests did likewise, for family prayers. The young Gaunts found it very uncomfortable to be prayed over separately. They had grown up with the comfortable anonymity of congregational prayers in the Church of England, and the thought of God's all-seeing eye called down upon them individually by these unusual people was extremely disconcerting. It was an experience not easily forgotten.

From this time on, a new confidence appeared in Mary's writing. In the past she had used the experiences of Ernest and Guy and her parents. Now she began taking adventures and characters that were part of her own life and building them into her writing. She used *Tooram* and its dairying in an article for *The Argus* not long after, and in her novel *Kirkham's Find*. A shooting incident some years before involving her uncle was stitched into the plot of a later story. And, more importantly, the sojourn with the fundamentalist family in their chaotic household became the focus of a book. She was using scraps of her own past to make a new patchwork quilt of her own design.

...oOo...

The Australasian paid £50 for 'Miles Dunlop's Mistake'. It paid another £50 for 'The Riot at the Packhorse'. For a young woman with an allowance of £25 a year, this was encouraging indeed. She was twenty-nine years old. Her first article had appeared in 1885; she had been writing now for four years. She wrote in her bedroom and was often interrupted by her mother to help with household chores. But she had earned £100 with two stories. A writing career now seemed like a real possibility.

There was a confidence, a spirit of striving. Had she not been among the earliest female matriculants and been one of the first at The University of Melbourne? Women were campaigning strongly for the vote and becoming more active in public life; they were working outside the home — some from sheer necessity and some, like Mary, fighting 'respectable' opinion for their own self-esteem. There were women telegraph operators and postmistresses and librarians. The old idea of marriage as the only way to a secure future was breaking down. The census for the following year — 1891 — showed that only 61.7 percent of women in Victoria aged 25 to 29 were married or had been married.[4] So Mary was not alone; being a young single woman was becoming a reasonable option.

When Mary started university in 1881, another radical change in the population was in evidence. The census that year showed that, of the 2,323,000 colonists, just over sixty percent were born in Australia. Her parents and their generation had come from elsewhere; Mary and her brothers and sisters, and sixty percent of the white population, were Australian-born.

Most of the books in the colonies were being published in England, and there was a flourishing market there for stories and articles in magazines and periodicals. Mary felt she needed to go there to make a name for herself. A visit now might improve her chances, give her useful contacts, establish her as a writer. Mary had dreamed for years about travel. Lucy was now engaged and planning to marry in 1890; for an unmarried elder sister, this could be a good time to go.

She went to visit David Watterston, a tall, gaunt, stern, grey-haired and grey-bearded man, the formidable chief at *The Australasian*, to ask for a letter of introduction to their agents in London. She hoped to write for newspapers as well as magazines, and even thought of a career in journalism, as she confided in a magazine interview some years later.[5] Watterston warned her not to expect to travel on the proceeds of writing in London, which was, of course, what she dearly wanted to do.

Nevertheless, she decided to go to England.

Chapter 8

A Voyage 'Home'

I had proved I could earn money and I went on doing it. My mother sighed over it for she was honestly terribly afraid. What on earth would men think of me?...Despite my mother's fears, I was beginning to enjoy myself as I had never in my life done before.[1]

The young woman who boarded the *Ballaarat* alone and sailed for England in February 1890 was one of a breed of colonial women who would make their mark on the 'mother country': she was independent, capable and determined. To her annual income she could add her £100 earnings; she could pay for a modest lifestyle and even afford to travel.

Life on board the *Ballaarat* was the beginning of freedom. Mary had always felt the disapproval of her parents, particularly her mother, very keenly and was often self-conscious and uncomfortable as a result. Now there was no-one to curb her natural enthusiasm and curiosity, and remind her about doing 'the correct thing'. She could — and did — enjoy the social life on board.

The ship stayed in Colombo for two days, giving Mary her first taste of the enchantment of the tropics. At Gibraltar she met Guy, who was serving his final year in the merchant navy, and at Plymouth there was Ernest, both brothers set on the long climb towards admiral status.

Ernest had a beard now, and looked older and more serious. He took Mary by train to London and she stayed with a woman who was a family friend. The moments of social discomfort were not behind her.

> The captain and doctor asked me to lunch on board the *Ballaarat* in the Docks. I accepted this invitation with great pleasure.
>
> Consternation. My hostess was horrified, so horrified she had to send for Ernest [who was now at Greenwich]…in order that he might show me the error of my ways.
>
> 'Don't you see,' said he, 'it looks just as if you were going to see those men.'
>
> 'But, of course! That's exactly what I am going for. You don't suppose I want to see the ship? I know her from stem to stern.'
>
> We were hopelessly at cross purposes. He thought it most improper to go and meet men in that deliberate manner. I thought it the most natural thing in the world. I had done it all my life. Defying the public opinion that surrounded me, I did it once again.[2]

But there were benefits to staying with her London hostess. She took Mary to a good London dressmaker and milliner, and with new and attractive clothes and hats she dressed for social functions with far more confidence.

She went to visit Cecil, now a sergeant in the 13th Hussars, in Edinburgh and Cecil took her to see her first castle. She began to discover that she could love home and love the 'old country' too. She discovered that what was socially unacceptable back in Victoria could be acceptable, even desirable, in Britain: 'People asked me to stay with them and, to my surprise, they carefully mentioned the day they expected me and the day I should go away.'[3] She learned that there were unspoken social rules. When she was out walking with Cecil, his colonel's wife deliberately ignored them and Cecil realised that it was because she had not been introduced; the colonel's wife did not know that Mary was Cecil's sister.

She visited friends of Guy's in Liverpool, her father's sister Mary and others of his family in Staffordshire. She went to Manchester, Wales, Kent and of course to London.

In London she joined the Society of Authors. There were well-known, successful members — Bernard Shaw, Rudyard Kipling and Sir Arthur Conan Doyle — and a considerable number from the colonies — Walter de la Mare, Ada Cambridge, Winifred James and Ethel M. Dell. The Society looked after the interests of authors generally, and was of particular help to those living overseas and dealing with British publishers when they needed to redress grievances and sort out problems involving their rights and incomes.

In London, the secretary at the Society of Authors was, like Watterston, cautious, suggesting that she begin modestly. She settled down to write, and sent out articles to lesser English magazines, but without success. It seemed they were both right — everything she sent out came straight back again.

Then she saw Guy, who told her about a hair-raising trip by torpedo boat across the Atlantic. It had been a dangerous journey in the parent ship and the torpedo boat, two small craft in heavy and dangerous seas. The crossing was a success and Guy was commended by the Admiralty for his efforts. Mary fell back on her tried-and-true formula: she wrote up Guy's adventure as if it were her own.

'Of all the craft that ever I sailed in, the torpedo boat is the worst…' she began. After a graphic description of the voyage, she described the dangers of their approach to the Newfoundland coast:

> On the evening of the second day the fog lifted, and right ahead, far away in the distance, we saw the land faintly marked on the horizon, while close around us were icebergs of all sizes. How near we had been in the fog we could never tell, but they towered up over us looking like great mountains from the deck of our little ship…They were very beautiful, those icebergs, and took all sorts of fantastic forms; some were spotlessly white with a great deep blue ravine down the centre, some had tunnels through them big enough for a far larger ship than ours to pass through, others had sheer precipices down into the water, and others were worked into minarets and towers, spires and mullioned windows, which caught the feeble sunshine till it dazzled our eyes to look at them.[4]

As she had done before, Mary gave herself a suitable pen-name: 'an Officer on Board'. In spite of the advice from the Society of Authors, she sent it to one of the most prestigious publications, *The English Illustrated Magazine*. She signed her letter 'M. Gaunt', hoping her mother was right and that her 'shockingly strong-minded' signature would look like a man's.

The editor, Kinloch Cooke, accepted the article. He wanted to make some minor changes, so he wrote to 'M. Gaunt' with an invitation to call and see him. He was working at home, in his rooms, and set out whisky and soda for his naval officer guest. Mary, who thought of editors as elderly and fierce, found herself in the private apartment of a pleasant man her own age. She got quite a surprise, as did Kinloch Cooke!

Cooke made tea for her and they discussed the changes amicably. He wanted to see more of her work, and took two other stories, 'Christmas Eve at Warwingie' and 'Gentleman Jim — a Story'.

Cooke was very interested in the British Colonies; he had travelled widely throughout the Empire, and had been for some years secretary to the Earl of Dunraven, Under-Secretary of State for the Colonies. He went on to become editor of a number of influential magazines and journals after the *English Illustrated Magazine* — a very useful connection. Cooke had some helpful advice to offer. If she was planning to go back to Australia, she would do well to get an agent in London who would look after her interests. He recommended A. P. Watt to her. Mary took his advice, and her long association with Watt began from that date.

Later in life, Mary reflected that it might have been wise to stay in England then. She was just beginning to make a name for herself at the centre of the publishing world. There had been disappointments — her new novel, *The Other Man*, had been refused by several publishers, but she left the manuscript of it with her new agent. Otherwise, she had made a good start.

She went home, as planned, before the English winter set in. She sailed on the *Massilia* in November 1890. In January 1891, the first of her stories appeared in *The English Illustrated Magazine*, followed in February by the torpedo boat article, which was graphically illustrated — like two friendly messages of farewell. The second story came out in August. In all, eight of her stories appeared in the magazine over five years.

On the voyage home, she stayed a while with friends in Bombay and came across the strange phenomenon of the English official abroad. Her host and hostess lived in magnificent style; they could seat sixty people to dinner, they danced at Government House balls, and her hostess went sailing most afternoons. Yet the hostess and her friends had nothing good to say about the country that provided them with such a luxurious living. In India they had status and wealth; in England or Australia they would have been nobodies. On Christmas Day, when they were singing songs around the piano and someone struck up 'Home Sweet Home', there were tears in more than one pair of eyes. Mary could hardly conceal her amazement.

> I venture to say not one of those people but would have been dismayed if, there and then, they had found themselves transported to the old country — without the salary that came with the 'land of regrets'...They all talked as if they had come from stately and luxurious homes and were putting up with unheard of hardships. The truth, I strongly suspect, was that none of them had ever been so well off in their lives.[5]

It was not confined to India, she was to learn — she saw the same artificial attitude later in other parts of the Empire. She never quite grew accustomed to it.

...oOo...

Back at home, Mary faced her fate rather differently than before. She was easier with her mother now, more mature and confident in herself. Because Mary was plump, her mother had always insisted on dark colours to make her look slimmer. With the help of women friends, Mary was learning that low-cut styles were more becoming for her shape, and she was choosing the light colours she loved and felt good in.

She bought a typewriter. She embarked on a novel — the love story she had heard from her father's old colleague some years before, now translated onto the goldfields. The heroine was Jenny, daughter of the publican at *The Lucky Digger*, who was in love with Black Dave, a miner and a thoroughly bad lot. Jenny, however, was loved by a police trooper.

Elizabeth did not like the idea of Mary writing at all, and found the excerpts she saw and heard, written in bush vernacular, rather vulgar. But Mary kept on; her whole future was at stake. There were still interruptions for household demands, and she had much to learn about writing, but she was loving it.

Because she was serious about earning a living, she continued to write short pieces. During her absence overseas, Edward Morris and a group of academic colleagues had begun *The Australasian Critic*, in October 1890. It was designed to cover an impossibly wide range of topics — botany, science, music, art, literature. Morris invited Mary to review Ada Cambridge's novel *The Three Miss Kings* for the new journal. Mary wrote the review and this time used her first name in her signature: Mary Gaunt. The review was printed in the issue of September 1891, which proved to be the final issue.

Importantly for Mary, though, she met Ada Cambridge:

> From that review started a friendship that lasted her life, a friendship that was no light thing. She showed me that the woman who wrote was not necessarily the awful helpless creature my mother always considered her. This woman was sweet and kind, neat, tidy, and very capable in her household. She was perhaps too sentimental judged by modern standards; but there was always a sweet reasonableness about her that must have made her a godsend to her husband and children…It was well her friendship loomed large in my estimation for it was all I ever did get out of the *Australian* [sic] *Critic* beyond the editor's kindly praise and encouragement. I was not even given the books I reviewed.[6]

Living in her parents' house was not always easy, but there were times when it was convenient. Once, while working on her book, she found herself in an impasse with the plot and could not make any progress. She needed a break, a chance to put the book aside and think about something else for a while. Her mother came to the rescue.

Elizabeth's brother Octavius Palmer had a dairy farm near Warrnambool. Mary was glad to accept an invitation from her Uncle Octavius and Aunt Emily, so she went off for a holiday to the Western District.

> Aunt Emily was in touch, according to my mother, with all the nicest people around her. Which, being interpreted, meant that she had some particularly eligible young man on hand.[7]

Aunt Emily was preparing to introduce her to one of the richest squatters in the district. Mary caught sight of him beforehand, 'walking along with a billy in his hand and his trousers tied with string just under the knees, a most unheroic and commonplace figure.' The man had no hope of making a good impression after that. But the break proved helpful and Mary went home to finish writing her novel.

Chapter 9

Consolidating

Ah, it's thirty years since the men used to ride across the ranges just to stay the night at Yanyilla, and I don't think it was wholly for your grandfather's society they came. Oh yes, I had lovers, like every other girl, but there was only one I cared about — and I cared — I believe I care still, for all I lost him three-and-thirty years ago. I used to look forward to dying and meeting him in heaven, dear, but I was young then, and after I passed thirty, and began to go down hill, I got to know that he'd never recognise in an old woman the girl he loved on earth…He died there in my arms, and at first I could not believe it…what can anyone do, when all the happiness has gone out of one's life. Then I began to grow old, dear, though I was not twenty, and I have been growing old ever They say love doesn't last, but I think they are wrong; I know it has lasted me all these years.[1]

Mary began her career at an auspicious time in Australian writing. Although the number of books being published in the colonies was fairly small, she was part of a wave of writers and artists who were beginning to express the idiom, the ideas, the aspirations of the generation born in Australia. A decade either side of her birth came writers Rosa Praed, Barbara Baynton, Victor Daley, Mary Gilmore, Andrew 'Banjo' Paterson, Henry Lawson, Henry Handel Richardson and Ethel Turner. In the same period, and also pursuing fresh new ideas, came the artists Julian Ashton, Frederick McCubbin, Tom Roberts, John Longstaff, Rupert Bunny, Agnes Goodsir,

Emanuel Phillips Fox, Arthur Streeton, Charles Conder and Ethel Carrick. With Federation in 1901, this was the generation of writers and artists for whom, in their thirties and forties, 'the colonies' became 'Australia'.

For many years the settlers in the bush, the outback and in country towns had been producing campfire songs and bush ballads which told of life in a harsh land. There were typically heroic images of the drovers, stockmen and timber cutters who were slowly taming the interior. Until the 1890s, these rough bush songs had been popular only in the bush; poets and writers were recording them, but they were considered inferior to the literature of England and Europe.

But the situation was changing; the voice of the working man was heard in the strikes of the early 1890s, the generation born in the colonies had grown up and was making a claim to its own literature and ideas. And the voice of the 'larrikin' Aussie, who did not conform to class expectations and had egalitarian ideals, was being heard in the cities and gaining acceptance as an authentic Australian voice.

The Sydney *Bulletin*, under Archibald and then A. G. Stephens, was the single most influential force in the acceptance of the new egalitarian voice in Australian writing. Stephens in particular had an ability to pick original talent; Vance Palmer called him 'the godfather of nearly every significant book issued during the period [of the 1890s]'.[2]

The Bulletin became the voice of bush people. Stories which in the past had featured Englishmen wooing squatters' daughters gave way to the writings of Barcroft Boake, Henry Lawson and Banjo Paterson, and from these emerged the developing images of the bush: the ideas of mateship, of the easy-going colonial cutting through social barriers, the man or woman battling and beating the vastness of the bush and coping with the dangers of heat, bushfires, flood and isolation. *The Bulletin* encouraged the larrikin writers; it was irreverent and racist. And although the image was often romantic and romanticised, it had a distinctly Australian flavour.

Mary's stories of the bush, of life on the diggings, of bushfire and mateship, fitted well with this growing image. Her one story in *The Bulletin*,

'A Dilemma', was set on the goldfields, where friendship triumphed for two men who found themselves on opposite sides of the law. It was mateship on a pedestal, although in this case the loyalty and courage belonged not to a colonial bushman but to an upper-class Englishman. Perhaps the fact that he was working on the goldfields in comparatively rough conditions excused his origins for *The Bulletin*.

As Mary grew in confidence, her stories began to emphasise the right of women to be independent, to have careers and equality. It was because of this she found herself in conflict with the publication; very few women writers shone in the firmament of *The Bulletin's* influence.

The colonies were changing fast: the population of the big cities near the coast was growing. With every setback in the outback — the petering out of the gold, the Depression of the 1890s, droughts, bushfires — outback people moved to the coast, to a very different lifestyle. The outback hero, and heroine, was under threat. *The Bulletin* writers, and Mary, were preserving an image of the world that was very real in the 1880s, alive in the memory of William Gaunt and his generation, but beginning to disappear.

Her story in the Melbourne *Leader* in October 1891 is a powerful statement about one aspect of a woman's life that Mary found hard to bear: the pressure to marry for status and security. In 'The Yanyilla Steeplechase', a woman reflects on her past with her niece, telling how as a young woman she was promised in marriage to a wealthy landowner though she loved the penniless young overseer of his property. The story does nothing for the myth of the likeable bushman — the father and his neighbour are unpleasant, scheming men, and the brutal humour of the one and the ruthless guile of the other bring misery and a lifetime of solitude and regret to the heroine as her lover is destroyed. It is a statement of the powerlessness of young women in such situations — her strongest yet and by no means her last.

...oOo...

William Gaunt was gazetted as a County Court judge in May 1891 and the Gaunt family moved to Melbourne, to a house in Malvern which was then on the outer edge of suburban development. This meant leaving Lucy behind in Ballarat; she had married in October while Mary was away. Only Mary and the two youngest boys, Clive and Lance, were at home to make the move. Clive was studying law at The University of Melbourne in October 1891, and Lance was following in his brothers' footsteps at Melbourne Grammar.

Mary finished writing her novel of the goldfields around Christmas 1892 and sent it off to Edward Arnold, publishers, in London. They liked the book and wrote back, offering to buy the manuscript for £50. She was disappointed. Edward Arnold wrote again, offering a royalty arrangement. It was a difficult decision, as she was unsure of how well the book would sell. Finally she chose the first option and sold the rights of the book for £50 — a fairly generous payment, she learned later, for a new writer's first novel. She hoped that if the book did well Edward Arnold would be keen to take the next one, which she was already writing.

There was some discussion about the title. Mary had called it *Deadman's*, but the publisher did not like the name. On the goldfields, 'Deadman's' was a place name with an interesting past, a lingering reminder of the hardship and heartbreak of the early days. She had used 'Deadman's Creek' already, in 'The Yanyilla Steeplechase'. For the English market, though, 'Deadman's' was not a good name: it had harsh, Wild West connotations. An alternative suggestion, *Black Dave's Girl*, was rejected as misleading, though Mary intended the 'black' of the title to be about morality, not race. There were letters to and from England about the matter. When finally the two black-bound volumes with gilt front covers arrived from Edward Arnold ('publishers to the India Office') and Mary hugged her first book to her at last, it was called *Dave's Sweetheart*.

Chapter 10

Warrnambool and Dr Miller

Our doctor's wife, a young woman of my own age — only a married woman, said my world, is always so much younger than an unmarried one — asked me to go with her to Warrnambool. I was to stay with her mother for the Races. The Autumn Steeplechase there was the great event of the year. The little town would be full of visitors.[1]

When Mary sat down at Mrs Chomley's dining table in Warrnambool she was meeting the charming Dr Miller for the first time, but there existed between them already a web of connections from a town scandal ten years before that entangled the doctor, Mary's uncle, Tom, and her father.

Miller, twenty-four and newly qualified, had been appointed the first Resident Medical Superintendent of the Melbourne Hospital in 1881, only months after arriving in the colony.[2] His brief was to reduce infections in the hospital and cut down the death rate. The hospital, said the Coroner, Dr Youl, 'was a contagious diseases hospital distributing diseases all over Melbourne.'[3] But even after Miller's appointment, the inquests and complaints continued. The hospital was overcrowded and patients with infectious diseases were treated beside the others. Wounds were treated and operations were carried out without modern antiseptic precautions.

Two years into his appointment, Miller resigned. The hospital records gave no reason. The *Australian Medical Journal* said it was because of ill-health. *The Argus* said he should never have been appointed in the first place. Whatever the reason, Miller left the hospital and took up practice in

Warrnambool at a much humbler salary. He served as Honorary Medical Officer at the Warrnambool Hospital until 1889, when he became Paid Medical Officer with a salary of £120 per annum.

One of the first calls on his services in Warrnambool came from Thomas Palmer's dairy. Through a Melbourne agent, Palmer had employed some foreign workers, described variously in the newspapers as coolie, Indian emeute, Afghan, Persian and Hindostanee. Palmer entered them in his records by number rather than name. Twenty-five men of different nationalities and religions who had no family with them and spoke no English were housed in one building on the farm and put to work milking cows. They were apparently led to expect a very different sort of work by the employment agent. There was unrest; Palmer took to sleeping with a loaded revolver by his bedside. On the night of 17 March 1883, a fight started, apparently between Muslims and Hindus, and several men were wounded.

Palmer gave evidence that when he arrived at the shed the Muslim leader, Sirdar Khan, was holding a pitchfork. It was after the evening milking. Palmer's eyesight was poor. There was confusion in the shed. Palmer said that Khan charged at him with the pitchfork raised. Khan's friends disagreed; so did the police sergeant.[4] Palmer fired several shots: one hit Khan in the arm, one in the stomach. The Honorary Medical Officer of the hospital, with the newly arrived Dr Miller, rode the eight miles to *Tooram* with the police sergeant. Khan was in shock and had no pulse. Miller did what he could for him, but Khan died the next day.

For his trial, Palmer retained the services of his brother-in-law William Gaunt and William's colleague Hickman Molesworth. Under cross-examination, he reiterated his claim that Khan was about to attack him with the pitchfork. Miller's medical evidence supported his case — a wound on the back of the right forearm and another further up at the front of the arm were consistent with a bullet having entered an upraised arm from the front. Palmer was acquitted. There was relief in the district that a solid citizen, Justice of the Peace, owner of what a Melbourne paper called 'the greatest dairy farm in Victoria, if not in Australia', had escaped from a deadly peril.[5]

It is unlikely that any of this was discussed at Mrs Chomley's dinner table. Mary had a particular interest in bee-keeping, and Dr Miller had beehives. He invited her over to see them the next day, with Mrs Chomley as chaperone.

…oOo…

The colony was beginning to feel the bite of economic depression. In December 1891, two Melbourne banks failed. Other banks and building societies followed, closing their doors without warning and disappearing with the savings of their customers. Land prices dropped; those with money invested in land went bankrupt, workers lost their jobs and sometimes their homes as well.

The organisations that cared for the less fortunate — the benevolent institutions of Melbourne — became places of interest to newspaper readers because of their vital role in caring for those who had previously cared for themselves. With her novel of the goldfields almost completed, Mary began a series of articles in *The Argus*, taking readers inside the institutions and showing how people were cared for there. First came the Austin Hospital, then the Deaf and Dumb Institution, the Institute for the Blind, and the Women's Hospital. Then she took readers on a tour of the slums of Melbourne with the Melbourne District Nursing Society, an eye-opener for Mary and for middle-class Melbourne. She followed this with a kindergarten, the Little Sisters of the Poor, the Old Colonists' Home, then the Nuns of the Good Shepherd at the Abbotsford Convent.

She was particularly concerned about the plight of women and children, and she found absorbing material at the Abbotsford Convent. She collected figures: 340 'waifs and strays' and 325 'penitents' — 'wayward girls', unmarried mothers, alcoholics, the destitute and the old.

> All the penitents wear a dress provided by the community. It seems, as a rule, to be grey, with a little white linen cap tied under the chin,

and, of course, a big apron…They are all hard at work, the penitents, and over every group is a watchful nun. It would not do that they should get talking together — that they should discuss the life they had led outside these walls. Some of them may have met, probably they have, but they must not speak of it; everything must be forgotten here.[6]

The tone is open, sympathetic to the work of the Convent, but there is a hint of distaste for the conditions imposed on the women and their necessarily tainted children. The nine articles, most of which appeared during 1893, all had a similar tone; Mary is learning about social conditions along with her readers.

She followed these with an *Argus* article called 'A Butter Factory', drawing on her visits to *Tooram*, Thomas Palmer's farm. The article is informative, the tone is pleasant and entertaining, not allowing too much information to clog up a light-hearted narrative:

> Of the internal mechanism of [the cream separators] I must frankly admit I know nothing. It was explained to me, of course, but the big room was full of the crash and whirr of machinery, and I lay the flattering unction to my soul that maybe I did not catch all the explanation, and that was why I did not understand what happened to the milk when it ran down through a pipe from the receivers into the separators to come out again through two different pipes skim milk and cream.[7]

In spite of the rather fey 'helpless female' tone in one spot, she manages to slip in some solid political thought as she reports the comments of a worker in the cheese factory:

> Oh, the cheese and butter factories are a blessin', a blessin',' said a young man, leaning up against the buggy, speaking in the slow speech of the countryman, and rubbing his thumb thoughtfully along the wheel. 'Specially to the women; before they started the women's lives was just wore out, makin' 'em old afore their time. Some men never thinks. Bless you, they don't care, all they wants is the money in their pockets, an' the cheese had got to be made some'ow, an' the women

had got to do it. But a woman's worth as much as a man now, more times than not.

Her next novel was to take up this theme — 'a woman's worth as much as a man now' — and build it into a story close to Mary's heart, and the most autobiographical of all her books. Life for women, for single women in particular, was an absorbing topic for Mary. This was to be a story about a young woman like herself who would achieve what Mary could not achieve — an independent life as a single woman. This heroine would find a way to earn her own living and enjoy the dignity and freedom that went with it; she would not have to marry in order to survive. She would do it by keeping bees.

She began with familiar characters: two sisters, the elder one sensible, restless, not very attractive, and the other pretty and socially successful. There are younger brothers who tease the heroine, Phoebe, about her ambition. There is a stern father who frequently refers to the girls' marriage prospects, a frivolous mother and a future in which there is not enough money to settle the girls in good marriages. It was to be the most autobiographical of all her books.

…oOo…

While Mary was still grappling with the plot, a woman friend invited her to Warrnambool for the races and Mary jumped at the chance. The two women stayed with Mrs Chomley, wife of a prominent bank manager, and Mrs Chomley had an acquaintance who knew about bees. He came to dinner the next day.

Dr Hubert Lindsay Miller was a tall, heavily-built man, a widower whose wife had died eighteen months before. He was pleasant and well-groomed. He was a fairly quiet man, but when he spoke his voice was deep and warm. He had blue eyes and a moustache. He also had twenty-five beehives.

Mrs Chomley went with Mary the next day to visit Miller and the beehives. He had a house on the street front — an ugly house, Mary found it — with a surgery and waiting room attached. But at the side was a large and lovely garden, with roses, fruit trees and beehives. As she made the acquaintance of the bees — 'Don't be afraid. They won't hurt you.'[8] — one of them stung her on the lip. The doctor gave Mary his distraught attention. Mrs Chomley strolled away and left them awhile.

The week in Warrnambool was a breathless week neither would ever forget. On Mary's last evening, they sat in Mrs Chomley's garden and talked until well after midnight and all the other guests had gone home. They were talking seriously about the future. Mary went back to Melbourne; Miller wrote every day.

Hubert Lindsay Miller must have been all that William and Elizabeth could have wanted in a husband for their daughter — he earned £1,000 a year from his medical practice and had an income from investments of another £800, as did his widowed mother. But fate took a hand: at precisely the time when he needed good prospects, he and his mother lost their savings when yet another bank failed. Miller was left with only his medical income of £120 from the hospital, plus fees from his patients, and his mother had nothing. He could not ask her to move out of his house to make room for a bride. And she was not inclined to move out on little or no money and leave the field to Mary.

After a lengthy and difficult impasse, Hubert insisted on setting the date; it was agreed they would marry on 8 August 1894 at St George's Church, Malvern. William, whose share investments were also in trouble, was moody and depressed and did nothing to help with arrangements. Luckily, Lucy was in Melbourne now and took an enthusiastic interest in Mary's plans.

On the big day, William insisted that all the family leave early for church, and when the family carriage came back he handed Mary into it. The town hall clock tower was beside the church, and as they drew close Mary could see that they were half an hour early. She pleaded with her father to turn back. 'We'll just have to go for a drive,' he said and, nervous, irritated and relieved all at once, she agreed. At last they got back to the church, checked that Hubert was there, and went in, and the ceremony began. Hubert was thirty-seven year old and Mary was thirty-three.

The *Warrnambool Standard* described Mary's dress:

> a stylish gown of pale grey covert coating, tailor made in Louis XIV style, with white moire waistcoat and brown colour lace cravat, finished at waist with mother of pearl buckle; Louis XIV hat in grey velvet trimmed with white wings and steel daggers.

Her mother wore black poplin silk.

The ceremony was a quiet one. William gave his daughter away, a woman friend and her daughters scattered flower petals in her path and Guy and Clive signed the register as witnesses. Back at home, as they ate wedding cake and drank champagne with their friends, Guy and Clive enlivened the celebrations with a kind of war dance of delight.

Mary and Hubert went by train to Bright for their honeymoon and returned to Warrnambool to take up residence in the house beside the surgery, with Hubert's mother.

Mary wrote later of her unhappiness at starting her married life with her mother-in-law in the house. It seems that the first marriage had not been a happy one, and his mother put it that Hubert should not desert her 'after she had sacrificed everything to come to him when he was in trouble because he could not live with his first wife'. She had then remained to care for him after his wife's death, thus establishing a claim to precedence. Widowed thirteen years earlier, she was, according to Mary, a clever, manipulative woman. But Mary only ever wrote of her long after Mrs Miller's death, in the autobiography that was never published.

Because of his mother's presence, Mary and Hubert seldom spent time alone together in the evenings, or had a meal alone together. At her first dinner party, the guests ate from Mrs Miller's china, the silver and the table linen was Mrs Miller's and it was Mrs Miller who sat at the head of the table, with Mary to one side. Hubert was grateful that Mary made no fuss and accepted the humiliating role, but she herself wondered later in life if it had been wise to be so submissive.

Mary and Mrs Miller clashed immediately over Mary's forthright views on women and their rights:

> Mrs. Miller, like my mother, held that the place of a woman of our class — daughter, wife, mother — was the hearth. She should be gracefully dependent on the man of the house, entirely subservient. She did not say openly, what was true in her case, that she had ruled her husband and her son by subtler methods.[9]

Mary had escaped one mother's oppressive views only to find herself enmeshed in another's. She disliked being petty, and bickering, and was anxious not to disturb Hubert's peace of mind by quarrelling with his mother, so she was forced very often into humiliating silence:

> I let her rail against the indecency of women being doctors, though why being a doctor was more immodest than being a nurse, who worked harder and earned less, I never could see. I let her take the head of the table and entertain the guests who should have been mine. I refrained from selling my eggs and chickens, when I had succeeded in demonstrating that poultry as a minor industry would pay. I said nothing, though I could never understand why it was to Hubert's credit to sell sixty pound tins of honey at a penny a pound while if I had made money out of my poultry I should have damaged his reputation irretrievably.[10]

A few years later she even taunted Mary when, after a reasonable period of time, she failed to become pregnant; to Mrs Miller it was clearly Mary's fault. There was a loneliness in having another woman in the house, one she could not talk to and whose company she could not enjoy.

When she was able to separate herself from all this, Mary was blissfully happy. She loved Hubert and loved being married. She loved Warrnambool — she loved the tall trees along the beach front, the wide streets, the harbour and the breakwater. She liked to watch the comings and goings of the little steamers that carried passengers to Melbourne and to towns along the coast. She loved the sea and the birds — black swans, pelicans, gulls. She liked to walk along the coast in stormy weather and feel the fierce, cold wind from the Southern Ocean and see great waves flinging themselves onto the shore.

Hubert seemed happy, too. They bought bicycles; Mary loved to ride hers around the town, although — or perhaps because — ladies who rode bicycles were considered by many to be 'forward'. Hubert liked to breed dogs, and they would ride their bicycles down to the sea together to take the dogs for exercise in the mornings.

And Mary loved the big garden. She had learned to make jam from the fruit trees at home in Ballarat, and now she had fruit trees — pear, peach, apple — in a garden of her own. She loved the freedom to keep chickens and look after a household, adding to their larder with jams, preserves and eggs so that, although Hubert's income was much reduced, they could still live comfortably and eat well. Even here there were conflicts with Mrs Miller, whose methods of housekeeping were a good deal less frugal than Mary's.

And Mary was also happy to continue with her writing. Life was busier now and she had no quiet room of her own, but she tried to sit down to write for a few hours each day. After 'The Butter Factory', she wrote about the grape harvest and the wine-making industry for *The Argus*. Slowly — more slowly than she would have wished — her writing progressed. There was even an opportunity to visit the Bakewells in South Australia again, and this time she went on an excursion to Port Vincent on Yorke Peninsula. She went on a five-hour crossing by small steamer one day, back on another one the next, and all the passengers were seasick. Determined to see the salt lakes, she hired a buggy and went out in search of them with the driver as her guide. They came to what looked like water — glittering white crystals of salt, with a few straggly trees, a ruined and abandoned house, and not a bird nor even an insect overhead. As she walked on the salt, the iron in the water seeping up gave her the feeling she was walking in blood. And in the air, unaccountably, was the unmistakeable perfume of sweet briar.

It was a strange and desolate place, not much in demand by visitors, she learned. But it was the only salt lake she had ever seen. She thought of the early explorers who had struggled through desolate country like this — 'it was like a little bit of Australian history placed before me.'[11]

...oOo...

If there was one cloud over her relationship with Hubert, it was that he said almost nothing to her about her writing. It was a disappointment that he took no interest in it, but he allowed her to continue without obstruction and she was grateful for that. When *Kirkham's Find*, her novel of independence, was published in 1897 she wrote at the front: 'To my husband, in loving acknowledgement of the tenderness and sympathy which makes these first days of our married life so happy, I dedicate this book.'

Chapter 11

Publishing and Praise

He tightened the arm around her waist, and then as the mare was sinking, he pushed her into the foaming waters. He caught a glimpse of her white face in the moonlight as she swept past to her death, and there was terror and reproach in it. Then the mare, lightened of her load, sprang forward. The report of a carbine rang out, but the bullet flew wide, and Gentle Dan was free.[1]

Dave's Sweetheart was published in March 1894. The attractive two-volume edition cost twenty-one shillings; and it sold so well that a second edition came out the same month. The critiques were positive. When Mary's mother Elizabeth read the two-column review in the Melbourne *Argus*, she apologised to Mary wholeheartedly and generously for having been critical of her and her writing. *The Australasian* gave a heartening amount of space to its critique of the book. Having affirmed her skills in general — 'Miss Gaunt undeniably possesses in no small degree the art of the storyteller' — and her powers with plot — 'Miss Gaunt has shown herself a literary craftsman of no common order' — the critic makes what must have been for Mary a very perceptive comment: 'The story…is an old one, though the characters and details are in a great measure new.'[2] The London *Daily Telegraph* called it 'one of the most powerful and impressive novels of the year'.[3]

Years later, in an interview in New York's *Strand Magazine* Mary said:

Had I come to England and pushed my way then, I dare say I

should have saved myself a lot of trouble in the future, but the Fates ordained otherwise. I met a tall, good-looking young doctor, and — what were literary aspirations to me? Though critics in London were putting on record that they considered me distinctly promising, I was content, and more than content, to make a home for one man in the little town of Warrnambool…[4]

The £50 payment for *Dave's Sweetheart* was almost half Miller's annual salary at the hospital. Mary was proud of the fact that the income from her writing helped the family budget, and grateful that because of it she never had to ask her husband for money. A further matter of pride was that by the end of the year, two Library of Australian Authors editions of *Dave's Sweetheart* had come out.

In the years after her trip to England she had a number of short stories published, and it was possible to earn more money from them by collecting and publishing them in book form. This became her next project. They were stories of the Australian bush, five of which had appeared in *The English Illustrated Magazine,* among them 'The Yanyilla Steeplechase' and 'Dick Stanesby's Hutkeeper', in which a 'decent' man treats a woman in the outback with casual cruelty. The stories were published by Methuen as *The Moving Finger* in September 1895. Once again, life in the Australian bush was presented for an English readership with, in the same year, an edition for colonial readers.

In her letter to Edward Arnold choosing single payment rather than royalties for the book that became *Dave's Sweetheart*, which she wrote in December 1893, she talked about the next story she was planning to send them. It would be more ambitious than the last, she said.

> The time is the present day — the scene the Western District of this colony and a pious — very pious, I drew them from life — squatter's family — who receive within their doors two ordinary everyday girls and try to make the Lord's own of this unpromising material.[5]

Mary was both fascinated and repelled by the family: she was sceptical of their religious commitment, critical of their missionary endeavours and uncomfortable with their fundamentalism. They were ideal subject matter for a book.

The story she made of them, she said in an interview, she left in England. Perhaps, after its rejection there, she took it back and was reworking it. It is Mary and Lucy on their trip to Warrnambool some years before, appearing as sisters Ruth and Dolly Grant — one mature and thoughtful, the other, a year younger, the prettier of the two. They are living on a very modest income after the death of their parents and have gone to stay with an uncle in the Ballarat area.

There are many other echoes here of Mary's life. In the story, the younger children make a raft and go sailing on a shallow lake on the property and almost drown. There is an assumption that girls who want to work will have passed matriculation. There are men who became friends at Melbourne Church of England Grammar School, and one who has lost his inheritance because he had shares in a company that collapsed during the Depression. And, perhaps the most convincing evidence of recent revision, there is a shy country doctor who finally wins the heroine's hand.

Mary wrote to Edward Arnold that she expected to finish the book by the end of January 1894. No Edward Arnold records exist for that time and Mary did not keep letters; presumably she sent the manuscript and it was rejected. But before the year was out *The Other Man* had been accepted by *The Argus* in Melbourne as the Saturday serial. The story is well-shaped for serialising, with sub-plots, bushfires and secondary romances. The readers wait week by week to find out what happens, and in particular if Ruth, the heroine, will see the light and accept, not the attractive but unreliable admirer but the patient and honourable doctor who loves her. After fourteen episodes, she finds she loves the doctor, and all ends well.

The episodes began appearing in October 1894 and continued through until January the following year. Mary still expected it to be published in book form in England and in fact — typical Mary — said in a newspaper interview for the Sydney *Mail* and the Warrnambool *Echo* in 1898 that this was going to happen, that Methuen would bring it out. It never did.

Nonetheless, Hubert Miller had married not just an enthusiastic amateur scribbler but a successful journalist and a published novelist.

...oOo...

As the Depression of the 1890s bit deeper, Mary turned some of the income-earning possibilities of her heroine into practical advice and began another series for *The Argus* called 'Little Industries for Women'. If women could not go out and get professional jobs, at least they could earn money from home. She researched and wrote the series, with practical down-to-earth information on how to get started, how to sell produce, etc., on a range of money-earning things women might do with little financial investment. The first was poultry farming, one that she knew first hand. Then came the silk industry — a long-term project because the mulberry trees needed to be three years old, though eggs could be bought and the silk cocoons sold for good return. Then came growing mushrooms and asparagus, and then scent farming — growing the flowers and producing the perfume.

Within a year the series was extended to a rather unlikely magazine. *The Tatler* provided theatre and literary news to a readership concerned with the nicer things of life — ladies' colleges, studio photographers, elocution lessons. In this magazine there appeared the article on poultry farming, followed by one on beekeeping:

> The girl who is the owner of a large and thriving apiary, who has thoroughly mastered its management, has in her own hands the means of earning her livelihood in the most delightful and interesting fashion, and need envy no one.[6]

Her friend and confidante, Edward Morris, produced a volume called *Picturesque New Zealand* in 1895, and Mary contributed a piece on Captain Cook and his explorations as they concerned New Zealand. Again she was in distinguished company and she was writing about a topic that was a favourite of hers — the early explorers.

By 1896, Warrnambool was beginning to emerge from the worst effects of the Depression and it celebrated with its Great Exhibition, which was opened by Sir John Madden, Chief Justice of Victoria. Local artists contributed to a beautiful tri-fold screen, destined originally for presentation to Lady Brassey, wife of the pleasure-loving Governor. Brassey's yacht, *The Sunbeam*, visited Warrnambool in 1896 and is featured on the screen. Because of vice-regal protocol, Lady Brassey could not accept the gift.

The delicate wooden screen was decorated on its six panels, front and back, with the work of local artists and writers. Ada Cambridge contributed a poem. Mary wrote a piece about a local scene: a water-colour painting of the mouth of the Hopkins River, one of the beauty spots of Warrnambool, an area that she knew and loved. In an excess of enthusiasm for her subject, and a distinct lack of careful research, she wrote: '…when the snow waters melt among the distant hills where the Hopkins has its source, the river gains the mastery…' But this was not the high country of the north-east where she had grown up, where rivers were snow-fed in the mountains. The Hopkins rose in the dry wheat-belt country of the Wimmera.

…oOo…

In August 1897, *Kirkham's Find*, Mary's manifesto for successful single womanhood, was published in London. The heroine is Phoebe, as close to a self-portrait as Mary ever came in her fiction. Her younger sister Nancy is the more attractive of the two. Stanley, the eldest of their brothers, is not as academically successful as the women students at 'The Shop', as The University of Melbourne was being called even then. Their father is a professional man in Ballarat. Phoebe envies her brothers' educational opportunities and their chance to earn their own living. Faced with living unmarried at home, Phoebe talks with her mother and sister:

> 'What do you want then, Phoebe?' asked her mother.
> 'I want to be able to do without marrying. I want to be somebody, to be something in the world…I really believe I just want to be able to earn my own living.'
> 'What nonsense you talk, Phoebe. You can't do any such thing.

A lady loses caste at once if she attempts anything of the sort.'

'Much that would trouble me if I could only earn £200 a year...I want to earn my own living — to be quite independent. I don't care how little I earn at first, if I can go on improving, like a man. I want to earn enough to be sure of being comfortably off in my old age. To be decently dressed, you know, and be able to travel about a little, and buy books, and have money to give away, and—'

'Anything else?' asked Nancy sarcastically.

'Well, no, that would about do me, I think,' said Phoebe, ignoring the sarcasm. 'If I didn't marry then, it wouldn't matter a bit. I'd be a great deal better off than half the women who marry because they must.'7

Nancy has two admirers, one of them Ned Kirkham, who goes off searching for gold with his cousin Allan Morrison. Allan Morrison is based firmly on George Ernest Morrison, Mary's fellow student at The University of Melbourne, and his larger-than-life exploits. After some remarkable walking feats, including walking from the Gulf of Carpentaria to Melbourne, George Morrison's adventures in New Guinea made headline news.

In Mary's book, Ned Kirkham and Allan Morrison are attacked by natives in Australia's Northern Territory and Morrison is speared. Kirkham cannot pull out the spear, so he cuts off the shaft, leaving the spearhead in the wound. With amazing tenacity they escape, but at last Morrison, who has lost a lot of blood and is in terrible pain, can go no further, and Kirkham goes on alone and brings back help.

After adventures and tribulations, Ned Kirkham realises that it is the practical, independent Phoebe he loves rather than her pretty but rather empty-headed sister. Love triumphs in the end, but only after Phoebe has established herself as an independent woman.

Kirkham's Find did very well. Two printings of the hardback Colonial Library edition, a paperback version, a School Presentation copy and the English edition came out in 1897. It was Mary's most successful book so far.

The *Argus* reviewer was complimentary, but felt that Mary had overdone the plain older sister's plight: 'Most of us will search in vain for a memory of any family in which the homely face of the eldest born, a girl of sterling worth, was the subject of such constant irritating and unnatural comment in the domestic circle.'[8] Her adaptation of Morrison's New Guinea escapade gained approval in a novel where there was considerable emphasis on the domestic: 'The flight from the treacherous blacks...proves that the authoress can describe hair-breadth escapes as well as the placid household life. It is an excellently handled piece of sensationalism.'[9]

The London *Bookman* said it showed 'an increase in strength and vitality [over her earlier books]'.[10] 'A really charming novel,' said the London *Standard*.[11] Overseas and in Melbourne it was received well. In Sydney, there was *The Bulletin*.

On 20 November 1897, the Red Page in *The Bulletin* reviewed three new books by Australian women: Mary's *Kirkham's Find*, Louise Mack's *Teens*, and *Miss Bobbie* by Ethel Turner. For *Miss Bobbie* there was kindly enthusiasm and only the faintest condescension: 'Ethel Turner's *Miss Bobbie* completes her round half-dozen volumes: she will soon need a whole shelf to herself; [it] quite maintains the author's excellent level...*Miss Bobbie* is pleasant and interesting throughout.' For Louise Mack, for whom a bright future was predicted, there was a short and rather dismissive paragraph about her output and how one had to 'admire the lady's industry'. *Teens* lost out in comparison to *Little Women* — 'that permanent standard of girls'-book all-but-perfection' — but nevertheless received considerable praise. Then the reviewer turned to Mary:

> About *Kirkham's Find* there is little to say. The author dribbles commonplaces over a vast number of pages through which lack-lustre characters walk slowly and gossip about nothing in particular. In *Dave's Sweetheart* Mary Gaunt left room for hope that she might become something more than the average fluent female penster. There is dramatic power in that book, and, so far as the women are concerned, a good deal of dramatic insight. But *Dave's Sweetheart* for the most part lacks intensity. The incidents are lost in a flux of flabby words. The author attenuates in ten sentences an impression which a vigorous writer would paint vividly in two. The collection of short

stories called *The Moving Finger* exhibited the same fault without compensating virtue. And *Kirkham's Find* touches the nadir of feeble flatulency. Scenes and people are indeed photographed minutely, with feminine precision; but, as the author's mind has no depth or scope or originality wherewith to glorify them, the whole is only a sorry small-beer chronicle. And the average woman's pre-eminence as a small-beer chronicler was already well established.[12]

It was a damning criticism from an influential paper.

While *The Bulletin* was doing its worst, an interesting opportunity came along for Mary in the form of a book to be reviewed for *The Argus*. She had long had an interest in Africa and this was a book by Rev. J. B. Thomson about the journeys of his brother Joseph, who had sailed down the African coast to the Niger delta, then travelled inland with commercial agreements and monopolies in mind. Companies like the National Africa Company saw German influence in Africa undermining their trade monopoly with inland tribes, and Thomson was doing what he could to bolster British trade interests. The article Mary wrote was little more than a summary of the subject matter of the book[13] but when she came to write about Africa herself some years later this was exactly the area she chose.

…oOo…

Through the years, Mary continued to write short stories. She was as fiercely proud of her colonial home as any and she saw, more clearly than most, that it was a very male-dominated society. In the world of Mary's fiction, the women are not pale figures in the background, but strong central characters. They hoodwink the local police sergeant in 'The Humbling of Sgt Mahone' (1901), they take justice into their own hands in 'Quits' (1898); they are feisty, courageous and extremely loyal, sometimes in the face of reason and common sense, as Gwen in 'Gentle Dan' (1902).[14]

Mary had also been working on another novel of the goldfields. Years before, William had ridden up to the Buckland River area in north-eastern Victoria after anti-Chinese riots there. Mary had made good mileage out of the event. She had used it in her article 'Gold' in *Picturesque Australasia* and she had used it as the setting for a story in *The Australasian* called 'The Riot at the Packhorse', which was serialised from January to March in 1890. It now appeared as a chapter of her novel, with Commissioner Ruthven, based on her father, dealing firmly with an anti-Chinese riot in the Buckland River area. It was a romanticised account but had a ring of authenticity about it. It also had the Commissioner involved in a dalliance with a young woman who is rough and illiterate and who he feels honour bound to marry — a bold, even risky plot device when the Commissioner was based on her father!

A few years earlier, Edward Arnold had not wanted to use *Deadman's* as a title. Methuen had no objection now, and the new book was published as *Deadman's* in September 1898. Two Colonial Library editions came out the same year and there was an American edition in 1899. It was the last book of Mary's to appear for five years.

Chapter 12

Disaster

One day, when Mary and Hubert were exercising the dogs at the beach, there was a frightening incident:

> One of the big Airedales disobeyed his master. To my horror Hubert held him under water till I thought he must drown and, rushing at him, I remonstrated. For a moment he looked at me curiously, then threw poor Rasp onto a ledge of rock where he lay gasping. When he recovered Hubert turned to me and said,
> 'I wouldn't have hurt him, but he must learn to obey.'
> For the moment I was satisfied. But not for long. It seemed to me such a savage thing to do. When we got home he tied him up to a tree, much too tightly, I thought. I gave the dog water and loosened the cord. I also spoke to my mother-in-law, not blaming Hubert, but troubled. She jumped on me.
> 'Hubert couldn't be cruel.'
> I had seen him so often gentle and tender I could not think it either.

But not long after, Mary and Hubert went down to the beach to swim. Mary was not a strong swimmer, but would tackle difficult swims with Hubert because she could put her hand on his shoulder if she was tired. On this occasion, she did not want to go in because the water was quite rough, but Hubert laughed and said she had nothing to fear because he would swim beside her.

> We went in and swam across a great pool, scrambling up on the reef on the sea side. There was a bright sun and a wild wind. The sea was magnificent — also very terrifying. The great waves kept sweeping across the pool, dashing themselves against the cliffs of the shore. I did not like it but was comforted to think that Hubert could get me back.

> He did not try! To my dismay he rose suddenly without saying a word, plunged in again and swam back to the shore. On the rocks on the other side he turned and beckoned to me.
>
> 'Come on,' he shouted. I heard him faintly above the roar of the sea and the wind. 'You can't stay there. Come on. The tide's coming in and the rock'll be covered presently.'
>
> It was true enough. But I was not at all sure I could swim across that pool with the water all foaming and churned up round me. However I had great faith in him. I slid into the water and, terrified as I was, managed to get across and hang on to the rocks just below where he was standing.
>
> I could not get out without his help because the strong undertow was dragging me down beneath the ledge where the rocks were all rough and spiky. Already I could feel them tearing at my skin. I knew I could not hang on there long. But he did not stoop to help me. He stood there laughing as if he found something amusing in my predicament.
>
> I was horrified and helpless. I could not even scream. I just clung there wondering how long I could hold on.
>
> It seemed ages till he stooped and pulled me out. Then he was pitifully sorry for what he had done.

Mary told no-one about what had happened. She had few confidantes, and in any case she did not want people to think Hubert was cruel to her. She hoped that as time went on it would be forgotten. But strange things began to happen.

One day, Hubert, who usually took very little notice of what she wore, bought her an opera cloak. He bought expensive horses they could not afford and did not need. He would have sudden moods of excitement and exhilaration for no apparent reason. He became restless. He sometimes broke into sudden bursts of laughter. One night he got up and began prowling, half-dressed and restless, around the house. He lit all the lamps, then dragged a large kerosene stove from the kitchen into the lounge, assembled all the cushions on the floor to make up a bed and urged Mary to join him there.

In a sad moment of oneness, Mary and her mother-in-law consulted desperately about what they should do. It was Hubert's mother who slipped out to get one of the older doctors in the town. He came, spoke a while with Hubert and persuaded him to go to bed. The next day he consulted with colleagues and gave Mary their verdict. Hubert had GPI — general paralysis of the insane.

Mary persuaded Hubert to go to Melbourne with her by saying that the eminent surgeon Sir Thomas Fitzgerald wanted to see him. Hubert went willingly, believing that Fitzgerald — Melbourne's leading surgeon — wanted to offer him a partnership, an unintentional deception that made Mary feel even worse about their trip. One of the Warrnambool doctors travelled with them. On the railway platform Miller attacked Mary and tried to knock her down, but his colleague managed to calm him down. In Melbourne, they booked into the Grand Hotel, later the Windsor Hotel, on Spring Street. The doctor took Hubert out to see the specialist, and Mary rang her parents' house. Her brother Clive, then a young law student serving articles with Mr Justice Hood, his father's colleague, came to the hotel. Two Collins Street doctors came, separately, and examined Hubert, who was pacing the room, talking erratically, bursting into sudden peals of laughter. The two doctors signed committal forms.

Clive took Mary home to spend the night in Malvern. Her father was in the country, but her mother — her tactless, well-meaning mother — was at home.

The next day, Lance went with her to the hotel and they took Hubert to the Kew Lunatic Asylum, where he was committed suffering from 'delusional insanity'.[1] It was Hubert and Mary's fifth wedding anniversary.

For a while, Hubert was physically well, and continued in the same excitable vein in the asylum. He said he was in the pink of condition, that he could jump, run miles, sing and play the piano, though a month before he could not.[2] A week after admission, he confided to them that he had just won £150,000, and began making plans about giving it away

Mary and Mrs Miller stayed for a time with William and Elizabeth Gaunt. Mary was going to see Hubert three times a week, and after a time the doctors felt he was well enough to go out for the day sometimes. Mary rented a little labourer's cottage not far from the asylum and she and Mrs Miller moved in there. They could bring Hubert there on days out.

Mary tried to keep working; she needed the money now. She put aside the novel she had begun the year before, and wrote articles and short pieces.

As Hubert improved, the doctors encouraged her to think of longer-term plans. She thought about taking him on a holiday — Tasmania, perhaps, or New Zealand, where Lucy was living now. With continued improvement, she booked passage for herself and Hubert and they went to Tasmania. They went to Launceston first, where Hubert was born, and where his father had practised medicine for many years, and then to Hobart. Hubert seemed calm. The sudden illogical outbursts and difficult behaviour seemed to lessen. They went on to New Zealand, but when the ship reached port they were not allowed to disembark because of an outbreak of bubonic plague. As the ship moved along the coast in rough sea, Hubert's mental state deteriorated: in the middle of the night he woke Mary to say they must jump overboard, that it was the captain's orders, and he seemed likely to drag her with him over the rails until in desperation she got the attention of a crew member and got Hubert back inside the cabin. When, after days of delay, the passengers were at last allowed to land, it was agreed that Mary might take Hubert ashore to see a doctor in Dunedin, but that he would not be allowed to stay in New Zealand. She found a kindly doctor who helped her get a return passage and deal with a recalcitrant Hubert, and by the end of the day they were back on board the ship.

Now Hubert was apathetic and silent. He lay on his bunk in the cabin and rarely stirred. They sailed back to Hobart and saw the early snow on Mount Wellington, but went straight on to Melbourne, where Lance met them at the dock. With Lance, Mary took Hubert back to the asylum.

As May lengthened into June, and the days grew dark and cold as winter came on, Mary was forced to accept the inevitable. She went back to Warrnambool to empty out their house and dispose of their belongings. It was a bleak and unhappy time, but the people of Warrnambool were understanding and generous:

> I have met most wonderful kindness on my way through life. Hands have been held out to smooth my path by people who most surely need never have troubled. But even then nothing could outdo the wonderful kindness of that little town of Warrnambool.
>
> …The auctioneer who sold my furniture would take nothing for his trouble. People came and bought, running each other up so that I should have good value for my household treasures, and every one I had ever known, it seemed, came bringing gifts — chiefly of things to be eaten. Sponge cakes and sweets, chickens and jellies, ducks and potted meats, and any amount of eggs, fruit and vegetables. One woman, a patient of my husband's, came forty miles, with a buggy stuffed full of viands, and flung herself on my neck weeping. Now, she said, she knew she would die, for never again would she find a doctor who understood her constitution so thoroughly.

Mary went through Hubert's papers. He was a man who kept every paper that came into his possession, and disposing of them, particularly his letters, was distressing.

> I swore an oath — that I have kept — that I would put every letter, once it was answered, into the fire. No one shall have the pain of going through my correspondence. But I do not think that now I have any one left but those who will smile tolerantly at all my follies. There is no one to be hurt.

Mary wrote this in her seventies. She kept her word; no letters she received have survived.

…oOo…

Back in Melbourne, Mary found board with a family in Princess Street, Kew, to make visiting easy (she had given up the cottage). She visited Hubert every day. The atmosphere of the asylum, and the stories of the inmates and their families, were depressing beyond description. She would go home from the asylum and sit in her room and try to write. She had started a novel about the earliest days of Australia, set in the colony of New South Wales in the days of Flinders and Bass, but she could not manage such a big project now. She kept doggedly at work, continuing to write articles and short stories.

Two poignant stories appeared during the time of Hubert's illness. One — 'And Three is Trumpery' — concerns a pair of young lovers and an older woman who drives them apart. The man is lost in the bush, thirsty and desperate and is slowly losing his mind. Her letter and his rescuer come just in time to save him.[3]

The second story, called 'A Missing Trustee', was published in *The Australasian* in July 1900. It is the story of a young wife concerned about her husband's absence and her frantic efforts to find him — he has been locked in a derelict building by an unscrupulous business colleague. Not prepared to give up, the wife searches frantically for her husband, and at last finds the means to set him free.[4]

It was a time of unease for all the Gaunt family. Their eldest son, Cecil, was fighting alongside the British against the Boers in South Africa, and Ernest, four years Mary's junior, was serving in the British Navy on the China Station. On 21 July 1900, the day 'The Missing Trustee' appeared in *The Australasian*, the Gaunts read the paper first with interest, then with horror at the news of a massacre of Europeans at the Legations in Peking by Boxer rebels:

> There was absolutely no sanctuary for the hapless Europeans. The men, including a few hundred marines, summoned to guard the Legations, could but fight till food and ammunition were exhausted, then devote their last revolver cartridges to slaying the ladies and children who, till a few weeks earlier, had dwelt at Peking in all happiness and fancied security.

In the same issue was news of the death, in the attack on the Peking Legations, of George Ernest Morrison, the man on whose exploits Mary had based those of the hero of *Kirkham's Find*.

Later, the family had word that Morrison was safe. The world learned that it was assumed Morrison had died in the attack, a story which was countermanded in later news bulletins. He was thanked by both the Austrian and German commanders-in-chief for his services during the Rebellion.

…oOo…

During this difficult time, an unusual writing opportunity came along for Mary. Joshua Lake, her fellow contributor to *Picturesque Australasia*, was gathering material for a limited-edition volume to be published as a fundraiser for the Children's Hospital in Melbourne. As Lake explained in the book, 'the Art and Literature of Melbourne' were being invited to donate their services for the project: Queen Victoria sent her picture and her good wishes; Lord Tennyson, Governor of South Australia, contributed a verse by his famous father; the Governor of New South Wales sent a few words; Banjo Paterson wrote a poem; Ada Cambridge contributed a delightful story of a nurse soothing a sick child; Edward Morris and Alexander Sutherland added their contributions.

Mary put in a story called 'The Light on Goat Island'. As a child she had spent holidays in northern Tasmania with her Archer cousins and their parents, Eliza Palmer and John Kinder Archer. Mary set her story on a small island off the north-west coast. It features the children of the lightkeeper, who climb up to the lantern and refill the lamp with kerosene every two hours through the night when their parents are prevented from returning to them. The story was beautifully illustrated by Arthur Boyd. Mary earned no income from the book, but it was good to have the writing opportunity and to be in such a prestigious volume. It was published at the end of 1901.[5]

At the asylum, Hubert was growing listless. The few friends who visited him gave up as bit by bit he gradually became unaware of them and of his surroundings. Mary had a little cocker spaniel, Sue, the last of the dogs Hubert had bred, and used to take her to the asylum each day. Then, unaccountably, she did not want to go near him.

> The only thing that roused him now was his desire to make Sue come and be friends with him and I used to make her go; but in a moment she would creep back to me with her tail between her legs, shivering and terrified.

The last few months dragged on. Hubert began to lose control of his bodily functions. He developed swellings that grew to be weeping sores. As spring came, he grew daily worse and at the end could not get out of bed. Mary watched helplessly as he slid further into dribbling incoherence and physical decay.

In the huge hospital case book where patient details were documented, a warder wrote his account of the final stage:

> The deceased…has been under my care since 8 April 1899. In April last he began to change rapidly for the worse, and some lumps appeared on both hips. Lately they began to break out. They were dressed regularly. During the last week he sank rapidly and died at 1.20 a.m. this morning. His wife was with him daily.[6]

It was 30 October, and the nightmare was over. The doctor who performed the autopsy wrote: 'The cause of death was disease of the brain and spinal cord'. Hubert was forty-three years old.

The painful details of his death were not advertised. The medical journals that had noted his registration, his promotions, his marriages, were silent. Mary put brief notices of his death in the Melbourne *Argus* and the weekly *Australasian*. The Warrnambool papers maintained an eloquent and embarrassed silence. At its regular meeting, the board of the hospital in Warrnambool moved that a letter of condolence be sent to Mary; the motion was supported by colleagues 'who spoke highly of the attention the late Dr Miller bestowed on his patients'.

Mary was numbed. 'I thought that I had lived my life, that no sorrow or gladness could ever touch me keenly again,'[7] she wrote later. She was alone, living in rented rooms, away from the kindly people in Warrnambool who had been her friends for the past five years. She felt responsible for

Hubert's mother, who was now also bereft and without income. William and Elizabeth, who had planned a voyage to England via America, had deferred their trip and, having already given up their house, were waiting in rented accommodation in St Kilda. They made it clear that Mary could go back home and live with them. But when Mary was again able to think clearly, she began to think of other possibilities.

Chapter 13

Days of Turmoil

My advice to any young Australian writer whose talents have been recognized would be to go steerage, stow away, swim and seek London, Yankeeland or Timbuctoo — rather than stay in Australia till his genius turned to gall or beer. Or failing this… to study elementary anatomy…and then shoot himself carefully.[1]

Hubert died intestate. Mary applied for letters of administration to deal with his estate, and swore the required oath that she would 'well and truly collect and administer according to law' what Hubert had left behind, and give an account of it to the Court within three months. She entered into the necessary bond for the value of the estate, and named as sureties Walter Manifold, a Warrnambool grazier, and her father William. The only people entitled to a distribution from the estate were Mary herself and Hubert's widowed mother. His assets were added up — a block of land in Warrnambool, a gold watch and chain, some shares and bonds just returning to somewhere near their original value, and some cash. He was owed a string of small debts, mostly by his patients, and his microscope and medical books were valued at £30. Bills had to be settled, including one to the Master in Lunacy for the balance of Hubert's 'maintenance' for sixty weeks and one day, at twenty-five shillings per week — a total of £75 3s. The total of assets for duty was £2,454.

…oOo…

Mary had a great deal of decision-making to do. Her parents were going overseas, her siblings were now living independent lives. When she began her studies at university she had moved down from Ballarat to a new life in a new place. She had begun a new life again as the wife of a doctor among the kindly people of Warrnambool, leaving Melbourne as a bride and returning a widow. Now she must build a new place for herself in a different world, and she had fewer resources with which to do it.

If she were to live independently, as she preferred to do, she needed an income. She looked for work that would provide a steadier return than writing, and considered clerical work, but William disapproved. She had begun to make a living from her pen — why not continue?

Mrs Miller suggested that they live together. They were both widowed now, and had Hubert as the bond between them. A shared life would help them both to live on their meagre incomes. William and Elizabeth were prepared for her to go back home too. In both cases she felt an obligation. In the end, she chose neither. From the suffering of the past year she had gained at least freedom — she was determined to make the most of it.

The need to earn money was urgent. On 4 December, newly into independent widowhood, Mary went into Melbourne to watch the troops march through the streets on their return from the Boer War. Mary watched as the crowds greeted the men, feeling the excitement and fervour of their welcome, not just because the soldiers were returning safely home but that, as she said, 'for the first time in history, Australia has sent forth her sons, citizen soldiers who are not a class apart but come from the very heart of the people to fight and die for the honour of the Motherland'. Kinloch Cooke, the *English Illustrated Magazine* editor she had startled ten years before, was setting up his own magazine, the *Empire Review*, and invited Mary to contribute. She wrote an article about the soldiers' parade through the streets, and sent it to him.[2]

With the Duke and Duchess of York due to arrive in May 1901 to open the first Federal Parliament, she wrote another article, this one on Melbourne — topical, down-to-earth and entertaining. Having described how the river approaches through dreary flats, factories and workmen's houses, she comments that arriving in Melbourne 'is like being shown into a grand palace by a very untidy back yard'. She calls it Australia's greatest city and speaks of its many impressive buildings, though she is not impressed with all of them:

> It must be confessed that, though spacious and comfortable, Government House is remarkably like a big factory with an ugly tower in the middle; that it is close to town, and that its grounds are very nice, is the most that its warmest admirers can say in its favour.[3]

She also contributed an article, 'Woman in Australia', with emphasis on the independence of Australian women. She discusses the servant problem:

> The average cook cannot cut a sandwich, or make brawn, or dainty cakes or jellies, so the daughters of the house make these preparations and then go to the races and enjoy themselves eating them, and seeing their friends eat them.[4] Many a shirt have I ironed, not because I could not afford to pay for them being done, but because I could not get any one to do them well for love or money.[5]

She mentions the friendliness of the people, particularly of the women:

> Should trouble come to you, friends will rise up on every side. They will give you money, they will weep with you, they will work for you, they will give you anything they have, they will put off the dance or the pic-nic because a deep sorrow has overwhelmed you and yours. It may be that in other countries people are just as kind, but it seems to me some of the hospitality and generosity of the pioneers, that hospitality and generosity that may arise of sheer necessity in a new country, still lingers among the women of Australia, and long may it stay there.[6]

She sent the three pieces to Kinloch Cooke, and all three appeared in the inaugural issue of the magazine — Volume 1, 1901.

When a newspaper article mentioned her planned departure for England, she received an unexpected letter:

A woman on a station in the north-west of the State wrote to me saying that they had always read my stories with keen interest and she hoped that, before I left, I would pay them a visit. Their station was on the Wimmera not far from the Grampians.

Mary went to see the Carters in January 1901, welcoming the diversion. They lived twenty-five miles out of town. At the last moment, when bushfire threatened, a friend urged her to cancel but she went anyway.

> The plains had been covered with mallee scrub; now the ground was one fierce glow. The bigger trees were still standing, each a blazing torch, burning from roots to crown…This was something worth seeing. I might never see such a sight again.

She reached Horsham safely and was met by kindly friends who took her to a bush race meeting, and then a drive in the Grampians over hair-raisingly steep roads. When she could forget about the bad, sad days behind, she enjoyed seeing a new and different aspect of the bush. She spoke of writing an account of the drive in the Grampians for *The Argus*; her hosts, who were educating their children at home and had only English schoolbooks full of daffodil poems and unlikely English adventures, urged her to write something suitable for Australian schoolchildren. Years later, in 1933, *The Golden Story Book for Girls* carried a story by Mary about a young English girl arriving to work on a dairy property in the Wimmera. Perhaps, in the quiet years in Italy, she got out her notes and shaped and polished a story based on her time with the Carters. The Carters would have liked that.

…oOo…

In 1894, Ethel Turner published *Seven Little Australians*. It was a popular success. Like Mary, Ethel had had a story published in *The Bulletin*, which many regarded as a sign of coming success. Ethel's publisher William Steele, on the other hand, urged a trip to England:

> If you are to make money as a writer to any extent, it must be by having many readers among the English millions…A little English

experience would help to (excuse me for so putting it) correct the free and easy, somewhat rowdy associations, due to atmosphere, climate, environment and the influence of *The Bulletin*...[7]

But the very influence that worried Mr Steele favoured the work of other writers. Henry Lawson's *Stories in Prose and Verse*, published by his mother Louisa, came out in 1894, and Banjo Paterson's *The Man from Snowy River* appeared the following year. Lawson's *In the Days when the World was Wide* followed soon after. 'I think we have struck a lucky time,' Paterson wrote to Ethel Turner, 'when…the feeling in favour of Australia is growing.' Even so, getting work published in Australia was not easy; the market was limited and the readership was small. Even the publishing companies with agents in Australia, like Ward Lock, publishers of *Seven Little Australians*, made their publishing decisions in the UK.

It was inevitable that writers in the Australian colonies would be drawn to London; they were, after all, sending their books to London publishers, as Mary was. Henry Lawson, already disillusioned, thought going overseas was the best thing to do. He left home in April 1900 on his second trip and was in England until 1902.

It would be a gamble for Mary to take off on her own — she would need to earn money from writing or starve. Using some of her capital for fares would reduce her already modest income. But Mary was a gambler. She took £100 out of her capital — which dropped the income to £26 — and paid for her passage to England.

When Hubert's affairs were settled and all debts were paid, there was £900 left. She gave this to Mrs Miller.

…oOo…

Now that the awful drama of Hubert's death was over, William and Elizabeth began to talk again about going overseas. Mary urged them to go. She could meet up with them in England. So William and Elizabeth left by ship for America on the first stage of their voyage.

Melbourne *Table Talk*, which carried social and literary gossip, printed an elegant studio portrait of Mary by Vandyck in its March edition, with a brief caption:

> Mrs. Lindsay Miller ("Mary Gaunt"), well-known Victorian novelist, wife of Dr. Lindsay Miller of Warrnambool, who is leaving Australia this month to settle in London, where she will devote herself to literary pursuits.

Clearly no-one at *Table Talk* realised Miller had died five months before.

Mary booked a passage for England via South Africa on the *Runic*, sailing on 15 March 1901. She packed up her belongings, her story ideas and unfinished manuscripts, and wrote farewell notes to her friends. She folded her marriage certificate and put it between the pages of her prayer book, where it stayed for the rest of her life. She was ready to go.

Chapter 14

A 'Dull and Stony Street'

Oh, the hopes of the aspirant for literary fame, and oh, the dreariness and the weariness of life for a woman poor and unknown in London! I lodged in two rooms in a dull and stony street. I had no one to speak to from morning to night, and I wrote and wrote and wrote stories that all came back to me… they were poor stuff, but how could anyone do good work who was sick and miserable, cold and lonely, with all the life crushed out of her by the grey skies and the drizzling rain?[1]

Mary began rebuilding her life in the loneliest place possible — the big city of London.

She wrote a number of times about the bleakness of that first long year in London, but she never spoke publicly or wrote about the main reason for it. She was not a woman to bare her soul to the press. This was not an age when people felt the urge to do that; there was gossip, but rarely confession. She would not tell the world that her husband had died insane. And the world would never hear from her what Hubert's medical colleagues knew, or guessed — that he died of tertiary syphilis.[2]

In an interview seven years later for *The Girl's Own Paper and Woman's Magazine*, Mary made the picture truly grim: 'Life was very, very hard for a beginner in London. I was practically a foreigner, I had no introductions, and I knew no one.'[3] She looked back on the stunning change to her life after Hubert's death: 'In a very few years the home life I had entered into with such gladness was over, my husband was dead, and I was penniless, homeless, and alone.'[4]

Her family and friends may not have agreed. It was the way Mary felt at her blackest times that was to become part of the saga of the aspiring writer moving to London, struggling, nearly giving up, then finally becoming famous and successful. But perhaps it is dangerous to trust writers such as Mary when they write about themselves. They have as generous a capacity for self-deception and as strong an inclination to look back with nostalgia or bitterness as other people, with perhaps a greater need to tell a good story. 'Homeless' meant Mary had given up the house that went with Hubert's practice, 'penniless' meant she had a modest income but no large capital, and 'alone' meant that she was a widow.

At forty, her hopes of happy married life and children were finished. She missed the sunshine and the tall trees of home. She had said goodbye, at least temporarily, to her family, and had left Hubert's mother back in Warrnambool. There were many ghosts behind her.

...oOo...

In 1900, London was the place to visit for Australians travelling overseas — the centre of the social world in the 'old country'. It was the stopping place on 'a trip home', where eager passengers docked after their six-to-eight week voyage on ocean liners. People who had never seen Britain — people who were born in Australia and even people whose *parents* were born in Australia — still spoke of a trip to Britain as 'going home'.

Among the many Australians who 'went home' in 1900 was a group of prominent leaders — Edmund Barton, Charles Kingston, James Dickson and Alfred Deakin — to conduct meetings about the federating of the Australian colonies. They spent three months meeting with the Colonial Office and, on the ship on their way home, got the news that Queen Victoria had given the royal assent to the new Commonwealth of Australia.

In London, artists could find galleries, musicians could find audiences and writers could find publishers. Young Australian artists, singers, musicians, actors and writers went there to pursue their careers and seek their fortunes. The artists Arthur Streeton, John Longstaff, Hugh Ramsay, George Coates, Rupert Bunney, George Lambert, E. Phillips Fox and Charles Conder were all in Britain — or in Britain and France — in 1901, when Mary arrived there. Tom Roberts, having painted the Australian faces for his giant canvas of the opening of the Federal Parliament, was on his way to England to finish the painting there. Nellie Melba, Ada Crossley and Percy Grainger were giving concerts there, and Florence Young had signed a contract with J. C. Williamson and was heading back to Australia on tour.

Writers from the Australian colonies were drawn to London, too. Many of their books were published there. Will Ogilvie was back in Scotland after eleven years in the colonies, and Louise Mack arrived in April 1901, the same month as Mary. The *British Australasian* put the hopeful new arrivals in touch with each other and helped them to settle in.

The *British Australasian* was a weekly newspaper that carried Australian and New Zealand stock prices, news of mining ventures and shipping arrivals, and snippets about colonial people coming, going and entertaining. If Lady Taverner had an 'at home', the *British Australasian* would let people know, to the chagrin of those who had not been invited. If there was a society wedding, the *British Australasian* would tell who was there and the gifts they gave, and now and then, if someone was missed from the list, publish an amendment in the next issue to smooth ruffled feathers. If Ada Crossley was giving a concert, or Percy Grainger a recital, the *British Australasian* would have the details. Like many other visitors, Mary would keep her London acquaintances aware of her doings through the pages of the *British Australasian*.

When she got to London, Mary went to see a family friend who arranged a room for her in a boarding house in Earl's Court Road. The stay was brief, the boarding house depressing. It was full of widows and maiden ladies, the sort she dreaded becoming. 'I have never been able to suffer fools gladly and thought I would be happier in rooms of my own,' she wrote. The friend helped her find rooms in Finborough Road. She was in Kensington, she told the *British Australasian*. Many visitors from Australia went to Kensington — the smart end at SW1, near Hyde Park and Piccadilly, close to the theatres around Leicester Square and the boutiques in Knightsbridge. Mary was in SW10 — too near the Thames to be Earl's Court, too far out to be Chelsea, but — administratively speaking — still within the Royal Borough. Finborough Road had long rows of four-storey Georgian terraces standing shoulder-to-shoulder, toeing the pavement, casting their long shadows across the street and up the facades of the houses opposite. No.17, Mary's house, was on the east side; it had a faded-elegant portico with three Greek columns and a wrought iron balcony above, and the long first-floor windows stretched up to catch the afternoon sun. She moved in just as building began on the Lots Road Power Station, which would serve the London Underground. Within a few years she would see its chimneys jutting up from across the Thames as she was walking home.

This was not a good address, she was told, but she could rent the rooms empty for only ten shillings a week. She shared a kitchen and the services of a daily maid with her landlady, who lived below.

> I was unwise to go to such a bad address even though the rooms were all I could have desired. I was still more unwise to spend £30 on furniture. But I did and began a most miserably lonely life. I have travelled in the interior of China, I have wandered up and down the Gold Coast but never anywhere have I been as utterly miserably alone as I was in 17 Finborough Road, Earls Court...I could not sell a single thing I wrote, and the silence of my rooms nearly drove me distracted.

...oOo...

William and Elizabeth travelled by train across North America. According to the *British Australasian*, the journey had not been dull:

> Judge and Mrs. Gaunt had a sensational experience on their railway journey across the American continent. Near Detroit, a collision occurred and the carriage caught fire. The occupants jumped out into the snow and watched the affair from the safe vantage point of a hillside.[5]

There was a gathering of the Gaunt family in London in the spring of 1901. William and Elizabeth arrived just before Mary. William was on leave from the Melbourne courts. He had family to see; his sister Mary, to whom William made a regular allowance, was living in Staffordshire, and he had cousins in Staffordshire and in Edgbaston in Birmingham. This was his first visit home since he left Staffordshire as a young man of twenty-three. Elizabeth had left as a two year old and remembered nothing of England.

While they were in London they stayed at a hotel near Mary when she arrived, who went to see them and have meals with them. After some time in England visiting family and sightseeing, they took the opportunity to do some travelling in Europe — to the south of France, among other places.

Mary was the next of the family to arrive in London, and the *British Australasian* announced it to the world:

> Mrs. Lindsay Miller, widow of Dr. Miller of Warrnambool, who recently died, has come to England, where she is best known as Mary Gaunt, the writer of several successful stories. She will supervise the forthcoming publication of a novel from her pen now in the hands of Messrs. Methuen and it is expected she will remain at literary work. Mrs. Miller is the daughter of Judge Gaunt of Victoria whose sons in the Navy have already won distinction for themselves.

Always optimistic and sometimes over-confident, Mary was telling the world — or those of it who read the *British Australasian* — that she was to be published by Methuen. Methuen had published her last three books and had no doubt shown an interest in the manuscript she had brought with her. But, according to Mary, 'Australia was entirely out of fashion' and they turned it down. She had nothing further published with them.

The *British Australasian* sometimes got the details wrong. In announcing the arrival of Judge and Mrs Gaunt in May, they mentioned that their daughter, Mrs Lindsay Miller, the popular Australian *vocalist*, had just arrived. They made up for it the next month by reporting: 'Mrs. Lindsay Miller has taken a flat in Kensington and has already commenced literary work.'

Mary had barely settled in when her brother Guy arrived in June, fresh from his exploits in Samoa, for which he was awarded the Distinguished Service Order. Soon afterwards, Ernest arrived; he had been made a Companion of the Order of St Michael and St George (CMG) in recognition of his service in China during the Boxer Rebellion. Louise — known to the family as Louey — Ernest's wife of two years, was a favourite with Mary.

Among the many Australian visitors to London that year was Mr Watterston, the redoubtable editor of the Melbourne *Australasian*, who was escaping the Australian summer. Watterston had published two long stories by Mary years before and in the next year he published six more. The stories might well have gone back to Melbourne in his suitcase.

There was much to see and do in London. Mary enjoyed the theatres, all only a bus or hackney ride away. There were libraries and exhibitions, lectures and shows. In May, there was a 'glittering' farewell for Sir George Sydenham Clarke, the newly-appointed Governor of Victoria. 'Glittering', the *British-Australasian*'s word, was perhaps not the best way to describe it; the women were all in black or half-mourning for Queen Victoria, who died in January. It was nevertheless an important London society occasion, and the Australian colonial sector of London society was well represented. Percy Grainger, at nineteen years old and making a name for himself in London's musical world, was there with his mother. William and Elizabeth Gaunt were there, and Ernest and his wife — and Mary.

So, during her first six months in London — the 1901 summer season — Mary had the company of her parents, two brothers and a sister-in-law, a flat in Kensington and a modest income of £26 a year, just enough to pay for the flat. She began work with her agent, was in touch with the editors Kinloch Cooke and Watterston, and by the end of the year had earned

£62 from her writing. This was the woman who 'knew no-one', who was 'homeless, penniless and alone'!

But the summer ended, visitors went back to Australia, and the chill days of autumn came. Mary faced the disappointment and dreariness of the London winter. She was asthmatic, and didn't like the cold. In the winter, when the sun was low in the sky, very little sunshine came in through the windows at 17 Finborough Road. Mary continued to write stories — stories with English settings — and send them off, but they came back again. She had one story in *Pearson's* in 1901, a story set in the Australian bush. A manuscript she had started in Warrnambool and put aside when Hubert became ill, a story set in Australia, lay neglected in her suitcase.

Building a writing career in England was not easy. It was one thing to *say* she was a writer, to tell the *British Australasian* about her writing plans; it was quite another to get the publishers and editors to make it happen. Louise Mack wrote back to the Sydney *Bulletin* in June 1902 about it:

> Australians…come here to get on. They feel Australia eagerly waiting to hear that they have got on…they rush to the *British Australasian* with pars about themselves…It must be an astounding thing to some Australians to read in the *British Australasian* of their fame, and to find that London continues not to know them, and that their bank accounts continue to decrease.[6]

On the market at that time were novelettes published by Newnes, bound in paper and on sale for one penny. Mary tried her hand at writing one, calling it 'A Sailor's Darling', and almost wept with relief when it was accepted and she was paid fifteen guineas. Now she could tell her parents that she was getting on with her writing work.

William had a year's leave from the Courts, and was considering retiring in England. He had never really approved of Australia; nothing in the colonies had been as good as what he had left behind. But he no longer felt comfortable in Staffordshire, where people seemed behind the times, and he felt lost in a crowd and lacking in influence in London. He and Mary went to look at the New Law Courts in London, having seen the new

Law Courts in Melbourne together a year before:

> He looked upon these Courts with the eye of an interested visitor, but a stranger.
>
> At last he turned and said with a little sigh: 'Well, I don't think they've much to teach us.'
>
> 'Us!' It brought the tears to my eyes. I thought how much happier he would have been could he have held that opinion years before…When the first snow came he went back to his own country — the country he had toiled for and, all unknowing, had learned to love. He never did retire. He had come to Australia to work fifty-one years before and he died in harness, the most ardent Australian of us all.

The cold weather came on as December approached and 1902 drew nearer, and Mary grew anxious. She had articles in the *Empire Review* that helped create the image of a writer, but she had written those before she left Australia and they did little for her confidence about England. £46 6s of her income for that first year was for work published in Australia and only the £15 15s from Newnes was English income. She had said she would pursue her writing career in London, but she was making so little progress. There was a new editor at the *English Illustrated* who was not interested in her work. The new paper, the *Empire Review*, did not pay nearly as well. If she did not earn money to live on, and preferably enough to travel on, she would have to go home to live with her parents again. She cut costs by giving up her share of the housemaid.

Her £26 income was just enough to pay rent. She had spent £30 — more than a year's income — buying furniture, and needed food, paper and stamps. There was a new editor at the *English Illustrated* who was not interested in her work, and what had been a fruitful market shrivelled away. The new paper, the *Empire Review*, did not pay nearly as well. She cut costs by giving up her share of the housemaid.

She got out the manuscript that Methuen had rejected. There were newspaper syndicates that bought stories and serialised them, and Cassell's was one of them. She sent her story there. Cassell's accepted it. It was not really the sort of story they wanted, the manager told her — it was set in Australia, and historical. They wanted modern-day stories set in England. Whether he objected to the fictionalising of historical characters like George Bass, marrying him to a girl in New South Wales in the story when, in real life, he had married before he left England, is not on record. He offered £40; Mary, not normally a bargainer but desperate now, asked for £50. They agreed on £45 and he gave her a cheque on the spot. Cassell's sent 'Mistress Betty Carew' to be serialised in Australian country newspapers: Maldon's *Tarrengower Times* and Heathcote's *McIvor Times and Rodney Advertiser*.

On her trip to England in 1890, Mary had visited the Horsfall family, friends of Guy, who were ship owners in Liverpool. Now they invited her to spend Christmas with them. They were wealthy people, kindly and welcoming, and Mary gained more from her visit than either party anticipated:

> ...here it was again presented to me, the land to which I had resolved to go when I was a little child, and everything in the house spoke to me of it. In the garden under a cedar tree was the great figure-head of an old sailing ship; in the corridor upstairs was the model of a factory, trees, boats, people, houses, all complete; in the rooms were pictures of the rivers and swamps and the hulks where trade was carried on. To their owners these possessions were familiar as household words that meant nothing; to me they reopened a new world of desire or rather an old desire in a new setting.

It was the world of Carlo, the little boy who was shipwrecked on the coast of West Africa and captured by savages, whose story she had read about long ago but never finished. It was the world of explorers and traders and the vast unknown. It was a dark, sinister world, as she learned from the old record book that she found at the Horsfalls. It was a record of the slaves kept on a Jamaican estate: their names, the note of their baptism *en masse*, their parentage. Births were recorded under 'increase', deaths under 'decrease'. A sudden and unusually high 'decrease', she surmised, may have represented an epidemic of some sort. The book did not say. It was a stunning record of pedigree lines, kept in the way people kept records of their animals. 'So, by its own record, is the institution of slavery condemned,' she wrote.

For a long time she had struggled to find a topic to interest the English market — and now there seemed to be an answer. Her first piece of writing about Africa appeared in *The Independent Review*[7] — it was called 'An old record book of slavery'. She wanted to write more about Africa. She wanted to *go* to Africa,

But for now, she was heading back from Liverpool to London, to her life in Finborough Road:

> One gloomy Sunday I went for a walk in the stony streets and Earlscourt is a dismal place to walk in, especially on a Sunday. I dare not spend even pennies on unnecessary buses…I came back…more depressed than ever. As I was mounting the stairs I was met by a small stream of greasy water descending, and I investigated. The kitchen sink was stopped up and the kitchen tap would not turn off. I sat down for a moment too sick at heart even to cry.
>
> I had to go out and seek a policeman to turn off that tap, for I found I was alone in that five storied [sic] house. I have always been afraid of an empty house. The walls have an uncanny way of whispering. I was often alone in it, I found. No words can tell the unutterable misery of those days. There was not a creature in the world who needed me.

At length, when her parents had gone back home, she left the rooms in Finborough Road and went to stay in a little hotel in Polperro in Cornwall, where she could live for twenty-five shillings per week. She sold her furniture at a huge loss — she got £3 for £30 worth — but she succeeded in selling a story set in Warrnambool to *The Sphere* for £8 8s, and left London somewhat heartened. Guy went to stay there with her while he was recuperating from the fever he had picked up in Malta, and his company was a tonic for her spirits. Together they ate pilchards, blackberries and clotted cream. They sat together storytelling in the evenings, and again she made use of Guy's ideas. Her only short story in *Pearson's* in 1902 — 'When the Colt Jammed' — was based on Guy's adventures. They went across to Britanny, where they lived even better for even less. Then Guy went back to the Navy and Mary went back to London, to Bloomsbury this time.

The Horsfall family owned small ships that traded to Italian and Spanish ports, and they offered Mary a passage south. She escaped more than one English winter on the Horsfall ships, usually the only woman on board, sharing the rough meals of the sailors. Thanks to the Horsfalls she could leave behind the cold and damp, and walk in winter sunshine in the streets of Florence and Genoa, and feast on the visual delight of the harbour at Taormino.

Thanks to Mr Watterston, seven of her stories were published in *The Australasian* in 1902, and in July a second edition of *Kirkham's Find* came out. In 1902, she earned £108 in all. The grim days of the 'dull and stony street' were gradually receding.

Chapter 15

The End of the Bleak Years

I could only write adventure stories, and the scene of adventure stories was best laid in savage lands. West Africa was not at all a bad place in which to set them. Its savagery called me.[1]

When Mary was growing up, Africa was a land of mystery for Europeans. In Britain and Europe, discussion and speculation about the source of the Nile had animated clubs and learned societies for years, and explorers' accounts of their travels were bestsellers. The world was reading with interest about 'the dark continent', the label popularised by Henry Morton Stanley, and about the exploits of missionaries like David Livingstone. Mary was ten years old when Stanley had his famous 'Dr Livingstone-I-presume' encounter. William Gaunt and his family, in faraway Australia, were no less fascinated than their cousins in England.

But it was not only the romance of exploration that focused British and European eyes on Africa. The explorers whose names were becoming household words were often at the head of a scramble for territory there. In West Africa alone, in the five-year period leading up to 1884, Britain established settlements along the Niger, the Belgians advanced up the Congo River and Germany was claiming protectorates in Togo and Cameroon, while the French moved inland along the Senegal, Niger and Congo Rivers. The vast natural resources of Africa were gradually being revealed to, and rapidly being exploited by, the outside world.

Travel writing about Africa was changing. At first, European travellers wrote about the coast, because that was almost all they saw. The latter half of the eighteenth century saw an increase of inland exploration, particularly by scientific expeditions. In the nineteenth century, explorers, traders, scientists, missionaries and adventurers set off into the interior of Africa, and a considerable number wrote about their travels. Travellers were eager to tell stay-at-home readers, scientists and government leaders about 'darkest Africa'; the adventurous packaging the mysterious for the curious.

She began to read about Africa. The Royal Colonial Institute in Northumberland Avenue, London, was only an omnibus ride away. There she could listen to lectures by diplomats, civil servants, traders, doctors and nurses, missionaries, adventurers and writers — people of all professions and interests who had been to Africa. The Institute had 'the most complete collection of Colonial literature brought together under one roof.'[2] It also kept newspapers from all over the Empire; like many a homesick colonial, Mary could go there to read the newspapers from home.

Mary loved to read about exploration in Africa. She read about it in her father's books as a child, and sometimes it got her into trouble:

> There was a book…that had a very deep and useful influence on my future life. It helped me in a way that no teaching I can ever remember helped me. It was, too, my first introduction to the world of travel, to other countries beside my own! It told at great length how Captain Speke and Captain Grant discovered the sources of the Nile.
>
> I used to play C scale, which I reckoned I could do mechanically, and prop up a book before me on the music rack.
>
> …
>
> But…that book got me into trouble many a time. It was heavy, and required a hand to keep it on the music rack. Even C scale requires two hands to play it properly. When I was far away with Captain Speke in Uganda or Unyoro, I am afraid often it did not get one.
>
> Presently a voice would call up the stairs: 'Darling, what are you doing? Wasting your time reading, I suppose. Do pay attention to your music.'
>
> My mother never seemed to realise my 'music' was a farce. I

'wasted' more time over it than I ever did over the most silly novel...
my 'music' never taught me anything at all.³

Now, a grown woman and in London, she could read about Africa as she pleased.

One publication she read regularly was *The Empire Review*, because it was a steady market for her. Her article about the soldiers coming back to Melbourne from the Boer War had been in the very first issue. 'Woman in Australia' had been in the second a month later and 'Melbourne' had been in the fourth. She arrived in England in time to read the last one on English soil.

The *Review* began life in a blaze of glory. Of the writers in its first volume of six issues, 45 of the 72 had titles. There were two dukes, two earls, a viscount, two bishops, five lords, eighteen sirs, three honorables, a rear admiral, four colonels, three clergymen, and thirty lesser mortals, listed in alphabetical order. Then came the four women contributors. Mary was second-last, Ada Cambridge was last.

The articles covered a wide range of topics. You could pick up the *Review* on a grey English winter afternoon, when the sun would be down by 4.30pm, and be transported to anywhere in an empire on which the sun never set. True, you might not be interested in military strategy or colonial expansion, but there was lighter fare. There was discussion of cricket reform and the LBW rule and there were Ada Cambridge's memories of her thirty years in Australia. And there was something else that caught Mary's eye.

Its first appearance was in June 1901. It was the beginning of a series of articles about Africa — and it was about the slave trade. The author established his credentials in the first paragraph. He had gained his information 'while accompanying, as a medical officer and naturalist, the expedition to West Central Africa sent out by the Hausa Association of London.' His claim of authenticity was impressive: 'I lived among the natives, shaved my head, wore their dress and adopted their manners and, as I speak their language, had little difficulty in seeing anything I wanted...'⁴

He had been in the huge slave market of Kano, and counted some of the dealers as friends; he knew the trade well. His name was T. J. Tonkin.

The Hausa Association was made up of missionaries, scholars, traders and politicians. Its stated aim was to continue the work of the Rev. Charles Robinson, who had died ten years before while translating the Bible into the Hausa language, and knowledge of the language was clearly a priority for the association. Its other priorities were not made quite so clear.

The articles were lively, graphic and well-written. Mary was intrigued. The Niger delta, the slave market at Kano, tribal rivalries, cruel and colourful customs; it was all familiar territory from the Thomson book she had reviewed five years before.

During 1902 she had two more articles of her own in *The Empire Review*. One was an imagined ending to the escape of two convicts on the coast of New Holland, strong on local colour and history, but fiction — something that had not been part of Kinloch Cooke's original plan. The second was 'Peace Night in London'. Although Melbourne had welcomed its returning troops more than two years before, England was only now celebrating the long drawn-out conclusion to the fighting in South Africa, and there were happy, noisy crowds in the London streets. Her stories continued to appear back at home in *The Australasian* — six in this year. And, thanks to her friends the Horsfalls, she escaped the worst of the winter with another trip to the Mediterranean.

The next year, 1903, began well. She had more fiction in *The Empire Review* in January — a short story called 'The Perils of Lucy Capel'.[5] There is tension and excitement as the young wife of a settler is threatened by blacks while her husband is away; they have set fire to the barn and killed the old manservant. Lucy will be next, but her husband arrives back just in time. It is set in Port Fairy, on the southern Victorian coast, not far from Warrnambool. Mary was finding a market in England for her adventure stories. By year's end she had sold three short stories to *Pearson's* Magazine and a few other small stories to less prestigious publications.

She broke new ground with her serial 'Susan Pennicuick: a story of country life in Victoria',⁶ which appeared in monthly episodes starting in February and continuing all year. Susan Pennicuick is courted by Roger Marsden and they are very much in love. But Marsden is tricked into marriage to an older widow and Susan is sent to cousins in the country, where she has Roger's child. England was less than two years out of the Victorian era, and having a baby outside of marriage raised questions of propriety and morality that must have made Kinloch Cooke hesitate over the story.

In the issue before, and in January of 1903, the articles by T. J. Tonkin started again. Mary came to a decision:

> I was always yearning to write about Africa, more especially about the Guinea Coast, and this seemed to be a heaven sent opportunity. I must still have been very Australian in those days for I wrote to this man asking him if he would collaborate in writing a book, the scene to be laid somewhere on the Guinea Coast. I suggested he should come to town and see me, for he was only in Stoke-on-Trent, which to my Australian eyes did not seem very far away. I felt sure he would come.⁷

Tonkin was interested, intrigued, but he could not leave his practice to come to London. Perhaps Mary would come to see him — and she did.

Thomas Tonkin was thirty-two years old, a doctor, good-looking and single. He was a poet and linguist, with a lively sense of humour, a fascination for the world around him and considerable writing skill. He had written medical articles on leprosy, but that was not all. He had, for example, written an article for *The Otago Times*, with an image of him as the swashbuckling adventurer, rifle over his shoulder, ammunition belt slung around his hips, telling the story of a naïve and unfortunate missionary rescued by the Expedition.⁸ Publishing his adventures in a newspaper in far-off New Zealand was one thing; doing it in England, where his patients might be reading his book in the waiting room, was quite different. He decided on a pen-name.

Tonkin grew up in the village of Ridgwell, in Essex, where his father was the Congregational minister. He took the pen-name of John, the universal man, as in 'John Chinaman' or 'John Company', and added the geography of his childhood — he became John Ridgwell Essex. Early in the twentieth century, the village name acquired an extra 'e' — and so did Tonkin. In 1909, his name appeared as 'John Ridgewell Essex'.

Tonkin never publicly acknowledged his authorship of the books he wrote with Mary. Even when she was writing her autobiography in her seventies,[9] she used only his pen-name when she spoke of him. In his lifetime, and in Mary's, his identity as co-author was never revealed.

Chapter 16

Collaboration

A lover has frequently to lacerate himself with a knife or otherwise inflict bodily injury upon himself, before he can convince his sweetheart of the genuineness of his intentions. 'Of course it is painful,' said an old gentleman who…was explaining to me this delicate matter, 'but the cuts are quite superficial. Do you not do the same?' I told him —No, our people sometimes cut their throats or hanged themselves *after* marriage, but it was not usual during the period of paying attention. 'Ah!' he replied, 'customs differ'.[1]

Dr Thomas Tonkin liked the idea of writing a book set in Africa. The Hausa expedition had been the most exciting, the most dangerous, the most exhilarating time of his life; this was a chance to re-live it. It would make a welcome contrast to his work in the medical practice. Tonkin was working in Hanley, Stoke-on-Trent, 230 kilometres north of London. He arranged lodgings for Mary with two respectable ladies who ran a girls' school not far from Hanley. She would be near Leek, her father's home; she could go to visit her relations on weekends.

Mary went north and settled into her lodgings, and the old magic began again. After years of ups-and-downs and uncertainty, she was writing again — really writing — and it was a full-length book about Africa. She worked hard.

The beginning of the story is pure Mary: a young woman is on a ship going out to Accra to marry Craven, the African doctor she met at home in England. She has a change of heart on the voyage, strongly influenced by Lindsay, the attractive Englishman who is her fellow passenger. There are interesting choices here: Lindsay, her husband's name, is commissioner, her father's title.

Then Tonkin's part comes in. Craven swears revenge, and Lindsay's life is threatened by the secret society of the leopard, whose arm can reach hundreds of miles to exert its secret 'ju-ju' power. There is plot, sub-plot and counter-plot, and much 'boys' own' adventure supplied by Tonkin, until at last the African doctor realises his revenge plan has got out of hand and many lives will be lost. He intervenes to rescue his former fiancé and hand her over to the Englishman she loves. The final drama — of Craven trying to rescue his beloved from cannibal savages and prevent large-scale bloodshed — ensures page-turning excitement to the end.

They finished the story in about four months — a considerable achievement. Mary took the manuscript, which they called *The Arm of the Leopard*, to Grant Richards and it was accepted. They signed their contract — under which no royalties were paid until the first 800 copies were sold — and waited for the book to come out.

The London book trade at that time was a cluster of companies; some shone like bright, constant stars on the horizon, some burned briefly and then faded into oblivion. There were companies on shoestring budgets that became big successes, and brilliant small companies that traded beyond their means and dissolved into bankruptcy.

When Mary and Tonkin placed their book with Grant Richards in 1904, the company appeared to be doing well, numbering George Bernard Shaw among its successful authors. But shortly afterwards, the business got into financial difficulty. When there was no progress, no word, Mary finally went to see them, and found the company's offices in confusion. The business had failed. Some copies of the book had been printed — perhaps a hundred — but the print run had stopped and was not going to resume. No more review copies were sent out, no press releases issued, no launch celebration happened. When Mary asked for the manuscript back the publishers said she could *buy* the printing plates — for £20!

One copy had found its way to London *Punch*. 'The Baron' wrote a glowing review. He called it original and exciting, and recommended it to readers. He talked about the difficulty of putting the 'veneer of civilisation on the savage', and suggested that a leading actor might like to consider dramatising such a 'stirring romance', especially the role of Doctor James Craven, the 'educated nigger'.[2] But if readers wanted to follow his recommendation, there were no books to be had. Apart from the *Punch* review, the book went quietly into the world and disappeared. The whole exercise — their time, the work, Mary moving house — had cost them money and achieved nothing.

Mary went back to London and to the publisher Smith, Elder & Co. Five years before, Mary's agent had sent some of her short stories to Smith, Elder & Co.'s *Cornhill Magazine*. In accepting a story, they had sent back an encouraging note saying that they 'would be glad [to] consider a book from Miss Gaunt's pen if she should think of publishing one'. Well, Miss Gaunt was in need of a publisher now.

She had an interview with Mr Smith, a tall, good-looking man with a kindly manner. Unfortunately, no other publisher would be willing to publish a book that had — in theory, at least — already been published by someone else, he said. He was sympathetic, though, and he liked the book. If there were to be a similar book available, he would be interested.

A similar book — Mary put the proposition to Tonkin. Yes, he was happy to write another one, but he was leaving Hanley and moving to another practice in the south of England. Mary would have to move there as well. She talked about it with Tonkin:

> He discussed the matter with his chief who said that, as he took paying guests, he would be very glad to receive me on reasonable terms, omitting to mention that the paying guests were lunatics.[3]

For all the strangeness of some of the residents, Mary was made very welcome by the doctor's wife and daughter, and was comfortable there. So she passed a lovely English summer working with Tonkin on the second of their books.

Now that they had worked out a writing relationship, the next story came on the heels of the first. The educated African, Craven, appears again;. Lindsay and his friend Durand are again comrades-in-arms, and are joined by James Brooke, a naval officer, in search of a rare African manuscript. They are in Tunis, North Africa, and they head south with a caravan across the Sahara in order to reach Sokoto, in the north of modern-day Nigeria — a route that the Hausa Expedition had considered far too dangerous. What Tonkin could not achieve in real life he could at least achieve in fiction.

Craven is again a fascinating character. The book opens with him addressing a dinner party:

> 'Gentlemen, I feel I must speak to you tonight. When I came back to my country I expected to be treated…well, as you white men do treat us whom you govern — at the most with a polite reserve, that I should have met with a reserve every whit as polite. But you have not done this; you have stretched out a hand to me tonight, almost as if I were one of yourselves, and it is this that opens my lips. I am a plain man. For years I have lived the life of a sham in Europe. Men have pretended that they thought me their equal. I have pretended that I thought I was…It is not me but my mission that you honour. You, Sir,' and he looked at the German Consul, 'are entertaining me because a great German society has given me a commission. You, Sir,' he bowed towards the Governor of the Gold Coast, 'are here because I am subject of your King. Even the mission with which I am entrusted has been given me, not because I am learned in the wisdom of the West, not because of the honours that stand against the name of James Craven in the lists of Cambridge and Heidelberg, but because I am a savage. Learned Europe wants this rare script that is hidden away among the savage hordes of West Africa …'[4]

So Craven and the white men cross Africa to find the rare parchment script, with all the edgy excitement of pursuit by 'the silent ones'. Craven explains to a white missionary:

> 'Do you see that?' he said. 'I used to kick them out of the way, but I'm

getting quite a collection now. That leaf is plucked from a branch that is carried by the party that shadows me. Every time I find one, it is to remind me that I am not forgotten. I tell you, Mr. Wilkinson, the constant finding of these things is sometimes enough to make men of my country go out into the night and seek for the destroyer...'[5]

The missionary, Wilkinson, is made a figure of ignorance and stupidity. He doesn't know the language; he preaches in English: 'It is the word of God, and somehow it will filter through into the darkened minds if the messenger be only earnest enough,' he explains.

When the book was done, Mary went back to London with the manuscript, and sent it to Smith, Elder & Co. Again she had an interview with Mr Smith, courteous and charming as before. He was sorry to disappoint them, but the book was so clearly a sequel to the first one that he couldn't take it. If, however, they were to write another one he might be able to help them.

Mary was almost ready to give up. She was getting short of money and they had earned nothing so far. In the end, though, she put the idea to Tonkin, and he was happy to take on another book.

...oOo...

Tonkin had now left the south of England and was working in Sheffield. Mary moved again. She took lodgings with a kindly woman in Pitsmoort, Sheffield, on the edge of the moors, and again she and Tonkin set to work. The lodgings were pleasant, the work was enjoyable, but funds were getting dangerously low. They were reaching the end of their third book and, while Tonkin had his income as a doctor, Mary was earning nothing. Then, out of the blue came a letter from her father enclosing £25. He felt sure that the collapse of her publisher must have been difficult for her and she might need the money.

She was touched by her father's kindly gesture. He was not a demonstrative parent, but he was clearly concerned, and she was grateful for his help.

It was only weeks afterwards that news came of William's death. He was seventy-five years old, but still active and had been enjoying good health until he caught a chill while conducting sessions in court at Port Fairy in western Victoria, He continued working until his doctor ordered him to rest. But he grew seriously ill, and over the course of a week declined rapidly until his death from heart failure. It was a sad time for Mary to be so far away from home.

William's property was to be held in trust for his children, with Elizabeth living on the income from his estate. Mary received £10 'with which to buy some article of personal adornment which she can wear in remembrance of me'.[6] Her mother packed up the house and set off to travel the world. If there was any remaining temptation for Mary to admit defeat and go back home, this would have put an end to it.

...oOo...

Mary's third book with Tonkin took up the image of the inept and ignorant missionary and turned him into a stupid and dangerous man whose character is often revealed through the eyes of his long-suffering wife. The missionary risks the lives of his wife and another young white woman out of stubbornness and ignorance. The young woman is almost abducted and raped, and finally the missionary himself is killed. The adventures and excitement build, as in the other books, and there is rescue, reconciliation and romance at the end. There is a poignant moment when the missionary's wife discovers she is alone — it is recognisably Mary's voice:

> Mrs. Webley sat down on one of the beds. For the first time since the death of her husband she had time to think; for the first time she had a mind to think with, a mind not burdened with the weight of a horrible fear. She realised she was a widow...The whisper seemed to grow to a shout and she put up her hands to shut it out. What was it to be a widow? She did not seem to be able to feel it. She would wear a black dress and white bands at her neck and wrist and people would lower their voices when they spoke to her of Africa...[7]

When Mary sent the third manuscript off to Smith, Elder & Co., there was a feeling of urgency about it. It was hard to believe the response. This book was 'a marked improvement' on the other two, but 'the shadow of dark-skinned lust lay over it' and it was declined. The authors were asked again if they would consider writing another book.

This time Mary had *really* had enough. She looked around for another publisher. She sent the manuscript to Heinemann, and they accepted it.

Fools Rush In came out in November 1906, with an edition in Heinemann's Colonial Library of Popular Fiction in the same year. Now Mary and Tonkin were in a strange situation. Their first book had been published, but no-one had heard of it. The third was published, and the second one was still waiting in the wings.

Then T. Werner Laurie (TWL) published the second book, *The Silent Ones*, in January 1909. TWL was a new, young publishing venture started five years before when Werner Laurie himself had left another publisher, T. Fisher Unwin, to branch out on his own. His treatment of Mary and Tonkin's book was all that they could wish for. It too had a Colonial edition. Copies were sent to magazines and newspapers; it was reviewed by a swag of prestigious publications, including *The Times*, and the reviews were good. No-one seemed to mind that Dr Craven suddenly reappeared in the final volume after not being involved in Book 2 at all, or that men who had been friends in the early book are meeting for the first time in Book 3.

But sharing the writing meant sharing the royalties. *Fools Rush In*, which had an English and a Colonial Library edition, earned Mary only £15 3s 6d. She was moving house and paying board, and had little time to write other things to earn a living. When work on the books was finished early in 1908, Mary moved back to London and went to live in a small private hotel in Brompton Square — a more fashionable address than Finborough Road. The partnership with Tonkin was over.

...oOo...

When *The Arm of the Leopard*, the first of the trilogy, was published, Mary sent a copy to her sister in Melbourne. She wrote in the front: 'Lucy Archer, with love from one author' and in a different handwriting was added 'and kind regards from the other'. It was obviously not proper for Tonkin to send love as fond as Mary's to a woman he had never met. There was a similar inscription in *Fools Rush In* three years later, but this time it was all in Mary's handwriting: 'Lucy — with much love from one of the authors and kind regards from the other — 29th Nov. 1906.' When *The Silent Ones* appeared just over two years later, the inscription read: 'Lucy, with love from her sister, one of the authors.' Nothing more. Did she write '…one of the authors' in the hope that the other would add his name? The book arrived in Australia with the empty space below Mary's name.

Chapter 17

The Adventure Begins

'You can't go to West Africa,' Lt. Collins said.

'Why not?'

'The British Government is tightening its attitude to free living in Colonial outstations. No woman alone is allowed to land in a British Colony there. I believe two missionary women were deported from Sekondi only last year. You can't possibly go!'[1]

During her early years in London, Mary joined the Lyceum Club. There she met with other professional women in the august clubrooms in Piccadilly, taken over, only a short time before, from the Imperial Service Club — a matter which it was said caused 'a shaking of bald heads and a gloomy rustling of *The Times* along Pall Mall.' Women could sit in the deep leather armchairs to read and talk, as men did in their clubs, or have traditional English tea in the dining room, or listen to lectures.

The Lyceum, which opened in 1904, was supportive of writers, particularly colonial writers. It was a meeting place, a place to make professional contacts, a place to get help. It was also a place where members could entertain friends and colleagues — blurring the boundaries between the professional and the domestic. When Mary wanted to entertain friends, she often invited them to tea at the Lyceum.

A few years after joining, Mary heard at the Club that a representative of the *Chicago Daily News* was looking for a mystery story to serialise in his paper. The length was to be between 50,000 and 150,000 words — full novel length — and there was to be nothing in it that could not be read aloud in a family circle. She hadn't written mystery before, but she was well-acquainted with the serial style. She decided to give it a go.

She spent a large part of 1907 on *The Mummy Moves*. She tailored the story to the specifications required — each episode of 3,500 words, with a 'curtain' to end each one.

A collector of African and Egyptian artefacts is murdered, and after this, and two subsequent murders, the mummy of an Egyptian princess is found, secure in its glass case, with blood on its hands. The plot is complex and clever, and the mystery is finally solved by a bumbling detective who is fond of quoting Latin. The story takes up a theme from the trilogy of books written with Tonkin: that an African might have a Western education but will feel the pull of forces from his homeland — the threat of secret societies and the power of the 'ju-ju'.

The story was set in London. Not long before she began the book, Mary had moved into a flat in Morshead Mansions, not far from the British Museum, so help with things like tribal knives and mummies was close at hand. It was not unusual for her to use her own settings and experiences to construct stories, but this time Mary excelled herself, using her own flat as the scene for a murder, with some of her characters even living in a block of flats called 'Marston' Mansions. It was published in book form in England in 1910, and had a Colonial Library edition and a second impression the same year. Mary asked for £250 for the serial rights. The *Chicago Daily News* offered £225; she accepted. The cheque, when it came, was a huge amount of money for her. The story was later published in book form. With the payment for 'The Love that was better than Gold', a story set in Western Australia which ran as a serial in *The Girl's Own Paper and Woman's Magazine* from March 1908, her income was looking very good. It was a pleasant novelty to think about how she might spend it.

A review of *The Mummy Moves* in the *Boston Transcript* when, years later, it was published in the US in book form, said:

> *The Mummy Moves* may safely be warranted to make a nervous person reading it on a gloomy evening glance sharply in dark corners before he or she goes to bed, and to jump when the wind rattles the window casing.²

This was the story the newspaper said should be suitable for reading aloud in the family circle!

…oOo…

Mary turned next to her plan for a love story — one that was to begin in England and end in West Africa. It would be mostly about what English people were doing in West Africa; if she could go and see the Coast personally, she could provide the setting for herself.

Mary had talked about West Africa, dreamed about West Africa, and written three books about West Africa. Now she determined to *go* to West Africa. She said, in an interview for *The Bookman* in February 1910:

> I wrote a pot-boiler, a mystery story for a big Chicago paper and they paid me well, and I thereupon set off for Africa.' It was, she went on to say, 'four months on the worst coast in the world…³

She went on:

> I…set off for Africa and the material for a novel which I fondly hoped was to bring me fame and fortune [*The Uncounted Cost*, published January 1910].⁴

When she got back to London the *British-Australasian*, which had faithfully printed her press releases, reported that 'her impressions of the West Coast will figure later in a series of articles, etc.' It was three years before she published any articles and she'd had another trip by then.

…oOo…

Lieutenant Robert Muirhead Collins, a retired naval man and an acquaintance of the Gaunt family, was acting as Australian High

Commissioner in London when Mary met him on The Strand one day. She told him of her plan to go to West Africa. She had money for the fare. She was ready to book her passage. There was an awkward pause.

For a long time, British Colonial officials had felt free to have mistresses and to take native women as concubines, as long as it was done fairly discreetly, but attitudes in Britain were changing. During 1908, a number of letters to the major daily newspapers called for change: 'those who represent us abroad should be clean-living men whose conduct may command the respect of the peoples they govern,' said a writer to *The Times*. Another complained of the behaviour of an official in Kenya who was keeping three girls, and demanded that the Government put a stop to the 'demoralising treatment of African women by British officials.'[5] It was not a view shared by the French, who felt that concubinage was 'as desirable for the health and hygiene, discipline and prestige of the French official as it was for his imperial authority and linguistic competence.'[6]

Collins explained the new British Government position to Mary. No woman travelling alone was to be allowed to land. Mary was stunned. What could she do? More to the point, what could Collins do? Collins agreed to speak to someone at the Colonial Office.

While she waited, Mary wrote to Sir Alfred Jones, head of Elder, Dempster & Co., the shipping firm that traded down the West African coast, and was invited to call and see him. She met Jones and several heads of the company, and talked enthusiastically of her plans. They listened, nodded and discussed. Finally, they not only agreed that she should travel to West Africa on one of their ships, they gave her a passage. She left the offices triumphant!

Collins also succeeded in his mission, guaranteeing her to the Colonial Office as a person of good standing. Sir Charles Lucas, head of the Colonial Office, gave her letters of introduction to all the governors along the Guinea Coast.

Now it was April, and in England Spring was coming. In West Africa in April, the mornings and evenings could be wonderful, but the midday heat was fierce. And that was during the good time. By May, when the rainy season set in, rain fell in torrents, dirt roads became impassable, and the air was hot and humid.

> 'No-one, not even black traders, stays up the river during the four months rainy season that begins in May; for most of this land, where the coarse grass grows eight and ten feet high, dense and close…is under water; the river is miles wide, and a very plague of mosquitoes and flies runs riot. The land is left to the natives…till September, when traders go back.[7]
> [Mary, writing after her *second* trip, when she knew better]

But Mary was determined to go. The way was clear. The first of the 'strange roads' that she travelled in her life was opening up before her. At the wrong time of the year, and perhaps for largely the wrong reasons, in April 1908 she left for Africa.

…oOo…

The whole sequence of events was like the beginning of a love affair: the anticipation, the excitement of starting out, the heading into unknown territory, the risk-taking, the uncertain future. It was a gamble, with high stakes. And, like every lover, every gambler, she was not to be dissuaded.

Mary packed her luggage for the trip. Conscious of the letters of introduction she carried, she packed lacy evening gowns, stylish hats, her best and most fashionable clothes. They were not at all suitable for the heat and for travelling. With the exception of one or two more modest cotton outfits, 'my dresses were the last word in discomfort,' she commented later.

She travelled by coastal steamer from Liverpool, edging south from the end-of-winter cold of England into the warm blue Atlantic. Her fellow passengers were going to West Africa because they must, because of their work — and she was amazed to discover that most of them did not want to go. She had boundless curiosity, and in every stop-over port was fascinated by the colour and life, the mixture of peoples, their living conditions, the sense of history everywhere.

She had set foot tentatively on the soil of Africa on her way to England in 1901, when her ship stopped at Cape Town and she watched Australian nurses disembark there to help in the war effort. She felt a certain connection to it; her brother Cecil had been with the British Dragoons fighting in the Boer War. Apart from that brief visit, everything about Africa was new, and it was strange and exciting.

Her first West African port was Bathurst on the Gambia Delta, almost 14 degrees north of the equator. The steamer stayed there for four days. She went on to Sierra Leone, which she found 'the most beautiful spot on all the west coast of Africa.' She was invited to stay at Government House while the steamer was there.

The first settlers in Sierra Leone were slaves that Britain had freed but did not want to house, along with white adventurers, misfits and traders on the make. From the strip of land around the mouth of the river in the original purchase, to a colony 300 kilometres by 400 kilometres across from its northern border with Guinea down to the Liberian border in the south, Sierra Leone had grown to be a multi-cultural colony of over a hundred ethnic groups. 'I know very little about Sierra Leone,' Mary wrote complacently later. But secure in her carrying hammock, she explored the town and promised herself that she would return one day to see it better.

Back on the steamer, she travelled down the shoulder and under the armpit of Africa, where the countries' coasts were labelled by what they produced for the colonial powers: Grain, Ivory, Slave, Gold. The closest she would get to most of the old forts would be a glimpse across the water, because landing from the steamer through the long Atlantic breakers was difficult and often impossible.

She landed at Accra and went to stay with Sir John and Lady Rodger at Christiansborg, the imposing castle on its rocky outcrop bought by Britain from the Danes in 1850. Now the real-life Mary was stepping into her imagined world; she and Tonkin had the two heroes in The Arm of the Leopard staying here. Tonkin had been there and now Mary was seeing it also.

Mary's First Trip to Africa – April to September 1908

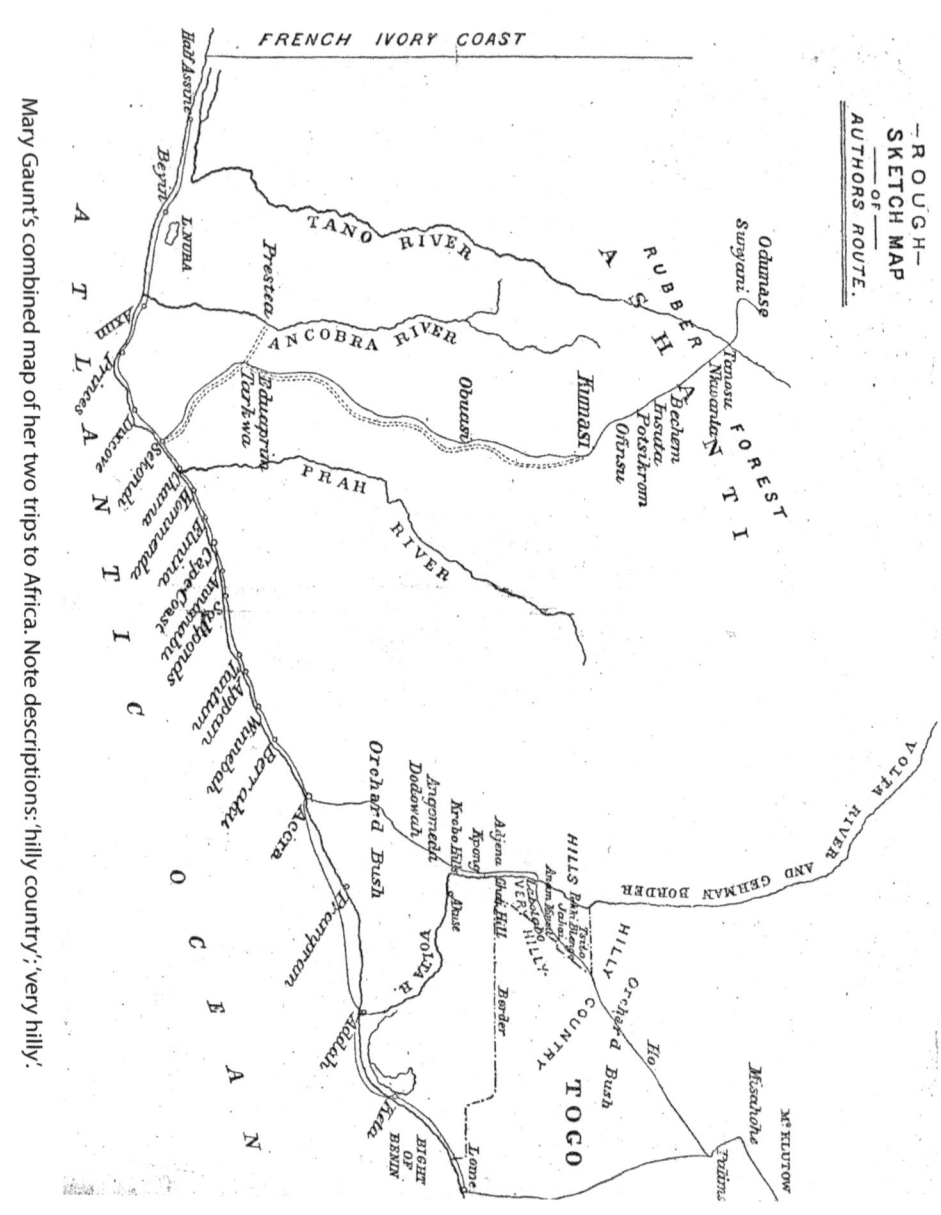

Mary Gaunt's combined map of her two trips to Africa. Note descriptions: 'hilly country'; 'very hilly.'

Mary loved the life of the VIP traveller. After the 'dull and stony street' in London, after life as an outsider, lonely and with little money, she was enjoying Africa from the deck of a steamer and staying in places most visitors would see only from the outside. She was being entertained by people of importance, who were politely interested in her travels. It was an entirely new world.

Travel conditions were often rough. Mary didn't mind that, but she wanted people back in the UK to be aware of the privileged position she enjoyed, that she was the guest of District Commissioners and Governors; that she was treated with courtesy and attention at each port of call. She reported it all in the *British Australasian*. Even in Ibadan, where she had to stay at the rest house, her meals were sent up from the Residence. Her readers and her London friends all knew about her status — Mary told them herself!

At Lagos, she stayed with Sir Ralph Egerton and his wife. Here she had her first opportunity to go inland, when Egerton made arrangements for her to go up country as far as Ibadan, one hundred kilometres inland. On the way, at Abeokuta, she visited a local Bale chieftain, the first white woman he had received, and they solemnly exchanged gifts. On the return trip, in a kind of heavy-duty rickshaw, travelling at a dangerous speed on a rutted and bumpy road, she was bounced out onto the roadway and her arm was badly gashed. Her host, the Resident, was very anxious — although it was only a surface wound, they were concerned about tetanus — and she was taken back to Lagos to be cared for by Lady Egerton. While her arm was healing she made plans about where to go next.

The steamer went on past the vast sprawling delta of the Niger to Calabar, the area Tonkin knew so well and where the adventures of their novels had been set. This was the area, more than any other, that gave the Coast its bad name: it was hot and extremely humid, a difficult climate for Europeans. In the Cameroons she saw slaves, 'hired labourers' they were called, a group of ill-clad men being crowded onto a riverboat, and some of them were in chains. In Calabar she met Mary Slessor, the indomitable

Scotswoman who had laboured for years as a missionary among the rejected children of the area, and was deeply impressed.

As her steamer went on down the coast, the colours on the map changed every few days: pink for the British territory she had just left at Calabar; orange for the German strip of the Cameroons; yellow for Spanish Guinea; mauve for French Equatorial Africa, where she stopped in Libreville, and on to the yellow-green of the Belgian Congo. They crossed the Equator and arrived at the mouth of the Congo at six degrees south latitude, and steamed up river as far as Matadi, starting point for one of Henry Morton Stanley's expeditions. According to the *British Australasian*, Mary went on down the coast to St Paul de Loando, another 300 miles further south, but she wrote nothing about it in her books and articles.

On her return trip northward, she left the steamer and stayed briefly at Cape Coast Castle with the Provincial Commissioner. He arranged for her to go by land along the coast the eight miles to Elmina, where she could pick up the steamer again. She was carried in a hammock: 'I know of no better way of seeing a country than going slowly through it borne on the heads of four men in a hammock,' she wrote.[8] It was also a chance to visit the huge, sprawling castle of Elmina, the greatest of the slave castles along the coast. There was a doctor in charge there who, after dinner, settled her into a pleasant suite of rooms in the castle overlooking the sea. She had a night there she would not forget:

> There descended on me a feeling of helplessness and terror that I could not shake off and could not explain. Sleep was out of the question. There was something brooding in that room, something that took all hope and happiness out of life. It seemed as if it must be threatening me — me personally. All the long dreary night the impalpable thing held me, crushed me with a foreboding that was beyond words terrible, with a fear that held me paralysed on the bed staring wide-eyed at the window space because I was afraid to look round the room, and yet still more afraid because I dared not look.[9]

She learned later that no-one could sleep in those haunted rooms. She did not waste the experience; later, she put her heroine Janey through the same experience in *Every Man's Desire*.

One of the few railways to penetrate inland from the coast started at Sekondi, a prosperous trading town west of Accra. The single railway line, completed five years before, made travel into the interior easy — an opportunity not to be missed. Fifty kilometres inland was Tarkwa, where there were goldmines. Mary knew from her childhood years how mines could scar the countryside and destroy the trees, but she was not prepared for the wide swathe of barren red earth she saw around the Tarkwa mines. The mines had made the town prosperous. She was sobered to learn, though, that the mahogany that had fallen in the path of progress was used as pit props and burned in the locomotives. Trees beside the lines were cut down to prevent them falling across the tracks; the timber was used to fuel the railway engines.

At the terminus of the railway, 270 kilometres inland and an all-day journey, was Kumasi, where the Ashanti queen had besieged the British fort and starved its residents. It was now a peaceful place, resigned to its colonial status. The native shops sold cheap imports from the factories of Europe. Mary was entertained at a dinner party by the Chief Commissioner, although a howling wind that blew through the open windows and sent the crockery and glass flying almost put an end to the evening. On the outskirts of the town, Mary went walking in the forest and found herself totally surrounded by, overwhelmed by, tall trees that shut out the sun. She wanted to explore them further; she wanted to go deeper into the forest, to feel that sensation again.

For her partly-written love story, she needed an African posting for one of her heroes. It could not be a cosmopolitan coastal town; she needed an isolated place in the jungle where the power of the 'ju-ju' could threaten the heroine. Kumasi, surrounded by the magnificent mahogany forests, would do the job nicely.

She loved the forests:

> We know not the meaning of the word forest. England's forests are delightful woods where the deer dwell in peace, where the rabbits scutter through the fern and undergrowth, and where the children may go for a summer's holiday; in Australia are trees close-growing and tall; but in West Africa the forest has a life and being of its own. It is not a thing of yesterday or of ten years back or of fifty years. Those mighty trees that dwarf all other trees in the world have taken hundreds of years to their growth. When a slight young girl came to the throne of England, capturing a nation's chivalry by her youth and innocence, the mahogany and kaku and odoum trees were old and staid monarchs of the forest. When the first of the Georges came over from Hanover, unwelcome, but the nation's last hope, they were young and slim but already tall trees stretching up their crowns to the brilliant sunlight that is above the gloom, and now at last, when the fifth of that name reigns over them, at last is their sanctuary invaded and the seclusion that is theirs shall be theirs no longer. For already the axe is laid to their roots, and through the awe-inspiring forest runs a narrow roadway kept clear by what must be almost superhuman labour, and along that roadway…flows a perpetual stream of traffic, men, women and children…
>
> The spell was upon me the moment I left the town.[10]

But Mary realised she could not see what really mattered from the deck of a coastal trader and the window of a train. She had been able to go inland briefly because officials helped her to get there, but this was not enough.

She wanted to write a book about travelling in Africa. It would have the novelty value of being written by a woman, and a woman from the colonies at that. But she would need to return, properly equipped; she needed land transport to go further into the magnificent mahogany forests, and to get to the castles on the coast. She needed a camera, camping equipment and supplies. She needed introductions to people who could help her move around. She would write her articles and her novel in the meantime, but she wanted to do more; she wanted to write a *travel book* about Africa.

Chapter 18

Writing about Africa

Now a crocodile drifting down in deep water, or lying asleep with its jaws open on a sand-bank in the sun, is a picturesque adornment to the landscape when you are on the deck of a steamer, [but] crocodiles can, and often do…grab at people in small canoes…On one occasion, one…chose to get his front paws over the stern of my canoe, and endeavoured to improve our acquaintance. I had to retire to the bows, to keep the balance right, and fetch him a clip on the snout with a paddle, when he withdrew, and I paddled into the very middle of the lagoon, hoping the water there was too deep for him or any of his friends to repeat the performance.[1]

After a round trip of some 20,000 kilometres, Mary arrived back in London in September 1908 and settled into her flat at Morshead Mansions. But she had not been back long when there was an unfortunate incident there. A drunken stranger who had followed her down the dark street accosted her at the door of the building. In her haste and panic, she couldn't get the door open. She ran her hand down all the doorbells of the building, but there was no-one else in residence — except for a most unlikely stranger on a short stay who appeared at the door and rescued her.

She developed a fear of going into empty buildings; she wanted to live where she could rely on someone else being there. She moved back to the house in Finborough Road where she had been years before. It was a less fashionable area, but she was more confident now. She had the upper half of the house — seven rooms and a bathroom for £10 less than at Paddington Green. She let the rooms on the top floor to a widow with a small boy, and both parties were content.

The Silent Ones came out in January 1909. After the premature death of *The Arm of the Leopard* and the silence that followed the launch of *Fools Rush In* — the Colonial edition had only one review, in *The Australasian* — the reviews of her new book were gratifying. 'Could hardly be improved,' said the *Academy*; 'striking story' said the *Athenaeum*; 'vividly written' said the *Glasgow Herald*; 'racy and highly impressive style' said the *Pall Mall Gazette*. It was a very different reception.

She set to work on her novel. She now had almost all the material she needed to finish it. She had not been able to get to the places that Tonkin had described, that they had used in the joint books; they were inland, away from ports, hard to get to. She set the novel in the area around Sekondi, where she had penetrated farthest into Africa. In their report of where Mary was going, the *British-Australasian* had mistakenly written Lekonde for Sekondi; it was a short step to turn it into 'Lesondi' for her book. Those who knew West Africa or consulted an atlas would recognise Fort Alim for Axim, Obusadi for Obuasi, and so on.

The plot of Mary's Africa novel begins with two young women in Kent. There is Kitty, whose husband is away in West Africa, and who is flirting with Captain Cunningham. And there is her friend Anne Lovat, a writer, serious, a little naïve, who is in love with Dicky Bullen, and who has just received a letter breaking off their engagement. Kitty is very practical about it:

> Let us look the thing straight in the face. You and Dicky Bullen fell in love with one another, as anyone could see, and as the pay of a lieutenant in the navy, even backed by the earnings of a novelist who hopes she is going to rise, would not justify you in openly setting up housekeeping together you decided to postpone the official ceremony.[2]

Anne is humiliated and ashamed. Kitty suggests that she come to West

Africa with her, as the holiday will do her good. Anne refuses at first, but then reconsiders: 'I might write a real adventure story,' she says. 'Mr. Cunningham said there was plenty of material for stories, and perhaps I could do a good book of travel…I think I'll go!'

In West Africa, Kitty and Anne meet up with Cunningham, whose dalliance with Kitty has cost him his naval post and who is now a civil servant on the Mahogany Coast. With Kitty's husband Pearce, they travel up-country to Ashanti territory, where through a series of clever plot manoeuvres they fall prey to African fetish, or 'ju-ju', propounded by a well-spoken native. *The Bookman*'s reviewer said: 'We can only… congratulate [Mary] heartily on her full-length portrait of Kudjo Mensa, otherwise the Rev. John Trotter, M.A., of Balliol College, Oxford, a type of Ashanti who, after taking Orders in the Church of England, returned to his native haunts, went savage, and practised fetish. He is great!'[3]

In an exciting climax, Dicky Bullen saves his friends and finds redemption by coming to a heroic but very nasty end. Cunningham, after a suitable period of exile in West Africa, falls in love with Anne. Anne, true to her first love for a long time, finally realises that life can go on, and the book ends with all four central characters well placed to enjoy life in the future.

Mary was part way through the book when she struck difficulties with the plot. She had a friendly relationship with her publisher Werner Laurie, and she talked to him about it. He suggested that she let his reader look at the manuscript and give Mary her advice. The report from the reader came back: faults listed squarely and the problem identified unerringly. Mary was taken aback, but very much impressed. She wanted to meet the reader. Laurie must have had misgivings about arranging the meeting: 'Wounded writer slays outspoken critic!' But he had no need to be concerned.

Elsie Lang was a small woman, bright and charming. She was talented and well-educated, with remarkable linguistic skills and a wide range of interests. She was working on a translation of Verlaine's poetry, and had already translated *The Book of Fair Women* by Luigina from 16th century

Italian. What was more, she had a professional approach to her craft and a good eye as an editor, and she was kindly and diplomatic. After meeting her, Mary realised that her advice was sound and that she would do well to follow it.

Mary sat down with Elsie's comments and started work again. The book has many touches that reveal Mary's authorship, but one detail in particular reveals the beginning of her friendship with Elsie Lang. As the story opens Anne, the writer, a single woman, goes to visit her married friend Kitty who lives in a cottage in Lettingbourne, Kent, which has a lovely garden. Lettingbourne is an hour by train from London's Victoria Station and the cottage is twenty minutes' walk from the station. In real life Mary, the writer, single again, went to visit her married friend Elsie who lived in Sittingbourne, Kent, an hour from Victoria and twenty minutes' walk from the station, with a lovely garden. Elsie would have smiled at the whimsical touch.

Sometimes Mary's authorship is stamped a little more firmly. The character Anne Lovat speaks about how important her work is for her now that her love affair is over. Mary abandons the voice of the all-seeing narrator to put her own view strongly in the first person:

> In the olden days when we baked and brewed and spun and wove at home, the woman who directed and those who carried out her directions were part of a community which could not do without them, and the feeling that they were essential to the well-being of those around them lent to womanhood a dignity which the rapid advance of machinery in the early Victorian days threatened to undermine. [With their skills no longer needed, women] fought an uphill fight against the theory that a make-believe work was all that was required of a woman, that idle feminine hands, idle feminine lives, were the ideal; and with the new century the change has come.
>
> The unfortunate women — and there are thousands of them in England — who lead careful, guarded home lives are being left to die in lonely, grey, unwanted maidenhood. The prophet of old was wrong — there is a new thing under the sun. It is the women who go out and work, and add to the wealth of the community, who marry and bear children.

> Even if they do not marry, their gain is great. Anne felt this now. True she had gambled with her life as she would never have dared to gamble under the old régime, and she had lost. Love was so much that the world was grey and cold without it, but she had her work, and her work had given her power, and power is by no means to be despised.[4]

Mary called her book *The Uncounted Cost* — a title that resonates in the relationships of her characters.

The details about Africa had had to wait until she went there. Later, when she was writing about her travels, she gave the most casually — if not cruelly — dismissive explanation of how she came to get the authentic African content for her books:

> Looking back, I smile when I think of the difficulties that lay in my path. Even after I had carefully read every book of travel I could lay my hands on, I was still in deepest ignorance, because every traveller left so much undescribed and told nothing of the thousand and one little trifles that make ignorant eyes see the life that is so different from that in a civilised land. But if you will only look for a thing it is astonishing how you will find it, often in the most unlikely places; if you set your heart on something it is astonishing how often you will get your heart's desire. I sought for information about West Africa and I found it, not easily; every story I wrote cost me a world of trouble and research and anxiety, and I fear me the friends I was beginning to make a world of trouble too. But they were kind and long-suffering; this man gave me a little information here, that one there, and I can laugh now when I think of the scenes that had to be written and rewritten before a hammock could be taken a couple of miles, before a man could sit down to his early-morning tea in the bush. It took years to do it, but at last it was done to some purpose; the book I had written with great effort caught on.[5]

She had moved house three times to be near where Tonkin was working, to write with him. His name — his pen-name, Essex — was on the covers of their three books; it was in the British Library catalogue with Mary's, in reviews of their joint work. Now he was ignored and Mary was triumphant, alone, writing about Africa.

When *The Uncounted Cost* came out in January 1910, the *Athenaeum* critic said: 'The writer's powers are considerable, as is her knowledge of the Mahogany Coast and its people'.[6] Mary must have been pleased about that.

She knew well that the book would be controversial. 'I submitted it to a literary lady, a clergyman of the Church of England, a naval expert, and to two West Coast officials', she wrote when defending it later. These would have included Elsie Lang, Elsie's husband Rev. Lewis Lang, who was also a writer, and one of Mary's brothers — probably Guy or Ernest. They all liked it. So did her publisher. But this was, of course, no guarantee of what the public reaction would be.

She took the novel to Werner Laurie. It was time for a break. Her brother Guy had married five years before in Hong Kong and since then his wife, Margaret, and Mary had become firm friends. When her lectures were over, and her novel was safely in the hands of her publisher, Mary and Margaret left on a motoring holiday through France to the Mediterranean.

Just before they left, Mary's mother arrived in London. A wanderer in her widowhood — 'my restless mother', Mary would call her — Elizabeth now had more family in England than in Australia: her three eldest sons, in the British forces, were based in London, and at present Lance and his wife were in England on extended leave from Singapore. Clive was in Burma. Only Lucy was in Australia; she ran a women students' hostel at The University of Melbourne, later to be known as Janet Clarke Hall. While Margaret and Mary were away on their motor tour, Elizabeth stayed in Mary's house in Finborough Road. The key to domestic comfort in their case: mother and daughter staying in the same house, but consecutively rather than concurrently.

...oOo...

After the holiday, Mary got to work on her travel book, writing it up from her notebooks. There were decisions to be made about what she should include. The places where she had stayed longest, and enjoyed herself the most, were high on the list. She concentrated on the strip from Sierra Leone to the Volta River mouth — a formidable 3,500 kilometres of coast. On her trip she had begun to see the contrast between British Colonial territories and French ones, an interesting follow-up to the lectures and debates on colonial administration she had listened to in London. She determined to add material about the French and German administrations, perhaps comparing them with the British. After all, she was a colonial herself, and had grown up in the household of a colonial official — she had good credentials for writing about colonial policy.

Now, back in England, she began assembling the notes she had made as she travelled, adding commentary, making a list of places to revisit. The castles on the coast were a must — the working buildings, the residences, the romantic ruins — were a must. She could write articles on them, as well as include them in the book. This would be a travel adventure set in Africa. Only thirty years before, the *New York Herald* had sent Henry Morton Stanley into Africa to search for David Livingstone and, such was the interest it aroused, Stanley was giving lectures about it for years afterwards. Exploration, hardship, adventure, captured the public imagination.

Women travellers in Africa were still rare. Mary Kingsley had published a witty and wonderful account of her travels in West Africa only eleven years before, and there were books like *Petticoat Pilgrims on Trek* reviewed in the Royal Colonial Institute's journal. Mary would be able to present the image of a gutsy but vulnerable woman, adventurous, willing to boldly go where — sometimes, at least — no white woman had gone before.

The trip would need careful planning. There were few railways, and the roads could be bad. She could take advantage of the great rivers, sometimes navigable for hundreds of miles inland. She would have to investigate travel by land, accommodation, what to take, and what it would all cost. She was still close enough to the grim early years in London to feel the cold breath of financial disaster at her back. But in the world of travel without brochures and bookings and tour guides, before cars and buses, adventurous land travel by a lone white woman in Africa would surely sell.

Chapter 19

London 1909–10

Australia is a new country, and the chances for those who are willing to go "out back" are great...

Woman's work is very highly paid in Australia, even unskilled work. I have before me a letter: 'A cook at last, thank goodness,' says the weary house-mistress, 'only £1 a week and she can't cook. But there's always some drawback.'[1]

As spring came to London in May 1909, Mary was home and hard at work. She had missed the last English summer; she arrived back from Africa as the days were closing in, bleak and grey and cold. Now summer was coming again, a gentle English summer, and she was in London to enjoy it.

The Royal Colonial Institute offered lectures on Britain's dominions, informing its members in England, and those throughout the colonies who received its journal by mail, of the endless variety, the great wealth, and the enormous potential of the British Empire. Its aim was to 'foster the love of Overseas Britons for the Motherland' and, as its Year Book proudly reminded its members, 'to cultivate in the breasts of residents of the Self-Governing Dominions, Colonies and India the feeling that neither the accident of birth overseas, nor the fact that a wider sphere has been chosen by a Briton born in the United Kingdom can in any way affect his British citizenship so long as his home is still under the British Flag.'[2]

Mary was not a Fellow of the Royal Colonial Institute, only an Associate. It was not the accident of her birth overseas, but the accident of her birth as female, which decided this. She was entitled to receive the monthly journal, and use the library and attend social gatherings and lectures, but not annual general meetings where decisions would be made about the Institute. Ladies could not be Fellows.

There was Frank Fox, the good-looking journalist, writer and man-about-town who had arrived in London some time ahead of his wife and family. He wrote in his journal article: 'The Australian…is the best raw material for an army in the world. He is purely British stock, bred too, from the most adventurous types of the British blood — the Chartists, poachers and agrarian offenders of one epoch, the gold and land seekers of another.'[3] Late in 1910, Frank Fox became News Editor of *The Morning Post*; Mary contacted him about sending articles back from Africa.

The editor of the RCI journal was Archibald Colquhoun. The interests of the women in the Institute concerned him; as editor of the new-look Institute journal, *United Empire*, he published the names of women Associates. Of all the books reviewed in the journal — pronouncements on British colonial policy (and German, and Belgian), accounts of voyages, missionary experiences and ladies' adventures — there is only one review of a novel, and it is Mary's. The central character of *The Mummy Moves* is a London detective; no-one travels or explores, no-one even leaves England. Perhaps the mention of African ju-ju theme and the mummy imported from Africa countered raised eyebrows in Northumberland Avenue.

…oOo…

In 1910 George Ernest Morrison, now *The Times* representative in Peking, was on an extended visit to London.

Mary knew him as Ernest, as most of his family did. She wrote to him, inviting him to dinner. It was her habit, on paper, to be rather formal — 'Dear Mr. Morrison', which in this case was odd, as she went on to write 'I dreamt about you so vividly, hence this letter.'

There is no record of whether Morrison accepted her invitation, but in the book on her travels in China she wrote: 'When [Morrison] came to England he used to come and see me', so perhaps he did come to dinner.

Morrison was a man on the move, preoccupied with other things. He had had a passionate affair in London on his previous visit in 1905; there was another and brief one on this visit. Mary might well have dreamed about him, but it is unlikely that he returned the compliment.

Mary had been interested for some time in the matter of emigration to the colonies, particularly to Australia. England was struggling to feed, clothe and educate its growings population; the old systems of parish relief were ineffective in the overcrowded industrial cities, and organisations to promote emigration were multiplying. Mary believed passionately that Australia was a great place for people to live — a healthy land of opportunity. She wrote to *The Times* in March, responding to the claim that married couples with children could not get work in outback Australia. Women were in demand, she wrote, and were well-paid for their work. A correspondent had claimed that it was hard to get work in Australia for married couples with children. There were simple solutions, Mary said: couples could put off having children for a few years, or they could have their children 'boarded out' for no more than ten shillings a week.

> Those who are not prepared to risk something, to face some hardships, to put up with some deprivations for their own future good, had better stay and starve comfortably in old England…[4]

Australia was the place for the adventurous, but the Mary who pleaded for the right of women to work on their own terms in *Kirkham's Find* had grown more conservative with the years.

A few months after the *Times* article, Mary was at a conference on emigration arranged by the Royal Colonial Institute. She and two other speakers recommended Australia for migrants; one had information on 'the great Victorian immigration-cum-irrigation scheme', another had a scheme for land settlement in Western Australia. Mary made particular mention of the opportunities for women, proud of how far forward Australia had moved since her struggle to find useful professional work thirty years before. She told the conference that 'no woman landing in Australia and willing to use her hands need be out of work for an hour.'

Morrison, also a member of the RCI, was writing articles for the *Morning Post* while travelling in Europe. Mary was also writing an article. 'I'm bringing my great mind to bear on the emigration question,' she wrote flippantly to Morrison in August, 'as I'm full of theories. When *The Times* rejects it, I will send it to *The Morning Post*.'

…oOo…

The Lyceum Club had a number of interest groups. Mary and her friend Margaret Baxter, also a writer and also Australian, were vice-presidents of the American Circle, an oddity which puzzled even the members of the Circle.

When invited, however, Mary spoke to the American Circle of the Lyceum Club about her travels. It required a slight deviation from the Circle's normal agenda; they would have to celebrate Washington's birthday at their next meeting. The president pointed out that, because of her position, Mary had practically *represented* the Circle while travelling in Africa — something for Circle members to be proud of.

So, on a February day of heavy London fog, Mary gave a lecture to the American Circle on her travels in Africa. The *British Australasian* reported that:

> Mrs. Lindsay Miller has the gift of attracting the attention of her listeners from start to finish, so it was small wonder, at the conclusion of her address, that she was enthusiastically applauded.

Margaret Baxter regularly organised 'at homes' at the Austral Club, of which she and Mary were members. In March, she varied the program to include a talk by Mary; it was to some extent a repeat of the talk to the American Circle. The meeting was chaired by Captain R. Muirhead Collins, Mary's intercessor with the Colonial Office. The members became engrossed in the map with which Mary illustrated her talk, and were amused at her accounts of being landed by mammy-chair — slung over the side of the steamer — along the surf coast. Among the friends who came to listen was her sister-in-law Margaret, Guy's wife.

Mary's home in Finborough Road was modest in both size and location. She gave an 'at home' for Margaret, and another for her mother at the Lyceum Club, so that they could meet her friends — the kind of social function she normally avoided so that she could get on with her writing.

One social function she *did* attend, however, was a reception in June at the Lyceum Club for delegates to the Imperial Press Conference. She was a co-host, with Margaret Baxter. The guests were entertained by Amy Castles, the young Australian singer who was taking London by storm. There were guests who were important to Mary. Sir John Rodger, Governor of the Gold Coast, and his wife, her hosts in Accra, were there. The Commissioner at Cape Coast, E. C. Eliot, was there with Mrs Eliot. Her brothers Guy and Lance were there, and their wives. Many of her friends in the Women Journalists' Club were there, along with other London journalists and writers.

There were relations and friends visiting London, too. Her eldest brother Cecil was in London for a time, and attended her Lyceum 'at home' in honour of Guy's wife. Lance and his wife Violet — Morrison's sister — arrived from Singapore in August 1909 and stayed until early 1910; Violet stayed on a bit longer than Lance, returning with their new baby. Claude Palmer, son of her mother's older brother Octavius and Mary's first cousin, was there with his wife Marjory through the summer of 1909. Major Carandini and his wife and daughter Estelle, after winter sports in Switzerland, were spending the summer in England. Carandini was the brother of Mary's aunt Rosina Palmer.

According to her niece, Ellinor Archer, Mary kept a diary all her life, but no diaries have ever been found. It would be interesting to know how she balanced the time needed for her writing with the need to be with people and enjoy her life in London. She didn't always get on well with people, including members of her family; she was prickly at times, self-important about her lectures and her books, and absorbed in her work. But she enjoyed company, and spent time with people.

...oOo...

Her third book with Tonkin, *The Silent Ones,* was being widely reviewed, and had also come out in a Colonial Library edition. The *British Australasian* had an article about her with a studio photograph, and readers could now buy her book — along with those of other Australians and New Zealanders — from the *British Australasian* headquarters in The Strand. Meanwhile, she continued with her writing. She sent a story to *Pearson's Magazine* whose likeness to *The Silent Ones* suggests an alternative passage or one the co-writers rejected. She also sold a story to *Windsor Magazine*, 'Sweet Briar in the Desert', that recalled her experience on the salt lakes in South Australia ten years before.

All the while she was working on her book about Africa and making plans for her second trip. She would go further inland. She would go back to Ashanti territory, deep into the forests, where the high canopy shuts out the sun, and experience the sensation of being totally overwhelmed by nature that she felt briefly at Kumasi. She would hire bearers to carry her along the coast where boats could not dock, so that she could see the old forts up close and learn their stories. She would write about what few other travellers could write about, and do what few travellers had done, and *very* few women. She would go into West Africa alone.

...oOo...

Mary was business-like; she had to cover her costs. She looked around for a possible market. In July 1910, she wrote to *Century Magazine* in New York asking them to buy the serial rights to her new book about Africa, to be published by Werner Laurie. In case they hadn't read any of her work — though she was *sure* they would know her name — she sent them a copy of *The Uncounted Cost* which, she assured them, 'has already gone into four editions numbering over 7,000 copies.'

> At the end of the present rainy season I propose to return to West
> Africa and journey along the Gold Coast with a train of carriers

> in order to write a series of articles upon the very fascinating old world Castles which are dotted along that coast from Half Assinie to Christiansborg. They are as you know mediavel [sic] but as far as I know have not yet been properly described — any body with any literary talent as a rule giving the Gold Coast a wide berth…[5]

The reply from *Century* has been lost, but it seems that they were disinclined to buy serial rights to a book she hadn't yet written, from a writer they had not heard of. She wrote again:

> I thank you for your courteous letter. It seems to me very natural that you do not feel inclined to commission articles from an author who is perfectly unknown to you…On the other hand, I know my own powers, am intent on building up a reputation and know that the articles will be good. I propose to spend some little time in Liberia, arriving there some time in November or December. Would you care for me to submit to you an article about Liberia, well illustrated by photographs. I use a Una Tropical Camera. I do not propose that you should commission it, but if you can promise to give me a decent price should it suit you, I am perfectly willing to submit the article on approval, the understanding being that you make your decision in a fortnight and pay me on acceptance. I only wish to sell the serial rights or the American serial rights only according to the price you offer.
>
> Does this seem to you a fair offer?[6]

There is no record of a reply, but no articles by Mary — either about Liberia or about the forts — appeared in *Century Magazine*.

Gradually, Mary found ways to finance her trip. Werner Laurie could see, from what she had written so far, that this would be an interesting book, and was willing to give her an advance to cover expenses while she was away. Her brother Cecil, an army officer, lent her his camping gear.

To one of Mary's teas at the Lyceum came Miss Oram, the nursing sister at Sekondi in West Africa, who invited her to share her quarters at the hospital there. The way was opening before her.

Chapter 20

The Storm Breaks

I was staying up in Liverpool when, shortly after the new year, I received a letter from my publisher, Mr. Laurie, saying he wished I would come back to London, as the libraries were banning my book, *The Uncounted Cost*, and *The Times* had refused to advertise it. Naturally I returned at once. By banning I found he meant that each library had only taken a few copies, so as not to give the unlucky author a grievance; for instance, of my last book, *The Silent Ones*, Smiths had taken 400, of this, they ordered 26, and the other libraries followed suit, and were pledged by that very action not to offer the book to their subscribers. My publisher, Mr. Laurie, was very depressed about it, and told me how *The Times* had refused his advertisement over the telephone. I could not believe it, but said 'Try again', and he did try again, and this time, since he demanded a reason, they wrote to him and gave one. The book was 'unsuitable'. Then I sent them my cheque and asked them to advertise the book for me, and very promptly was the cheque returned: 'We have already explained to your publisher that we cannot advertise this booklet.'[1]

In a world where co-habitation before or without marriage is widely accepted, it is hard to imagine the shock effect this topic had on some readers in 1910. *The Uncounted Cost* caused a storm. Edwardian England was not ready for it; certainly *The Times* and the circulating libraries were not ready for it.

Mary was not one to take their response lying down. She called on the Society of Authors for their help, and got the ineffectual response that distribution bodies other than the current company — Smiths —would be sure to arise. This sort of campaign had happened before and would no doubt happen again; she would just have to wait until the storm passed. This was cold comfort to a writer trying to make a living — 'I shall remember that against the Society if ever I get the chance'.[2]

One of her friends at the Lyceum, Mrs Spencer Wilkinson, was more positive. Her husband was, apart from his academic position, a leader writer for *The Morning Post*. He suggested writing a good letter to *The Observer*.

> I took his advice…The book was practically dead, my publisher told me, killed by the libraries. *The Observer* put in my letter of protest and so did the *Westminster Gazette* and some other papers, and such an effect did it have that by Tuesday the libraries were buying freely
>
> and in ten days the whole first edition of 1,500 copies was sold out.

The Times relented and took the advertisement for the book. But the conservative *Times* got its revenge with a review: 'Mrs. Gaunt introduces us to two young women holding views of life and love which neither of them, if generally adopted, make for the greater sanity of women and men.' It went on to outline the plot, which the reviewer made to sound interesting in spite of himself, and concluded: 'Mrs. Gaunt seems to have worked conscientiously at her rather inconsequent story…We learn nothing from any of her characters. They are flat and uninteresting, and have none of the dimensions.'[3]

Mary responded with wry humour. 'It is lucky for me most of the other papers have been enthusiastic, but *The Times*! How are the mighty fallen! I feel—

> It is all very well to dissemble for love,
> But why did you kick me downstairs?'

Regardless of *The Times* review, the book was a huge success. Laurie printed more copies. The Colonial Library edition and the US edition came out later in the year.

Other reviews considered the book within a wider scope. The *Daily Graphic* called it 'a perfectly clean and sincere attempt to deal with certain fundamental truths from the woman's point of view'; the *Manchester Courier* called it 'a clever, serious novel, well worked out, conceived in high moral strain, and beyond all question entitled to claim as a work of genuine purpose'. Others praised its clever plotting and its local colour: 'You can hear the crack of the rifle,' the London *Bookman* exclaimed; 'real terror walks through the pages. You get the genuine atmosphere of the tropics.'

The Bookman review must have pleased Mary. It was her first book to come out in England since the break with Tonkin, the first she had written where the African background was all her own. 'To those who have helped me, I dedicate this book with grateful thanks,' Mary had written at the front of her manuscript. Undoubtedly, the people who helped her travel in Africa in 1908 were included in the general thanks. But perhaps Tonkin was getting a covert 'thank you' here, too. She could afford to be generous now.

She made good use of the controversy created by some reviews. On 1 March 1910, Margaret Baxter scrapped the usual musical program of the Austral Club's weekly 'at home' and arranged a 'causerie' on censorship, at which Mary spoke. She was passionate and amusing on the banning itself and on the lame backing down of the libraries and book distributors.

The controversy increased the sales of the book. It got her interviews. There was an article, with portrait, about her in *Bookman* in February, and in it she put her point about the integrity of her book and the mistaken attacks on it:

> My means of livelihood are thus taken away from me, and it is cold comfort to reflect that on the same principle *The Scarlet Letter* and *Adam Bede* would be banned, for Hawthorne and George Eliot are dead and no longer need bread-and-butter.

No doubt she wrote to the *British Australasian*, telling them about the trouble she'd had with the circulating libraries. Perhaps she sent them a copy of the article because, when they reviewed the Colonial edition in May, they gloated about the boost in sales caused by the ban, and said:

> This shows how liable to make mistakes are those who set themselves up as literary censors.If *The Uncounted Cost* is to be considered an improper book, so also are *The Scarlet Letter* and *Adam Bede*…[4]

The Uncounted Cost came out trailing its own clouds of glory — fifteen excerpts of reviews of *The Silent Ones* were quoted in its endpapers. They are reviews of a work by two authors, used to promote a book by one.

With the controversy dying down, reviews of *The Uncounted Cost* continued to be encouraging — there were nineteen recorded in the bibliography. So when the serial *The Mummy Moves* was published in England in book form in August and went into a second impression within the year, along with a Colonial Library edition, it must have seemed a good time to return to Africa.

The days when she had felt 'homeless, penniless and alone' — the early days in London when she had had little success — were behind her now. Apart from her faithful publicists the *British Australasian*, who carried a delightful portrait of her, she had an interview in *The Girl's Own Paper and Woman's Magazine* to coincide with their serialisation of her story 'The Love that was better than Gold' in 1908. They too included a picture; a business-like, book-reading, too-busy-to-look-up picture. There was a piece in *The Bookman* in February 1910, with a social portrait in evening dress. She had published short stories in quality magazines too — *Windsor* and *Pearson's*. And these days there were always reviews.

On this second trip, she would need introductions even more because she would be blazing her own trail. She wanted to go where there were *some* people — British and European people, that is — but she would not be on well-trodden paths. This time she wanted the mystery, the mystique of Africa, the secrets waiting to be revealed, the strange people with strange practices to be written about. If she were to write a successful book about her experience, it needed to be a very different experience from the ordinary.

Some time after the dust had settled on the controversy, Mary met the head of Boots' Library at a lunch:

> 'We owe you an apology,' said he. 'We mixed *The Uncounted Cost* with a pernicious book published by ---. When we found out our mistake it was too late.'

And Mary responded with:

> 'Do it again,' said I. 'I'm going back to West Africa on the proceeds.'[5]

Chapter 21

Back to Africa

Such a walk it was. Never have I met such a road. It was steep, and it was rough, and it was stony as a mountain torrent; now after the rain it was wet and slippery and the branches of the overhanging trees showered us with water as we passed…[T]he jungle was thick on either hand…and there were mysterious rustlings as small animals forced their way through the bush or fled before us. My host offered me his stick to pull me over the steepest rocks, and also supplied the interesting information that round the Consulate the deer came down to lick the salt from the rocks, and the panthers, tigers they called them there, came down and killed the deer. I made a mental note not to walk in that path by night; indeed I made a note not to walk in it ever again, as drenched and dripping with perspiration we emerged into a clearing and saw looming up before us a tropical bungalow…

    Next morning I told my host I would go and see the town.
    'But I shan't go by the short cut,' I added emphatically.
    'What short cut?'
    'The way we came last night.'
    'That's not a short cut,' said he…'That's the main road.'[1]

Mary stood on the platform of London's Euston Station, ready to catch the boat train to Liverpool, a short, stout woman surrounded by a formidable pile of luggage. In the studded leather suitcases, along with a straw hat, sensible shoes and serviceable skirts, there were hats, gloves, evening dresses, silk stockings and dainty shoes, but not quite as many as on the last trip. In the boxes were a portable dining table, glassware, cutlery, crockery and cooking equipment. The Una tropical camera with a supply of glass plates nestled safely in its specially constructed carrying box, and in another was her metal typewriter. There was a box with her papers, including a typewritten carbon copy of her half-completed travel book on Africa. There was a bedding roll and camp bed and, courtesy of her soldier brother Cecil, a portable bath. Mary was going to Africa again.

Ernest, Mary's second-eldest brother, was at the station to see her off. 'Have you any directions for the disposal of your remains?' he asked her.[2] It was a joke they both enjoyed. Travel came naturally to them. 'I cannot remember when anyone of us would not have gone anywhere in the world at a moment's notice,' she wrote at the start of her book.[3]

The Elder Dempster line was one of the Liverpool-based shipping companies that had wrested dominance of the slave trade from Bristol and London by the middle of the eighteenth century. All around Albert Dock and the Port of Liverpool area, and up along James and Water and Dale Streets, stood the imposing offices of shipping companies, banks and insurance companies that had continued to prosper after abolition in 1807 of what came to be called 'the Atlantic trade'. Mary had a get-on-and-off-anywhere ticket with Elder Dempster for the West African coast.

She had, too, in her replenished collection of letters of introduction, a letter for Sir George Denton, Governor of the Gambia. On the ship, good fortune presented her with an unusual opportunity. She discovered that Sir George was a fellow passenger and presented her letter of introduction to him. She asked him about the colony, and he invited her to disembark with him — there was a wharf at Bathurst — and stay awhile and visit. She abandoned her plan to make French Senegal her first stop, and disembarked with Denton, getting caught up in the pomp of his official 'welcome home'. So it was in the Gambia that her second African adventure began.

She stayed with Sir George Denton at Government House for three weeks. It was a delightful place, every room benefiting from cool breezes.

She had a large, simply-furnished bedroom, equipped with the one item in the house she disliked: a wire mesh enclosure like a room within a room which kept out the mosquitoes — and the fresh air as well. She sat outside on the wide verandahs to write during the day. It was a 'womanless household', so she employed a servant. He was Ansumanah Grant, mission-educated in Liberia. He was twenty-three years old; she spoke and wrote of him as a 'boy'. She dressed him in a white shirt, khaki knickerbockers and a red cummerbund. He went with her as guide, interpreter and helper for the next nine months.

With Denton's help, Mary had a trip up the Gambia River into the peanut growing area in the hinterland. The British gained a toehold there when one bank was held by the French and the other by the Portuguese; Britain built a fort on the island of St James 'to protect their interest in the great trade in palm oil, slaves and ivory that came down the river'.[4] She knew very little about the Gambia River. Now a whole new, fascinating world was opening up.

She travelled on the French Company steamer, the *Mungo Park*. The deck was a jumble of cargo for the settlements up river, along with ninety deck passengers with bedding, cooking pots, babies, live chickens and even a goat. They spoke a jumble of languages, including 'that bastard English which is a lingua franca all along the Coast'.

> [The captain] remains in my mind as the most unique specimen of the genus I have ever seen. He wore a khaki coat and very elderly tweed trousers, split behind; his feet were bare; he did not pander to that vitiated taste which demands under-linen, or at least a shirt, but, seeing it was the cold weather, he adorned his black skull with a woolly cap with ear-flaps.
>
> The siren gave wild and ear-piercing shrieks; there were yells from the wharf, more heartrending yells from the steamer, a minor accompaniment from the lighters, bleating of goats, cackling of protesting fowls, crying of children, and we were off without casualty, and things began to settle down.'[5]

The wide, wide river narrowed as they came near the ruins of the old Fort St James. The place had been small, cramped and desperately unhealthy.

> Tradition…says that the gentlemen of the company of soldiers who were stationed there were for ever fighting duels, and that the many vacancies in the ranks were not always due to the climate. But the heat and the long monotonous days would conduce to irritability, and when a hasty word had to be answered for at the sword's point it is no wonder that they cursed the Coast with a bitterness that is only given to the land of regrets. All honour to those dead and gone Englishmen. They upheld the might of Britain and her trade, and if they died — now, at last after many weary years, their descendants are beginning to realise the value of the land for which they gave their lives.[6]

The romance of history could seduce Mary completely, as with the bored and drunken men who 'gave their lives' for Britain's right to occupy and exploit the land.

> …As we moved up the river we could plainly see the shore on either side, the dense mangrove swamp, doubled by its reflection, green and beautiful against its setting of blue sky and clear river. Crocodiles lay basking in the golden sunshine on the mud-banks, white egrets flew slowly from tree to tree, a brown jolah-king, an ibis debased for some sin in the youth of the world, sailed slowly across the water, a white fishing-eagle poised himself on high, looking for his prey, a slate-blue crane came across our bows, a young pelican just ahead was taking his first lesson in swimming, and closer to the bank we could see king-fishers, bright spots of colour against the dark green of the mangrove.[7]

There were few English women on the coast — they were regarded as 'heroines and martyrs' if they went there with their husbands. 'Possibly it is because I am an Australian and have had a harder bringing-up that I resent very much the supposition that a woman cannot go where a man can,' Mary wrote. The French trader she met was scornful of the English attitude; his wife was due to arrive soon with their month-old baby. Mary was becoming convinced that the nations whose colonial officials took their women with them were far more likely to hold a colony.[8]

She was also becoming convinced of the vast wealth that Britain could exploit; the fertile soil could produce every tropical crop, and could provide raw materials for the workshops of England for years if properly managed. She would show the British people how to enjoy the wealth of West Africa — how careful husbandry and diligent administration would bring enormous rewards. This was not just a journey, but a crusade!

The steamer unloaded passengers and cargo, and took on a load of groundnuts — peanuts — for the return trip down river. Mary wrote about the mangrove swamps, the settlements, the climate and the whole ambience of the mighty river. It was a journey she loved.

She had Christmas and New Year in Bathurst with the Dentons. December was the dry season, when the cool Harmattan wind blew — a comfortable time to be there. While there, she wrote about Gambia and the groundnut growing, and sent her article back to London on the fortnightly mail steamer. It appeared in *The Morning Post* in March 1911, while she was still away. It would be a continuing theme of her writing; that Britain and the Britons knew all too little about their colonies around the world. A second theme was alluded to by a French trader on the river. The colonising powers had been frustrated by the refusal of native people to work; they were self-evidently lazy. Now they were discovering that the natives would work if there was something they wanted and 'we are making him want', he said.[9] To Mary it seemed like sound good sense, and good business, to turn native people into consumers.

She planned to go to Liberia, because she wanted to write articles about it to send to *Century Magazine* in the US. The steamer crew advised her against landing there, assuring her there was nothing to see. Like Sierra Leone, it had been set up to accommodate freed slaves. Taken from all over Africa, deracinated and brutalised by years of servitude, the slaves have been resettled here — back to anywhere in Africa was near enough. Mary was determined to go.

From the deck of the *Zaria*, the coastal steamer, she was slung over the side by mammy-chair into a surfboat already half-full of water, and her gear dropped down with a splash beside her. She saw, as she drew closer to the shore, that 'man's handiwork was tumble-down, dirty, dilapidated, unfinished'.

> I stepped from the boat to a narrow causeway of stone; it is difficult to get out of a boat five feet deep with grace, more especially when your skirts are sopping, and I stepped from the causeway — it was not above a foot wide — into yellow mud…There were negroes in all stages of rags round me, and then out from amongst them stepped a white man, a neat and spick-and-span white man with soldier written all over him…[10]

The British Consul offered her a choice of accommodation: there was a boarding house in the town, not too uncomfortable, he understood, or 'If you will stay at the Consulate I will be delighted, but it is a mile and a half from the town, and I have no wife.' It didn't take Mary long to decide: 'There could be but one answer to that. Of course I accepted his invitation; there are but few conventions and no Mrs Grundy in out-of-the-way spots, thank heaven, and in the growing darkness we set off for the Consulate.'

As this was a 'negro republic', there were no bearers to carry her, and she had to walk up the steep path to the Consulate:

> '…[T]he jungle was thick on either hand, the night birds cried, the birds that loved the sun made sleeping noises, the ceaseless insects roused to activity by the rain made the darkness shrill with their clamour, and there were mysterious rustlings as small animals forced their way through the bush or fled before us.'[11]

She spent close to a fortnight in and around Monrovia, declining the invitation of the President's wife to see the area upriver because, in the land of freed slaves, she would have to walk. The President's wife had declined to be photographed, and Mary accepted that, but when the congregation of the church she attended also refused, she was annoyed: 'they need not have reviled me in the blatant, coarse manner of the negro who has just seen enough of civilisation to think he rules the universe'. 'The Liberian is only a travesty of the European,' she decided, 'arrogant without proper dignity, boastful with absolutely nothing in the world to boast about unless it be the amazing wealth of the country he mismanages so shamefully.'

She went on by coastal steamer eastward towards the Gold Coast. She wanted to land at Half Assinie, at the border with the Ivory Coast. This was the part of the coast she had been looking forward to, where the forts and castles began. But there was no dock or safe landing place, and she had a great deal of equipment to get ashore. The alternative was to go on to Axim, fifty miles further on, and travel back overland.

It took some time to assemble the necessary team of carriers. She would need eight men to carry her in two shifts in a hammock, two servants, and seventeen men to carry her equipment on their heads. A Forestry Officer from Axim was travelling the same way, and his team had to be assembled too. Mary watched with wry amusement:

> There is a family resemblance among all travellers on the Gold Coast. They all try to reduce their loads to a minimum and they all find that there are certain necessaries of life which they must have, and certain other things which may be luxuries but which they cannot do without, and certain other little things which it would be a sin not to take as it makes all the difference between comfort and savagery. So the procession comes along, a roll of bedding, a chop box, a kitchen box with pots and pans, a bath, a chair, a table, the servant's box, a load of water, a certain amount of drink, whisky, gin, and if the traveller is very luxurious (I wasn't) some claret, a uniform case with clothes, a smaller one containing the heavier things such as boots and the various goods that pertain to the European's presence there. Before the Commissioner goes his orderly, carrying his silver-topped stick, the insignia of his rank.[12]

For much of the coast they followed the shoreline, walking on the firm sand high up the beach. When they came to a waterway inland, she reluctantly got out of her hammock and was carried over piggyback by a brawny carrier. At the end of a hot day, they settled in a small fishing village for the night. Mary had a bath and changed into fresh clothes, and dined with the Forestry Officer — *hors d'oeuvres,* soup, fish, chicken, sweets and fruit.

They travelled along the coast back to Half Assinie, and Mary had a chance to look around. When it was time to start back, Mary's carriers, who came from the area, demanded money before starting out. But, warned the Forestry Officer, if they are paid now they will run away. Mary refused to pay them. In the morning, the carriers failed to turn up. The Forestry Officer went to the village headman. 'If they do not come,' he said, 'we will leave all our loads, and you will be responsible for them, and we will go on without the carriers, and no-one will be paid.' The carriers reappeared, and the little party set off back to Axim.

Mary visited Prince's, an abandoned fort 'tumbling into ruins', with the Commissioner at Axim then, via small boat, got back onto the steamer heading east to Sekondi. She sensed the Commissioner's relief when he saw this demanding woman safely into the boat.

At Sekondi, Mary stayed with Miss Oram, the nursing sister at the hospital. 'No-one who is not absolutely driven to it by stern necessity stays in a West-African hotel,' she noted. Sekondi was the terminus of the railway line into the interior, to Kumasi and the Tarkwa mines, and miners on leave were rough men and hard drinkers — the hotels would not be suitable for her.

The doctor at Sekondi told her, as so many did, about the unhealthy climate, but Mary noticed that his patients were in a hospital, which kept out not only the mosquitos but every breath of fresh air. The nurse's airy bungalow — free of the wire mesh favoured by the doctor — was far more comfortable.

> 'I've packed [our women] back home — ill, most of 'em.'
>
> 'Yes,' the scornful nurse told me, 'the men came out first and some of them lived with the native women. The women of the Coast are just riddled with disease — well anyhow, many of them. The women did not know what was the matter with them,' went on the

nurse. 'The doctor said it was the coast, and back they had to go. The climate indeed!'[13]

Instead of the easy route by coastal steamer, Mary went eastward overland from Sekondi eastward to Accra, staying in village resthouses, visiting the crumbling fort at Kommenda and seeing the legendary castle of Elmina again. She wrote about them all for *The Morning Post*: Beyin, the smallest of them; Axim, where the footsteps of the old Dutch governor could be heard at night; Elmina, the finest on the coast — built by the Portuguese, bought from the Dutch by the British, with moats that bred mosquitoes; the mighty fortress at Cape Coast and the smaller, well-preserved Annmabu. She titled her article 'Ring of ancient forts: ghost-haunted castles', and sent it off by steamer to England. It was published in April 1911.

She recorded details of the castles in her diary, but felt she hadn't seen enough of them, or spent long enough in them, to write a book devoted to them. The attitude towards them was disheartening too; many people on the coast saw the castles as 'heaps of crumbling stone that were best allowed to decay for they only recalled a time that was best forgotten.'[14] She was seeing at first hand the horror, rather than the romance, of the slave days that she had dwelt on since childhood. Her publisher, Werner Laurie, never got his book about the castles, although they appeared briefly in later books.

The journey along the coast was eventful. At Winneba her carriers were tired and she could not get a new team, so she was forced to go back to the sea and take the steamer to Accra. But there was one more castle she wanted to see, and she could do it by leaving all her luggage and taking only the 'hammock-boys' and her luncheon, and making it a day trip. It should have been simple:

> There was a river to cross just outside the town of Winnebah…a big undertaking in West Africa, even when you have only one load. I'm afraid I must plead guilty to not knowing my men by sight; for a long time a black man was a black man to me, and he had no individuality about him. Now they all crowded into the boat to cross the river, and it was evident to my mind that we were too many; then, as no

one seemed inclined to be left behind, I exercised my authority and pointed out the man who was to get out, and out he got, very reluctantly, but cheerily helped by his unfeeling fellows. It took us about a quarter of an hour to cross that river, for it was wide and we had to work up-stream, and once across they all proceeded to go on their way without a thought for the man left behind. And then I discovered what I had done. I had…put the unfortunate ferryman out of his own boat, and…my men were quite prepared to leave him on one side of the stream and his boat on the other…I declared they must go back for him, and my decision was received with immense surprise.

'You want him, Ma?'…when they found I really did, and moreover intended to pay him, two of them took the boat and he was brought to me with shouts of laughter, and comforted with an extra dash [payment].[15]

Unable to get carriers to go further by land, Mary reluctantly went on by coastal steamer and was landed by mammy-chair at Accra. She stayed a few days at Christiansborg Castle, where at night two ghostly Englishmen, one with 'eyes like bright stones',[16] walked along the corridors. The Acting Governor and his wife had no wish to entertain her but gave her hospitality for a few nights, then, when she insisted that she must stay in Accra awhile, found her a tumbledown bungalow which suited her well as there was plenty of fresh air. She made daily sorties into the town, engaging a cart and 'boys' to take her about.

Once again, she could not get carriers to continue along the coast. She wanted to get to Keta, where there was an old Danish castle. She settled for an interesting alternative. A motor lorry was going up-country to the Basel Mission Station at Dodowah, and from nearby Akusa the Acting Governor could arrange carriers to take her to the Volta River, and she could travel downstream to Keta. She had been a month in Accra; it was April and time to move on.

Bearers were waiting at the Basel Mission Station as arranged, and she set off late in the day to go the twenty-seven miles to Akusa in one march. When the bearers wanted to stop, she insisted they keep going, and they did — singing, stamping their feet and clapping their hands and calling, to make it sound like they were a big party. They were passing Krobo Hill, and 'on Krobo Hill was one of the worst, if not the worst blood fetish in West Africa. Every Krobo youth before he could become a man and choose a wife had to kill a man, and he did it generally on Krobo Hill.'[17] The bearers went faster, not stopping for anything until they were safely past, and then threw themselves panting onto the ground to rest.

Help for Mary's inland travel came this time from the Swanzy trading company's representative. No-one else he knew of had ever done it, but he could get her to the German border by going upriver and cutting across to Ho, in German territory. From there she could get to Palime, and there was a railway line from there down to the coast.

She was rowed upriver by six men, in a canoe with a canopy over her chair.

> It is something of an adventure to go up the Volta, for as soon as we started its smooth, wide reaches were broken by belts of rock that made it seem well-nigh impassable. Again and again from the low seat in the canoe it looked as if a rocky barrier barred all further progress, but here and there the water rushed down the narrow chasm as in a millrace. Wonderful it was to find that a canoe could be poled up those rocky stairways against the rushing water…I really had not time to be afraid till it was all over.[18]

'The Gambia is interesting, the Congo grand, but the Volta is entrancingly lovely,' Mary wrote. The river twisted and turned, and there were tall green-covered peaks on either side. There was brilliant sunshine, then wind, then the mist rose up and swallowed all sight of the river.

> Sometimes its great, wide, quiet reaches are like still, deep lakes;… sometimes it is a raging torrent, fighting its way over the rocks, and beneath the vivid blue sky is the gorgeous vegetation of the Tropics, tangled, luxuriant, feather palms, tall and shapely silk-cotton trees bound together with twining creeper and trailing vine in one impenetrable mass…Always there are hills, rising high, cutting the

sky sharply, ever changing, ever reflected faithfully in the river at their feet.[19]

She went overland again, stopping to visit the British Cotton-growing Experimental Farm, where it was far easier to grow cocoa so the natives refused to co-operate. Then on to enjoy the hospitality of the Basel Mission staff and a rest house on Anum Mountain, a night in her camp bed on the floor of the cocoa store in Tsito and, after more wrangling with bearers, on to Ho, and the German territory of Togoland.

The roads were better, the gardens were neater and prettier, and the hospitality as warm as it was undeserved, since she had no letters of introduction. Through neat streets and orderly towns she made her way, always with curiosity, through to the railroad at Palime; then as a lone first-class passenger, down to the coast on the narrow-gauge railway. Lome was the capital, 'the most charming town I have seen in West Africa,' she said.[20] Another surfboat, another hazardous landing on the beach, another trek along the coast to Keta, and the District Commissioner arranged for her to stay with the Bremen Mission Sisters. She was back in British territory.

By surfboat and steamer, she got back to Addah, swinging in a mammy-chair into yet another surfboat with her servant and all her gear.

> We were going straight into a furious boiling sea with white, foam-lashed waves that flung themselves high into the air…Then the Custom-house officer, a black man, edged his way close beside me, and stretching out his hand put it on my arm. I did not like it. I object to being touched by black men, so I promptly shook it off, and as promptly the boat was apparently flung crash against a stone wall; she had really hit the beach, and over I went backwards and head first into the bottom of the boat. The man's help had been kindly meant; he would have held me in my place. But there is no time for apologies when a surf boat reaches the beach. Before I had realised what was happening, two Kroo boys had dived to the bottom of the boat, seized me without any ceremony whatever, and raced me up to the shore, where they put me down in all the blazing sun of an African afternoon, without even a helmet or an umbrella to protect

my head. Grant followed with the helmet, and I endeavoured to smooth my ruffled plumes.[21]

There was a long wait in Addah for a steamer, then another surfboat and another hazardous boarding. She was drenched to the skin trying to take a photograph from the deck of the steamer, and in the tumult of getting out across the bar the superstructure of the boat, along with much of Mary's luggage, was damaged or destroyed, but at last she was on the coastal steamer and headed back to Sekondi.

From Sekondi, where she stayed again at the hospital, she had the chance to go along the land route to see the castles at Dixcove. But in Dixcove it began to rain — heavy, torrential rain — so that what were small waterways on the way out were torrents on the way back. The rainy season was coming.

From Sekondi she took the train up to Tarkwa, the bleak gold-mining area, where she stayed for two weeks in the Swanzy bungalow. Again she mourned the trees:

> But a short time ago the whole place had been dense forest, very difficult to work, and after the usual fashion of the English everyone set to work to demolish the forest trees as if they were the greatest enemies of civilisation.[22]

At the end of the railway was Kumasi where, two years before, she had experienced the magic of the vast forest. She was met with a hammock and taken to the house of the British chief commissioner and his wife. Here she heard the story of how the British had deported the Asante king and some members of his government in 1894, and demanded the Golden Stool, symbol of the Asante people, and how Yaa Asantewaa, their Queen, had led a rebellion and besieged the Kumasi fort. It was several months before the Gold Coast governor sent a force to put down the uprising. The small band of British soldiers and their families, and Swiss missionaries, had almost given up hope of relief when they heard the sound of guns and saw a little fox terrier, the mascot of the relief guard, come out of the forest.

Kumasi's roads — named 'Kingsway' and 'Stewart Avenue'— were wide and tree-lined and its houses were well spaced-out, with gardens around them. It was a peaceful place, resigned to its colonial status. The native shops sold 'European goods of the commonest, cheapest description supplied apparently with the view of educating the native eye in all that is ugliest and most reprehensible in civilisation.'[23]

Mary recorded her views on colonial government:

> What a negro community requires is a benevolent despotism, but as a rule the British Government, with its feeling for the rights of the individual, does not see its way to give it such a Government. But Ashanti was conquered at great cost, wherefore as yet England has still to think of the rights of the white men who dwell there as against the rights of the black man...[But] The Ashanti himself, the truculent warrior of ten years ago, has under the paternal and sympathetic Government of this Chief Commissioner become a man of peace... and is pleased, nay eager that the white man should dwell in his country.[24]

Whereas officials down on the coast hated their life, here in Ashanti territory they found it good, and were anxious that Mary should find it so.

Now time was growing short, and she wanted to go into the forests again. These were rubber trees, and the hammock and the carriers were dwarfed by the great roots and vast trunks which let the sunlight in only in the middle of the day:

> The forest remains in my mind as the most wonderful and awe-inspiring of my experiences. It was difficult to take photographs, for the trees day after day stood in close phalanxes, straight as Nelson's column, never breaking into branches till they were possibly 150 feet from the ground, and between the trunks was a dense undergrowth of fern and creeper, and jungle of all sorts, so closely twined that it was impossible to step a foot from the path, which must have been kept open by an infinity of pains. Never in the world have I seen such mighty trees.

She loved the sensation of being enveloped and overwhelmed by the forest, of being the only white person there to sense it and feel its power. It was a feeling expressed by another woman traveller, Freya Stark, who wrote about having a landscape to herself as being 'a pleasure exclusive, unreasoning and real'.

Further north she came to the mahogany forests.

> '[We] travelled in a pathway that wound beneath the great trees, travelled mostly in gloom, for neither sun nor rain could penetrate, and yet…it had a wonderful charm. I do so hope and pray the British will not rashly cut down and destroy that forest. A mahogany tree is just as well worth preserving as an oak, and though it takes two hundred and fifty years to its full growth it is often rudely cut down and destroyed in a single day.'

She went 258 kilometres to Sunyani and back. In one small town, Bechem, in the heart of the forest, she caused a minor sensation. The chiefs for some distance around had come together to celebrate the coronation of King George V, and the town was full. Now came another amazing event — the arrival of a white woman. No white woman had ever been there before. She was presented with gifts — a sheep, some chickens, plantains, yams, eggs and other foods. She stood while the crowd stared, and solemnly received these offerings. She had to, of course, offer suitable gifts in return, and having nothing similar sent an English pound to the chief. She gave most of the food to her carriers.

With the rainy season beginning, she hurried back to the coast. The little streams she had been carried over on the way up she now had to cross by canoe, or in one case by climbing across a slimy fallen tree trunk. She watched the Wangara women, with loads on their heads and babies on their backs, negotiating the crossings as best they could. 'For perhaps the first time in my life I was more than content with that station in life into which it had pleased my God to call me.'

There was a final train journey down to the coast, a stay with Miss Oram at the hospital, and she was out through the surf to the steamer, bound for England.

Chapter 22

After Africa

[In] her pretty flat…everything was cosy and delightful. I found myself in an ideal sanctum; a bright fire (an item indissolubly connected with comfort in England, somehow), plenty of easy chairs, well-filled bookcases, a business-like writing desk, a table with typewriter and paper, and on the mantelpiece a beautiful grinning blue deity, looted from some Chinese temple or other.[1]

Alice Grant Rosman, the Australian journalist living in London, and later a well-known novelist herself, interviewed Mary for *Everylady's Journal* in June 1912. The 'pretty flat' sounds a far cry from the 'dull and stony street' of that first bleak London winter. Mary had moved up in the building and had more room, but it was the same address!

Mary had moved out and sold the furniture years before, and stayed at a hotel in Cornwall with Guy for a time. She had been back in London, she had moved around the country to co-write with Tonkin, she had been to Africa — now she had returned to Finborough Road. She had the upper half of the house — six rooms, a kitchen and bathroom, on two floors. She let the rooms at the top of the house to a woman and her child, so she was no longer alone in the building.

Rosman was favourably impressed with Mary:

Mary Gaunt left Victoria for London more than ten years ago, but she is still a thorough Australian, energetic, enterprising, with a keen, quick sense of humour and a charming manner…

She did not describe Mary's physical appearance, but the article was illustrated with a pen sketch based on Mary's debutante-like studio portrait in *Alone in West Africa*. In real life Mary was fifty-one; in the Lallie Charles portrait for the book she looked much younger, and the sketch made her look slim, naively attractive and about twenty-one years old.

Mary had arrived back from Africa in the autumn of 1911. The glass plates were developed, the last changes to the text made, and *Alone in West Africa* came out into the world in January 1912. A second edition, a Colonial edition and a US edition come out in the same year, with a third edition in 1913. It was even, in 1917, translated into Ashanti. After the disappointments of the past, here was a book that the English market was ready for — and the US and colonial markets too.

The 'alone' of the title suggests a heroic and solitary figure — if not a Marco Polo in savage foreign lands, at least a Gulliver finding quaint and wonderful things. But while she was sole planner of the expedition and took on the whole adventure alone, she had the comforting presence of British officials and traders along the way. And she had Ansumanah Grant and teams of native bearers. 'Alone' was a relative term.

The reviews were long and mostly complimentary. The *Daily Telegraph* said: 'She is rich in feminine intuition, in vivacity and in narrative skill. She aims always at the vivid personal impression; actuality is of the essence of her temperament…the general reader will rejoice in its spirit, energy and vision.'[2]

The reviewer for *The Spectator* pondered the places she had travelled to. '[Her] personal courage…took her into places singularly ill suited for wandering white ladies and where, it must be added, she cannot have gone without causing a considerable measure of anxiety and inconvenience to others.' He liked the comparison of German and English methods of administration; he quoted her comment on leaving the forest track in British territory: 'The Germans make roads as the Romans made them, that their conquering legions might pass.' But, he pointed out, 'it is necessary to bear in mind that the writer is an Australian…It is in all senses an open-air point of view, fresh, healthy, virile (even when it is a woman's), seeing weak points and sometimes making good ones, but, on the other hand, rough and ready, over-confident from want of adequate knowledge and training…'[3]

The *New York Times* said: 'the best feature of the book is the photographs of scenes in West Africa, which she took herself.'[4] And *Bookman*: 'The book is illustrated…with many novel and striking pictures of scenery and people.'

The Times, however, was disparaging:

> She travelled overland along the coast which few Europeans ever do, and she also struck inland to places where no white woman has ever gone before. Her courage was a thing to wonder at, for she was ignorant of the very elements of African travel; she forgot the most necessary details, could not control her carriers, and suffered in consequence much discomfort and fatigue. But her womanhood, the one fact which makes her journeyings remarkable, is also the fact which made them possible. Mrs. Gaunt was never out of touch with civilisation and was helped along wherever she went. Her methods were extremely simple: she deposited herself helplessly on the doorsteps of the various Provincial and District Commissioners and awaited developments.

And, adding insult to injury:

> Much prominence is given in the text to the taking of photographs and many are here reproduced, but they are invariably indistinct…[5]

There was no question that Mary could put forward her point of view with precision and humour, as many critics pointed out. Her insight into the colour issue is a case in point:

> Tall, stalwart, handsome as is many a negro, no white woman may take a black man for her husband and be respected by her own people; no white man may take a black girl, though her dark eyes be soft and tender…and hope to introduce her among his friends as his wife. Even the missionaries who preach that the black man is a brother decline emphatically to receive him as a brother-in-law.[6]

Mary accepted that she put demands on her hosts as she moved about, but regarded it — as did other travellers — as reasonable. When Mary Kingsley, a single woman of thirty-one, went to West Africa fifteen years before, she acknowledged her reliance on British residents, although she preferred traders and agents to government officials:

> Thanks to 'the Agent', I have visited places I could never otherwise have seen; and to the respect and affection in which he is held by the native, I owe it that I have done so in safety.[7]

Mary Gaunt was also quite willing to acknowledge that she was not only a worry, but a nuisance, to some of her hosts:

> I noticed that at first those who took charge of me were dreadfully afraid I would die on their hands. After a little they were dreadfully afraid I would not!

Readers welcomed the image of a healthy woman travelling in West Africa. Few British officials took their wives out there with them, and even fewer British women went there for pleasure. Reviewers commented on this novel point of view. Some officials in West Africa did not approve, though: '"Spoiling our leave and docking our pay," was what a rueful young man on the Gold Coast told me I was doing six months later. I ought to have kept up the reputation of the country as the White Man's Grave, instead of being in such rude health.'[8]

She was invited to give a lecture at the Royal Colonial Institute — her first — and it was advertised in the Institute journal. In the audience were Liverpool people with African trade interests who engaged her on the spot to go up and lecture in Liverpool, and paid her to do it. The book, and the journey itself, got her into *Who's Who*. It also made selling stories much easier for her. And — greatest honour of all, according to some members of her family — she had a racehorse named after her. Although *Mary Gaunt* (sire: *John of Gaunt*) never raced, her progeny were very successful, and one of her brothers sent her newspaper clippings of their successes from time to time.

At the end of the year she was in Aberdeen, lecturing to the Scottish Geographical Society. She used her talk, which was published in the journal of the Society, to make a plea for the preservation of the mahogany forests.[9]

Altogether, she spent over a year in Africa — five months on the first trip (April to September 1908) and eight months (November 1910 to July 1911) on the second.

...oOo...

During the year that followed, Mary was working on another novel about Africa: *Every Man's Desire*. She set the story on the Gold Coast, making small changes to the names of real places as she had done with *The Uncounted Cost*. She used the castles she had visited and the stories she had heard, especially the story of Letitia Landon.

Letitia Landon's story was still told along the Gold Coast, although she had died seventy years before. She was a gifted poet and a beautiful woman, married to George Maclean, a much older man and governor at Cape Coast Castle. She died at thirty-six of prussic acid poisoning, and the circumstances of her death were never adequately explained. Could it have been suicide? Murder by her husband or by his mistress? In Mary's story, a woman is poisoned at 'El Capo d'Oro' — the setting is Elmina, the placename is Mary's and the story is Letitia's.

Pieces of Mary's African travels abound in the story: a servant is dressed in a white shirt, khaki knickerbockers and red cummerbund, exactly as she dressed Ansumana Grant; the benefits of fresh air in the houses are emphasised; the carriers will not obey Janey, the heroine — 'we be no fit, Ma'; she goes for a walk in the vast mahogany forest that so impressed Mary:

> It seemed the village might so easily oversleep itself one morning and wake to find that the trees and greenery had conquered; the forest had resumed its sway and the human beings overwhelmed...

Mary had an instinct for a good plot, and she constructed the story well.

She used material from her travels, and also from her own life. Janey is twenty-nine and single, by her own assessment pleasantly attractive but not beautiful. She regrets her lack of education: 'no-one had ever thought her brains might be put to any use at all'. Her mother keeps on about her marrying. And when a friend catches the eye of the man Janey likes, she comments: 'these little soft purry women get everything'.

She dedicated the book to the town of Warrnambool and 'to the people whose kindness will never be forgotten and can never be repaid'. In a foreword, she thanked Elsie Lang for 'the interest she has taken in, and the trouble she has gone to, over this book'. Elsie's editorial skills had become very important to Mary.

The official publication date was February 1913.

While Mary was working on the book, her niece Ellinor, Lucy's daughter, came to stay with her. Ellinor was seventeen; she had finished school in Melbourne and was planning to study science at University. She was a rather shy, awkward teenager, given to sweeping and rather childish dismissals of people and things. She was glad to meet two friends when she boarded the ship, 'the rest [of the passengers] being a very shady lot'.[10] A few more days on board did nothing to improve her opinion; she found most of them boring, rowdy and vulgar. Within days she was regretting having deferred her studies for the trip; she was 'seasick, homesick, shipsick, miserable'.

Ellinor kept a diary during her stay in London; there are interesting glimpses of Mary, now fifty-one, through the eyes of her gauche and sometimes disagreeable niece.

> Got up for 9 o'clock breakfast, then started off with the Aunt to shop. [They disagreed violently over clothes.] We then went and tried blouses, and as our tastes are entirely different it was hard to agree on one. We finally got one which neither of us liked much; she called my choice 'dowdy' and I thought hers vulgar. I shall wear the one we did get very seldom…[11]

Ellinor found lectures at the Colonial Institute 'deadly dull'. She didn't like literary people. When she met Cecil, her uncle, she found him 'cross and rude and a regular Gaunt'. They 'had a most exciting fight about wearing [a] white evening dress, but had to give in or be rude. For [the] first time in my life I took former alternative and don't intend to again as it doesn't pay.'

But occasional glimpses of Mary are enjoyable:

> I will refuse dinner parties with Aunt M. in future. Going there she slipped and fell in the mud, frightening the life out of me, but she only giggled in her usual fashion and proceeded all over mud, hat on one side, etc. but as cheerful as ever.[12]

In May, Ellinor started at a school in Upper Norwood, giving her a chance to study English, German, French and chemistry, and giving Mary a chance to work. In June Lucy, Ellinor's mother, arrived in London on leave from Trinity Women's Hostel at The University of Melbourne. Elizabeth Gaunt, now seventy-seven, was also staying in London, and for a time indisposed because of 'a fall on the Underground' which the Underground said was caused by her jumping onto a moving train. Ernest and Cecil visited them all and invited Ellinor and Lucy to go and stay with them. Mary took a hotel room in Brompton Square and the family ebbed and flowed through the rooms in Finborough Road.

She took time off from writing to take in the unique spectacles of pageantry that London offered. She was in the streets to watch the funeral procession of King Edward VII, who died on 6 May 1910. Nine kings followed the coffin to its resting place, including the new King George V, Ernest's former shipmate. It was the last great gathering of the crowned heads of Europe.

Mary had writing friends and acquaintances also, among whom she numbered Alfred Deakin. She corresponded with him about newspaper articles, and knew his secret about writing articles for *The Morning Post* while he was Prime Minister of Australia.

She had a visit from Ethel Turner, who gave her a signed copy of one of her books.

When her Africa novel, *Every Man's Desire*, was gone to the publisher, Mary's thoughts turned to the next project. Her travel book was her best yet — perhaps she should write another.

When Mary reminisced about her childhood on the goldfields, she remembered her grandmother in a lace cap, sitting beside the open cabinet of curios, handling objects which Mary and the other children were not allowed to touch. There was the china spoon for measuring out the tea, carved ivory chessmen, delicate fans, lacquer boxes, a brooch made of mother-of-pearl, and the shoes — the tiny, beautifully decorated satin shoes. Baby shoes, Mary had said. No, her grandmother had said, these were the shoes of a lady with bound feet.

These were the curios brought home by Mary's grandfather, purser of East India Company ships, who had died in London before she was born. As the age of industrialisation rolled on into Mary's lifetime, it became easier for people to travel, and for travellers to take home not a curio but a 'souvenir' of one country that was mass-produced in another. Mary had discovered this in Africa — cheap, ugly, printed cotton goods from Manchester being sold in the markets of the Gold Coast.

But the things in her grandfather's collection of curios, with all the power of story and the mystique of the Oriental past, had begun for Mary a fascination with China. She remembered, too, the Chinese miners who came to the door to claim her father's protection on the goldfields. They were patient, hard-working men from southern China, taunted and feared by turns by the white community around them. They were separate, different, strange. And somewhere behind them — back in some distant and exotic land — there were women who waved exquisite ivory fans and wore tiny shoes on bound feet.

...oOo...

By the middle of 1912, Mary was beginning to think of going to China. She talked to Werner Laurie about it. The sales of *Alone in West Africa* were good; he would be happy for her to do another big trip, another 'A Woman Alone...' travel adventure. He encouraged the idea. He made the standard offer of an advance for her expenses, but an advance was only that — it would be deducted from royalties when the book was sold. As she relied on royalties for her income, she began to ponder other ways to finance a trip.

She went to visit her friend and fellow writer Mrs Basil Hargreaves — who wrote as Parry Truscott — who lived in the pretty village of Ditchling, near the Brighton line. Having found her compartment on the train, Mary stood looking out of the window at the bustle of the station and saw a porter bringing hot water bottles. Sharing her compartment were two reserved English ladies. It was cold; she asked if they would like hot water bottles. 'They gave me to understand that they required neither the hot-water bottles nor my conversation,' Mary wrote. She retired to her corner and gazed out of the window, lost in thought when, to her amazement, she saw a train of camels and elephants going along the road. Forgetting herself, she cried out, 'Oh look, elephants and camels!'

> Those two ladies were a credit to the English nation. They bore themselves with the utmost propriety. What they thought of me I can only dimly guess, but they never even raised their eyes from their papers. Of course the train rushed on, the camels and elephants were left behind, and there was nothing to show they had ever been there. Then I regret to state that I lay back and laughed till I cried, and whenever I felt a little better the sight of those two studious women solemnly reading their papers set me off again. When I got out at Hassocks they...literally drew their skirts around them so that they should not touch mine and be contaminated as I passed.[13]

There was a short setback to her daydreams about China when she was knocked down by a cyclist near her home and had to spend ten days in bed. Her brother Ernest observed drily that he thought she might be safer if she went to China.

Chapter 23

'Why Not a Book about China?'

One thing seems certain, between us Westerners and the Chinese, is a great gulf fixed. We look across and sometimes we wonder, and sometimes we pity, and sometimes we admire, but we cannot understand.[1]

In August 1912, George Ernest Morrison was back in London. Mary wrote to him on 20 August and invited him to dinner. Already becoming known as 'Chinese' Morrison because of his role with *The Times*, he had just been appointed political adviser to the Chinese Government. She wrote jokingly, 'May a sister-in-law once removed bid the new Emperor of China welcome and wish him a good time in England.' She was rather tentative; she invited him to a meal 'either to have a quiet chat or to meet friends' — that is, alone or with others. She did not know the main purpose of his trip to England. A week later, on 26 August, in a ceremony attended by only a few family and friends, Morrison married Jennie Robin, his long-time secretary and twenty-seven years his junior.

With the news made public, Mary wrote again on 31 August with good wishes on his marriage and sent him a copy of her travel book, *Alone in West Africa*, as a wedding gift. She invited *both* the newlyweds to dine, and declared her ulterior motive:

> My publisher thinks a book of Chinese travel — written by me, save the mark! — would pay far better than this one has done, and it has done most excellently well, or I should not dare to offer it. And he has given added impetus to the thought at the back of my mind

that I should like to go to China. Would you help me with advice or introductions. I mean insure me letters of introduction from the Chinese Government or any facilities for travel such as they undoubtedly could offer.

I assure you I hesitate very much about asking you because I am asking what to me is a very big thing and it may be impossible for you to grant it, but if you could it would put what to me is a big sum of money into my pocket. To begin with, could I go to a paper and say I had your influence behind my power to write travel articles, my fortune would be made…[2]

Morrison's name would open doors; it would give her work prestige and sell books. So she urged the invitation to dine during the next week; she would keep all days free.

But Morrison didn't have much time. His new position made him an important political figure; members of the British Government wanted to talk to him, the press wanted to talk to him, old friends, job seekers, people with business propositions, fortune hunters — everybody wanted to talk to him. Morrison and Jennie invited Mary to come and dine with *them*. Over dinner, Morrison suggested that she rough out the sort of letter she'd like him to write. He and Jennie invited Mary to come and stay with them in Peking.

Mary went home and did as Morrison suggested, and sent her draft letter to him the next day. Time went by, and soon Morrison and Jennie would be leaving to go back to China. There was no letter from Morrison. Mary went to call on them. On the day she called, there was a note from Jennie to say they wouldn't be able to come and see her, as they were almost out of time. Mary wrote another urgent note — she knew Morrison was busy, but she needed to have his letter. She needed to be able to tell her publisher, and the newspapers, that she started 'with his interest and good wishes'.[3] Next day, Morrison sent the letter, apologising for the delay.

She was elated. She would go to China. She would write another big travel book. She would see the land her grandmother spoke of long ago in Beechworth, the land where men spoke a strange foreign tongue and women with exquisite fans tottered on tiny feet.

She began writing regular letters to Morrison, who was now back in Peking. Either he had suggested she take a pistol, or someone else had and she had told him about it. She wrote to tell him she was delaying her departure to see her novel *Every Man's Desire* launched into the world and to write something for *Harper's*, who had asked to see some Africa articles. She told him *Century Magazine* had ordered two articles on China at £30 each and 12s 6d for every photograph used. Publication in two such prestigious magazines would be very good for her. She added a postscript: 'I believe I'd be safer with a dummy revolver.'

She was clearly planning a trip similar to her second Africa trip: she would hire an interpreter, who would hire bearers when needed; she would use public transport when it was available, and after that she would be carried across China, stopping with missionaries and government officials on the way and relying on them for local knowledge and help to get to the next stopping place.

It was an amazing, eccentric, British upper-class approach to travel. She would arrive at outposts of the Empire — the posts of British civil servants or of religious missionaries — with letters of introduction from impressive people, and be welcomed and offered hospitality, and settle back to be received and made comfortable among strangers.

She was anxious to impress Morrison with her plans — as no doubt she impressed, amazed, her acquaintances in London. Morrison's replies were polite, helpful and brief. After all, what Mary did in Africa, with bearers, an interpreter and a train of porters, Morrison had done in China on foot and alone.

She sometimes adopted the tone of the helpless little woman:

Forgive me for troubling you, but this is going to be a big book and my publisher is wildly excited about it…I have never travelled armed, so I do not see the necessity of doing it now…what bank had I better send my money through, and how much should I have for the journey from London after all the expenses, ticket, sleeping car and meals are paid? I am always an easy prey to those who ask tips, so an idea of how much I should give conductors would make me most grateful. I am afraid I am bothering you a great deal, but as every penny is earned by hard labour you will understand I feel I am bound to take a little care of it.[4]

This is the woman the *Literary Digest* called 'a woman slave-driver' because of her account of travelling at night past Krobo Hill.

There was a lot of serious planning to be done. She wrote again to Morrison. Should she send her heavy photographic equipment by sea? Would she need the portable bath? How could she arrange money matters across Siberia? Would he think it worth her while to linger in Siberia, or go straight on and 'give all her mind' to China? (In the end, she rejected the canvas portable bath she took to Africa in favour of an india-rubber one given to her by a friend, which proved to be much better.)

She was preoccupied with the cost of the journey. Morrison — like her brothers, like many men — travelled because of his work. He earned a professional salary and his expenses were paid by his employers. Like many women travellers, Mary had no such advantage. Some travelled with independent means; Mary had to earn the money for the trip.

She told Morrison in a letter that she had 'a nice little sum' coming to her in September of 1912. William Gaunt had for many years been paying an allowance to his unmarried sister Mary in Staffordshire which, by his will, was continued after his death. The elderly Mary Gaunt died in January 1912; she may have responded to William's generosity by providing for his two daughters in her will, particularly as Mary and Lucy were now both widowed.

Mary wrote to Morrison that the prestigious US *Harpers* magazine had shown interest after seeing *Alone in West Africa*. The London newspaper, the *Daily Chronicle*, had also expressed interest. She corresponded with *Century Magazine* in New York, apparently using Morrison's name, about writing articles for them. She would write articles for them all. She talked about photographs with Sinclairs, in the Haymarket, London, who normally developed her pictures. She arranged to send pictures back to them to be processed, if she was not able to get quality work done in China.

During her preparations came awful news from Guy. As captain of the battleship HMS *Centurion*, he was supervising speed trials on the night of 12 December in the English Channel when his ship collided in darkness with an Italian ship, the *Derna*. The next day there was no trace of the *Derna*. The ship and all thirty-six of her crew had disappeared, apart from the body of one seaman washed ashore in a lifeboat. Guy was to be court-martialled for putting his own ship in danger and for failing to do everything possible to help the other ship. The court-martial would be months away, but the shadow of it, and of the lives lost, cast a cloud over Guy and all the family.[5]

With her plans almost finalised, Mary spent Christmas with her family at *Gauntswood*, Guy's home near Leek, in Staffordshire. Back in London on 30 December, she signed a contract for a book to be called *Alone in China*, and collected £100 advance on royalties. With *Every Man's Desire* launched, on 31 January she boarded the train for China.

Elizabeth (nee Palmer), Mary Gaunt's mother.
Photo from the Athenaeum, Chiltern

William Henry Gaunt, Mary's father.
Photo from the Athenaeum, Chiltern

The sale notice for the Gaunt home in Chiltern, *Woodlands*.

Black Dog Creek, on the diggings near Chiltern, in summer. Photo by the author

The Ballarat Club, where William entertained his friends. Photo by the author

The Lyceum Club, London. Photo by the author

Mining race cut into the rock, Beechworth. Photo by the author

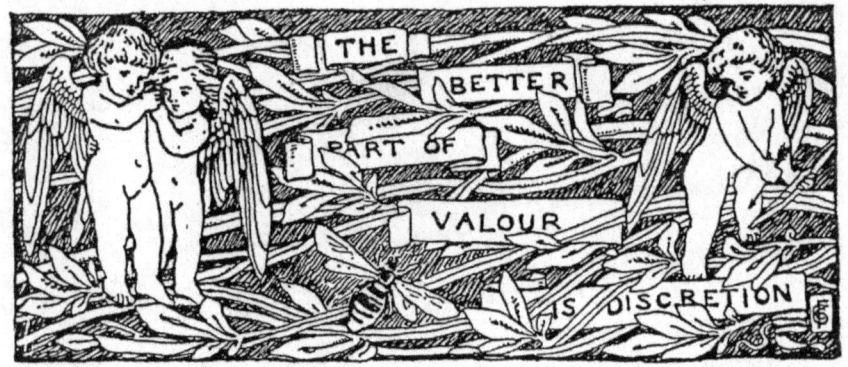

"LOST."

A Story of the Australian Bush.

By MARY GAUNT.

With Illustrations by E. F. BREWTNALL, R.W.S.

"HELM, old man, we've lost the track!"
"Don't be a howling idiot, man. Lost!
Why, there's the track right ahead, an—
But Anderson flung himself off—
grass and covered his face wi—
"I tell you," reiterate—
and shading his ey—
might have bee—
"They were made yester—
my dear fellow, we mad—
"What!"
Helm raised—
stooped ove—
again cr—

"ANDERSON FLUNG HIMSELF OFF HIS HORSE ON TO THE DRY CRISP GRASS."

'Lost', illustrations of the story from *English Illustrated Magazine*, 1892.

Marry's house in Finborough Road — the doorway on the right.
Photo by Susan Kerr

Finborough Road, London — the 'dull and stony street'. Photo by the author

Down to Polperro, Cornwall, where Mary and Guy spent a holiday. Photo by the author

Playing draughts, Cape Coast. Photo by Mary in *Alone in West Africa*

Mary Haven in New Eltham, Kent, Mary's home during World War II. Photo by the author

The Rectory in Frinstead, Kent, home of Elsie and Rev. Lewis Lang. Photo courtesy of Howard Rigney

The church in Frinstead, Kent, where Elsie and Rev. Lewis Lang are buried. Photo by the author

Hotel de Paris, Mary's first home in Bordighera. Photo by the author

The English Library, Bordighera. Photo by the author

Dr Thomas Tonkin, Mary's co-author for three novels, as pictured in the official report of the Hausa expedition.

Dr Thomas Tonkin had himself photographed later for a magazine article.

The Gaunt house. Photo taken about 1890. Possibly one of Mary's younger brothers in the foreground. Photo courtesy of James Read

The Gaunt house today. Photo by the author

Mary ready to leave the Wagons-Lit Hotel in Peking with her two Peking carts.

Mary at the Ming Tombs, outside Peking.

The courtyard of Mary's rented temple, San Shan An, outside Peking.

Mary (left) entertains — tiffin at San Shan An.

A street in the old town, Bordighera.
Photo by the author

An archway in the old town, Bordighera.
Photo by the author

A woman on her balcony, old Bordighera.
Photo by the author

The Moreton Bay fig tree at the Bicknell Institute, Bordighera, already destroying the brick wall at the entrance. Photo by the author

La Roseraie Vence, where British refugees from Bordighera, including Mary, stayed from 1940–41. It is now a fashionable small hotel. Photo by the author

Sunny Bank, the English hospital in Cannes — Mary's last refuge.
From a watercolour by the late Cdr. Ken Buckel

The site of Mary's grave in the cemetery in Cannes, France.
Photo by the author

The English section of the cemetery, Bordighera.
Photo by the author

The chapel of Saint Ampelio, patron saint of Bordighera.
Photo by the author

Chapter 24

China of the Ages

I looked out of the carriage window as the train ran through the Chinese city on its way to the Chien Men railway station, and wondered what the future was going to be like, and I wondered aloud.

'How will I get on?'

Opposite me sat an amusing young gentleman with a ready tongue.

'Oh, you'll be all right,' said he. 'The Chinese'll like you because you're fat and o--' and then he checked himself seeing, I suppose, the dawning wrath in my eyes.

The Chinese admire fat people and they respect the old, but I had not been accustomed to looking upon myself as old yet [she was fifty-two], though I had certainly seen more years than he had, and as for fat — well, I had fondly hoped my friends looked upon it as a pleasing plumpness. With these chastening remarks sinking into my soul, we rolled into the railway station.[1]

As the steam engine of the Trans-Siberian Railway slowed on the outskirts of Peking, Mary watched the houses and buildings, and had a few moments of sombre reflection about what lay ahead. So much depended on finding adventure, on shaping a story, on achieving success.

The train journey had been exhilarating. She had drunk in the 'clear, cold windless air' in a week in Moscow, she had crossed the ice-bright Russian steppes and seen Siberian birch forests twinkling with frost flowers in the sun. She had felt 'joy — joy that such beauty exists, that I was alive to look upon it'. Then the train had curved south, down through the Tartar cities and lonely graves into Northern China. It was a memorable trip, but after twelve days on the train, she was happy and relieved to be in China at last. It was 23 February 1913 — a momentous day for Mary and, as she learned later, a notable one for China as well.

The day was cold and an icy wind lifted grit from the streets and hurled it into faces and eyes. Once again, she stood on a railway platform surrounded by luggage. Gradually the passengers dispersed, and still she stood there. She understood nothing in the voices around her, the signs above her head. She was alone in an alien land. The Morrisons had not come.

She managed, with the help of one of the few remaining passengers, to get a handcart for her luggage and a rickshaw for herself, and went to the Morrisons' house. Neither Ernest Morrison nor Jennie was at home. A servant received her; her luggage was piled in the courtyard, and she was given tea and offered a bath. She had not been able to take a bath on the train, so she accepted the offer gladly. The Morrisons came home and welcomed her, and all was well — and a week later the letter announcing her arrival turned up.

She stayed with the Morrisons for two weeks. She rode out with Jennie in a rickshaw, but saw little of George until dinner in the evenings. She learnt of the death of the Empress, which had happened on the day of her arrival. The unloved wife and widow of the former Emperor was gone, and the last great dynasty of China was represented by a small child. Morrison was plunged into meetings and discussions; he had a demanding schedule and little free time. He was courteous to Mary, but his diary showed an attitude rather different:

> Feb. 25, 1913: To lunch came [several people]. Mrs. Mary Gaunt makes a very poor impression — very fat, almost hunchbacked, imperfect manners and for ever discussing herself, and her mind a blank about China.

It wasn't only Mary. In the same week Morrison wrote of one visitor as a 'brainless nonentity', a doctor's sister as 'a woman of weak intellect', and another guest as 'looking very sodden and alcoholic'.

A few days after her arrival, Mary wrote a testy letter to the *Central China Post*:

> My attention is drawn to a leader in your issue of 22 February which is written round the following astonishing text:
>
> 'From a paragraph going the rounds of the Press, it appears that Miss Mary Gaunt, the well-known Australian traveller, is about to start an expedition to unknown China and that by the advice of her brother-in-law Dr. Morrison, she is busy as an indispensable preliminary in practising with a Mauser pistol in order to become an expert shot.'
>
> It would be difficult to compress within one short paragraph more mis-statements of facts. I have never had the remotest intention of starting on an expedition through 'unknown China'. Like yourself I have no idea on what section of the map 'unknown China' is to be found.
>
> No such advice as that suggested has been given to me by Dr. Morrison. I have never carried a pistol in my life, nor have I ever in my life fired a shot from a pistol. Dr. Morrison is not my brother-in-law.
>
> Thanking you…[2]

It is difficult to say whether Mary was seeking publicity, hoping to get more mileage out of the coverage or just travel weary. As her brother Lance had married Morrison's sister Violet in 1906, Morrison was in fact her brother's brother-in-law. The description hardly mattered. She was certainly planning to take a little-known route across China, and she carried a small pistol and ammunition on her trip.

Mary moved into the Wagon-Lits, a hotel in the Legation Quarter which was popular with Western travellers. Around her, the life of the streets went on, but the Chinese were adjusting to a new world without the emperors who had ruled them for two thousand years — there was uncertainty, opportunism, anxiety everywhere.

Mary wandered the crowded, dirty streets. She saw how the glories of the past had faded into dusty temples where the gods had died. Slowly, gradually, time and China worked their magic on her. Along the tree-lined streets of the Tartar city, and beside the pinkish-red walls of the Imperial City, she saw the delicate lattice work of windows, the mysterious doors leading into secluded courtyards, the rich carving and gilding of the shopfronts. Gradually, the charm of the old buildings overcame the strangeness and she became absorbed in the past, the people, the stories, the whole weight of history around her.

In March, the funeral ceremonies for the Empress began. She had been a minor figure in the Palace, without the importance of Tz'u-hsi, the Dowager who had wielded power for almost half a century until her death in 1908. This woman had instead been wife and widow of the late Emperor. Still, the funeral formalities had to be held.

Their timing was fortunate for Mary. Embassies could get entrée for their nationals into the Forbidden City to pay their respects. A small window onto Imperial China was open to the prying world.

Mary lined up to be received by the military commandant, along with Manchu princes in white mourning sheepskins and black Tartar caps, Manchu women in high head-dresses and brilliant silk coats; Chinese ladies tottering on tiny, bound feet with flowers and jewelled pins in their sleeked-down hair. She took her turn in the line of dignitaries to bow three times to the picture of the dead Empress. A band and a choir sat in a circle intoning the funeral rites, beating drums and striking bells. There were refreshment marquees in the courtyard with oranges and ginger, tea and cakes. The crowd peered into corners and chattered together at this unexpected sightseeing opportunity. Over the chatter, over 'the weird, archaic Eastern music' came the sound of children from an American mission school singing 'Down by the Swanee' and 'Auld Lang Syne'.

Conditions were unsettled in China, and it was not a good time to travel abroad. Acquaintances, and the Embassy, urged Mary to stay awhile in Peking. While she did, Mary the businesswoman was at work. Before she left London she had talked to Sinclair, the firm that processed her photographs and slides, about the pictures for her magazine articles. She was concerned about the standard of work in China. She wanted to send some articles to *Century* in New York, and pictures with them. Why not send the pictures direct to *Century*? they asked. This was not the usual practice; a writer who offered illustrated articles was expected to send the pictures ready for use. Mary sent a note to *Century*: would they be willing to accept the undeveloped photographs? They appear to have suggested that she get them at least developed.

Six weeks after Mary had paid her respects, the funeral cortege of the Empress left the Forbidden City and passed through the Chien Men gate to the railway station. Mary climbed forty feet up the steps onto the wall of the great gate and watched the procession — the camels, the white ponies, the palanquins filled with flowers, the mounted cavalry of the Imperial Guard, police, attendants, Buddhist lamas carrying incense sticks, their yellow robes crossed with crimson sashes, and finally the Empress's bier draped in yellow embroidered satin — dragons for the Emperor, phoenixes for his consort. Then the coffin was loaded onto a train — the symbol of the Western intrusion so resented by the Manchu rulers — and taken to a tomb among those of the Ch'ing emperors in the eastern hills.

On 25 March Mary wrote to *Century*, using the Chinese-and-English, dollars-and-cents postage stamps of the new republic. The tone of her letter was curiously condescending:

> I went to the funeral ceremonies of the Dowager Empress of China and though a funeral does not inspire me I have thought that it might possibly be of interest to you. It certainly was bizarre…[3]

She went on in a more positive tone:

> I am in hopes of doing you something much better when I get into more unknown parts… I'm going up to Jehol, the hunting lodge of the Manchus…before I go away down to Szechuan, on the borders of Tibet, so I hope to give you something really interesting.
>
> …

> I am sending you some films[4] for you will see by those I have had printed they are so badly done that it is hardly worth while and you will probably get much better results in New York…I think I shall send my plates or films to be developed by Eastman Rochester, New York [as an afterthought, she has added 'or else to London'] who will probably do it better than I can get it done here, and they will send them on to you.

But, thinking of the current ones, she added as a postscript: 'I am sorry to trouble you to get the films printed, but what can I do?'[5]

If *Century* didn't want the article and photos, and they had made no commitment, she asked that they be sent to her New York Agent, Francis Jones. Whether they used the material or not, she wanted her originals back to illustrate her books and lectures.

She was planning to write the next article about the walls of Peking and send it — with pictures — via Francis Jones, but she supposed they might want something about 'more unknown parts'. She wrote, 'There is a great deal of unrest and rumours of wars and risings, but still I expect to get into the interior. I shall have a good try for it.'

Unfortunately, no articles by Mary about China appeared in *Century Magazine*. The walls of Peking were demolished in the 1950s because they obstructed the traffic; an article on them, and pictures, would have been an interesting, perhaps memorable, record.

While she waited in Peking, Mary studied the people around her with growing interest. She went to a theatre performance where she watched the audience more than the stage, and noticed particularly the way the women used make-up. Manchu women, she decided, 'put on the colour with such right goodwill that every woman, when she is dressed in her smartest, looks remarkably like a sign-board.'

She grew restless. She wanted to get out and explore China, but with rumours of war all around, Morrison warned her that she must stay near the capital. She learned, however, that there was a section of the Great Wall fairly near to the capital, and she was determined to go there. She met a few people at the hotel who also wanted to go, and together they took the train out to the Nan-k'ou Pass and were carried in chairs from the station to the pass itself.

> If the country round was desolate, the sunshine was glorious, the air, the clean dry air of Northern China was as invigorating as champagne, and I knew that I could go on forever and feel myself much blessed. It was well and more than well to be here in the open spaces of the earth, to draw deep breaths, to feel that neither past nor future mattered…I had all that I could ask of life.[6]

She was travelling for the sheer exuberance of it. At the pass, the travellers got a stunning glimpse of the Wall. It was neglected and falling into disrepair, but still breathtaking in its size and conception. They stayed at an inn nearby, and went to see the Ming tombs the next day, and the following day returned on the train to Peking.

Chapter 25

Peking and the Summer Palace

If there is any mode of progression more wearying and uncomfortable, I have not met it. It is simply a springless board set on a couple of wheels with a wagon tilt of blue cotton, if you are not imperial, over it, and a place for heavy luggage behind. [The passenger] packs his bedding and all the cushions he can raise around him, and then resigns himself to his fate…I cannot recommend a Peking cart, even on the smoothest road. And the roads in China are not smooth.[1]

Now that she had seen something of Peking, Mary wanted to go further afield. Again she was advised to wait, but she was not good at waiting. She had read the account of Lord Macartney's embassy to the great Chien-Lung emperor in 1793; she wanted to go to Jehol, to the hunting palace of the Manchu, and see what Macartney had seen. She also wanted to see the Tung-ling, the eastern tombs of the Manchu where the Empress had recently been buried. She asked around; no-one else had plans to go to Jehol, nor did she find any Europeans who had been there. The staff at the Legation were concerned, but they did not stop her going. It would be close to 500 kilometres in a Peking cart — a covered seat-for-one on wheels, without springing. Undaunted, she hired an English-speaking servant, Tuan, who engaged two carts, each with a driver and two mules. All along her route she would create an impression of unimaginable wealth — a foreign woman with a cart for herself and one for her servant and luggage.

She started out from the Wagons-Lit Hotel in a long serviceable cotton dress, with her hair pinned up under her straw hat, and taking stout boots for walking and climbing. The travelling was dusty and uncomfortable. The cart bumped and banged her about: 'the new nightgowns and chemises in my box were worn into holes with the jolting'. But this was the way to learn about China — meeting people, hearing the stories, seeing the countryside. She met a German girl who heard that, just after she left Peking, the German Consul sent around a message cancelling her passport because the country was far too disturbed for her to travel to Jehol. She met a man who worked for the British American Tobacco Company, who told her hair-raising stories of Boxer atrocities. She heard tales of Pai Lang, the White Wolf, whose robber band was roaming in Honan, to the south, and terrorising Chinese and Westerners alike. And, as they went through the villages, she heard the crying of children:

> Morning and evening, the little girls cried because the bandages on their feet were being drawn more tightly. Always it is a gnawing pain, and the only relief the little girl can get is by pressing the calf of her leg tightly against the edge of the k'ang. The pressure stops the flow of blood and numbs the feet as long as it is kept up, but it cannot be kept up long, and with the rush of blood comes the increase of pain — a pain that the tightening of the bandages deepens.[2]

After several nights at wayside inns, usually full of poor travellers and carters, she was relieved to find that there were Western missionaries in Ch'eng-te, the stopping-off town for Jehol. She had made no arrangements beforehand, but the missionaries made her welcome, and she stayed several days with them. It was a Brethren mission, and was to provide her with useful material for her Chinese novel, and a few unusual experiences for herself.

The hunting lodge of the Manchu was not as Macartney's party had described it. No-one had lived there for sixty years, and the paving tiles were cracked, the pathways overgrown, and the whole magical pleasure grounds neglected and sad. It took two ceremonial calls on officialdom to get the necessary permission to go there, but when it came it was permission for Mary and a generous retinue. So with missionary women and mission servants, Mary went on a grand picnic in the grounds. Behind the high walls, groves of trees and overgrown pathways led to temples, pagodas and pavilions reflected in ornamental lakes. The women crossed abandoned courtyards to peer through latticed windows into palace rooms where the red and gold of lacquered chairs and sumptuous interiors gleamed in the dust and desolation. Unoccupied as it was, the Republican Government continued to guard it and its treasures.

For the return trip to Peking, Mary paid off her servants and floated down river, and got a train back to Peking. It was a longer distance but a much more comfortable journey.

...oOo...

Mary saw quite a bit of Christian missionary work in China. She needed to make contact with Westerners — people who spoke English — and Westerners were mainly missionaries, since there were few British Government officials outside Peking. She learned to recognise the faith missions, where missionaries went out 'in faith' — not supported, or not supported completely, by funds from home. Often these missionaries wore Chinese costume and lived as the Chinese did. Mary was uncomfortable with this concept. She believed it was important to set a good example — to fly the flag, to always remember that they were British and not sink to the level of the poor, sick, dirty people around them. And she was uncomfortable with the fundamentalist branches of the church. She valued the standards of a good conventional Anglican upbringing: wearing clean clothes to church, limiting oneself to one wife at a time, respecting women, speaking English. Passing on these standards could only benefit the Chinese. She was completely taken aback at the Brethren mission in Jehol when:

> ...my hostess bowed her head, and thanked God openly that I had come through the dangers of the way, and been brought safely to

their compound! For a moment it took my breath away, and so self-conscious was I, that I did not know which way to look. My father was a pillar of the Church of England, Chancellor of the Diocese in which we lived, and I had been brought up straitly in the fold, among a people who, possibly, felt deeply on occasion, but who never, never would have dreamt of applying religion personally and openly to each other.³

She felt much more at ease at the well-funded missions, where the missionaries lived in reasonable comfort, and was particularly impressed with the work of the medical missions. She noticed that converts were often employed on mission compounds, and observed shrewdly that their choice of allegiance might be economic rather than religious. Stories she heard of Chinese workers deserting the missionaries when the Boxers came reinforced this opinion. She was inclined to agree with Morrison's cynical comment that 'their harvest may be described as amounting to a fraction more than two Chinamen per missionary per annum.'⁴

Still, she admired the medical work that was being done, and in particular the missionaries' attempts to rescue girls and women from the horrors of foot-binding. She could see that many poor and desperate people were helped in the mission hospitals and clinics, and was proud — if a little amazed — that Westerners would choose such a noble and selfless endeavour.

…oOo…

Summer came to Peking — dusty, airless and hot. Martial law had been declared, and travel across China was out of the question. She must wait — but waiting in Peking was unbearable. She went to stay for a short time with friends in Tongshan, near Tientsin, in a house which had been defended against the Boxers and whose occupants had another fund of stories. There was still no end to the unrest, but there was much she could write about.

She could not, for the present, go across China as planned, but she was not ready to give up. She had been writing a diary as she travelled; the next step was to settle down and write a book. She rented a small unused temple called San Shan An, about the size of a suburban house, in the foothills on the outskirts of Peking, and began work. She had two servants, and there were the coolies who looked after the temple, but there were no Westerners about. James Buchanan, a k'ang puppy bought at a street market in Peking, kept her company, followed her on walks and barked at real or imagined intruders. She set to work, shaping the diary entries into a narrative about her travels. She wrote about China in a state of turmoil for Britain in its last days of peace; she could see the day coming when 'the need for change, the desire for better things, the power to insist on a higher standard of living shall have come to [China's] lower classes'. She ended her account with speculation:

> ...surely the spirit of those men who built the wondrous courtyards and halls of audience of the Forbidden City, who planned the pleasure-grounds at Jehol, who stretched the Wall over two thousand miles of mountain and valley...must be alive and active as it was a thousand years ago. And when that spirit animates not the few taskmasters, but the mass of the people, when it reaches the toiling slaves and makes of them men, the nation will be like the palaces and altars they built hundreds of years ago, and the rest of the world may stand aside, and wonder, and perhaps fear.[5]

The summer faded — the last peaceful summer of the world. The November days grew chill. It would be too cold to spend the winter at San Shan An. She arranged to go and stay with her friends the Lewises — Dr Lewis was in charge of the hospital at the Presbyterian mission in Pao Ting Fu, 150 kilometres south-west of Peking. She had not quite finished the book when the weather closed in. She packed up her manuscript and books, and all her belongings, and turned her back on the little temple, on Peking, on the old year, and caught the train to Pao Ting Fu.

The day after her arrival, she went to the station to collect some pieces of her luggage which had gone astray:

> Nobody could speak a word of English. In the course of five minutes I should say, the entire station staff of Pao Ting Fu stood around me, and vociferously gave me their views — on the weather and the latest

political developments for all I know. If it was about the luggage I was no wiser. Some were dressed in khaki, some in dark cloth with uniform caps, and most had the wild hair that comes to the lower classes with the cutting off of the queue. There were about a dozen of them with a few idlers in blue cotton, patched, dirty, faded, and darned, and some of these wore queues, queues that had been slept in for about a week without attention, and they were all quite anxious to be nice to the foreign woman, and took turns in trying to make her understand. In vain. What they wanted I could not imagine. At last a lane opened, and I guessed the vociferating crowd were saying: 'Here is the very man to tackle the situation.' There came along a little man in dark cloth who stood before me and in the politest manner laid a dirty, admonitory finger upon my breast. He had a rudimentary knowledge of English but it was very rudimentary, and I remembered promptly that this was a French railway.

'Parlez-vous Français?' said I, wondering if my French would carry me through.

He shook his head. As a matter of fact English, pidgin-English, is the language of China, when another tongue is wanted, and my new friend's English was not at all bad — what there was of it. Though why I should go to their country and expect these people to understand me I'm sure I do not know.

'Your luggage is here,' said he very slowly, emphasising every word by a tap.

'Thank Heaven,' I sighed, 'take me to it,' but he paid no heed.

'You' — and he tapped on solemnly '— must — send — your — husband.'

This was a puzzler. 'My husband,' I said meekly, 'is dead.'

It looked like a deadlock. It was apparently impossible to deliver up her luggage to a woman whose husband was dead. Everybody on the platform, including the idlers, made some suggestion to relieve the strain, and feeling that it might help matters, I said he had been dead a very long time. I was a lonely orphan and I had no brothers. They probably discussed the likelihood of my having any other responsible male belongings and dismissed it, and the man who knew English returned to the charge.

'Where — do — you — stay?' and he tapped his way through the sentence.

'At Dr. Lewis's.' I felt like doing it singsong fashion myself.

'You — must — tell — Lu Tai Fu — to — come.'

'But,' I remonstrated, 'Dr. Lewis is busy, and he does not know the luggage.'

There was another big confabulation, then a brilliant idea flashed like a meteor across the crowd.

'You — must — go — back — and — write — a — letter,' and with a decisive tap my linguist friend stood back, and the whole crowd looked at me as much as to say that settled it most satisfactorily.

I argued the matter. I wanted to see the luggage.

'The — luggage — is — here' tapped my friend reproachfully, as if regretting I should be so foolish — 'you — must — go — back — write — one piecey — letter.'

'I'll write it here,' said I, and after about a quarter of an hour taken up in tapping, I was conducted round to the back of the station, an elderly inkpot and a very, very elderly pen with a point like a very rusty pin were produced, but there was no paper. Everyone looked about, under the benches, up at the ceiling, and at last one really resourceful person produced a luggage label of a violent yellow hue, and on the back of that, with some difficulty, for as well as the bad pen, there was a suspicion of gum on the paper, I wrote a letter to 'Dear Sir' requesting that responsible individual to hand over my luggage to my servant. I signed my name with as big a flourish as the size of the label would allow, and then I stood back to await developments.

Everybody in the room looked at that valuable document. They tried it sideways, they tried it upside down, but no light came. At last the linguist remarked with his usual tap:

'No — can — read.'

Well, I could read English, so with great *empressement* and as if I were conferring a great favour, I read that erudite document aloud to the admiring crowd, even to my own name, and such was the magic of the written word, that in about two minutes the lost luggage appeared and was handed over to my waiting coolie! Only when I was gone doubt fell once more upon the company. Could a woman, a masterless woman, be trusted? they questioned. And the stationmaster sent word to Lu Tai Fu that he must have his card to show that it was all right![6]

Chapter 26

'A Sunday Walk in Hyde Park'

You have not yet forgotten your trip to Jehol, I hope, and the roughness of the road. The trip you contemplate will make the little journey to Jehol look like a Sunday morning walk in Hyde Park, particularly as regards travelling comfort, to say nothing about the danger of the journey as regards hostile tribes on the southern and western borders of Tibet. You will be passing near the Lolo country, and I can assure you that the Lolos are *not* a set of gentlemen within the meaning of the Act. They are distinctly hostile to foreigners, and many murders have taken place in their country that have not been published…

If you have really made up your mind to go, however, just let me know, and I will endeavour to hunt up all the information that it is possible to collect as to the best route to take, etc., though I repeat I would not advise the journey, and the Geographical Society can go to the deuce.[1]

For centuries merchants from China travelled west, out along the arduous road that led over the mountains, across the vast Asian plateau, and down into Europe. Routes from all over southern China converged on the walled city of Hsi An, the old capital. Travellers from the coast would follow the valley of the great Hoang Ho (Yellow River) for a thousand kilometres from its vast delta, and rest awhile at the pass of T'ung-kuan, gateway to the mountains. Here they left the Yellow River, climbing slowly past the old capital until at Lan Chou, the old city at the crossroads, the Yellow River crossed their path again. Now they were at the edge of the unknown. From here the trade routes shifted with water supplies, tribal alliances and the political power of China. The main route went out due west, with the last of the Yellow River tributaries giving travellers a pathway into the mountains. They followed the Kunlungshan, the mountains on the border of China and Tibet, and skirted the southern edge of the great Taklamakan Desert, and swung in a wide arc northward to the walled city of Kashgar.

During the T'ang Dynasty, in the 7th, 8th and 9th centuries AD, Chinese control extended right out to Kashgar. By the late 1800s, Kashgar had become a prize in the 'Great Game' between Britain and Russia for control of Central Asia; they set up trade agencies and consulates there. The oasis at the crossroads between east and west was now the terminus of the Caspian Railway — as far as most European travellers wanted to go.

Towards Christmas 1913, Mary wrote to Morrison that she wanted to follow the route he had taken in 1910, across Asia via the Silk Road, to Kashgar and into Russia. Replicating any of Morrison's amazing journeys would have given her a traveller's tale worth reading, and the name 'Silk Road' had a magic of its own. Although it had existed for nearly two thousand years, few travellers went along its whole length. Merchants travelled in relays, selling goods on to be carried by others over the next stage. A Westerner travelling its full length would be remarkable enough; a Western woman would be assured of massive book sales if she could make it through.

Morrison had completed his trip in 1910. At that time China was decadent, but relatively safe despite an unwieldy provincial government system. But in 1911 had come the revolution. Sun Yat-Sen had established a Provisional Republican Government, but needed the strength of the army to force the abdication of the infant emperor. He called on the army leader, Yuan Shih k'ai, for help. Before long the army and the Provisional Government were contending for power, and China — especially in the rural areas — slid into chaos. Warlords gathered followers around them and roamed the countryside, imposing their own law, stealing and killing as they went. The authorities could do little to stop them.

And now, in this time of uncertainty, Mary was ready to go. At the American Presbyterian mission at Pao Ting Fu she had been finishing and proofreading the story of her trip so far. Here, near the capital, things were relatively settled, and she was secure and comfortable among friends; it was easy to feel confident as she waited for her chance to go home along the Silk Road to fame and fortune.

She expected great things of the trip. She wanted to impress the Royal Geographic Society and be offered membership — women had only been accepted as members since Isabella Bird in 1894. She wanted to be invited to lecture on her amazing journey back from China, and if there was danger, so much the better. She wanted to write an account of the journey, of course, but she wanted to write a novel too, with a British or American heroine, which she knew would sell. She was gathering material for it, and a few risky encounters would be good for a novel.

And there was something else. She had been away from Australia for twelve years. In an interview before she left England, she talked about how much she wanted to go home, but that her work was keeping her in England. She wanted to find a writing assignment to take her back. She was daydreaming about a journey across tropical Australia, and would need sponsorship and assistance from the Australian Government. A trip alone across Asia and accolades from the Geographical Society would clearly be very useful in such a scheme. The whole plan was about prestige and the 'fancy that!' factor that would sell her books and build her reputation.

Mary confided her plans to Morrison. In such troubled times, he could no longer recommend the trip. She did not have to risk her life for the Geographical Society. 'I will make you a fellow of the Royal Geographical Society whenever you care to invest £5 entrance fee and £4 per annum,' he offered.

> 'I would be glad to do anything I could to help you, but it seems to me that the journey in the present unsettled condition of the country is one which it would not be wise for you to enter upon. There are, however, lady missionaries as far as Lanchou, and where they could go there is no reason why you should not be able to go, except that they can speak the language.'[2]

Mary declined with thanks his offer to nominate her for the Society. 'A bus ticket from London Bridge to Putney is qualification enough, isn't it?' she answered brightly. She went on:

> My publisher wants me home for the publication of my book [the one about her journey out and her impressions of China], and I am trying to make him see it is to his advantage and mine to postpone the publication and advance me enough money to cross Asia. Whether he will take my views after I tell him you cannot recommend it I do not know, but I have put it to him that if I was killed it would be a most excellent advertisement for the book he will have to hand.'[3]

For the present, she was going nowhere. The anticipated commissions for magazine articles had not been forthcoming, and she did not have enough money for the overland trip. Also she had caught the flu, along with many others on the compound. But while she was recovering, a London newspaper offered her payment in advance for articles. On 19 February 1914, she wrote to Morrison triumphantly: 'I have the money for that trip I consulted you about, and that you don't recommend.'[4]

She caught the train up to Peking and went to the British Legation to apply for a passport, and to talk to Morrison about the practicalities of the trip. She was also hoping for letters of introduction, particularly to Sir George Macartney, British Consul-General in Kashgar.

The missionaries at Pao Ting Fu, particularly the women, were not keen for her to go. 'If I wanted to die,' said one, 'I would choose some easier way.'

Caught between different opinions, she wrote to another friend in Peking who had been in China for ten years and knew the language. He was against it.

At this crucial time two Westerners, William Purdom and Reginald

Farrer, came along the road and stayed at the mission. They were collecting botanical specimens for Harvard University's Arboretum. They knew China well; they were going west as far as Tibet. They thought it would probably be alright for Mary to do the same. It was spring — a good time of the year to travel, before the daytime temperature rises too high, before the dirt roads turn to mud with the summer rains. Mary started to pack.

She posted the manuscript of her book to her publisher in England. She had planned to call it *Alone in China* (echoing her *Alone in West Africa*), but by the most liberal interpretations it was hardly that. It became *A Woman in China*, echoing Morrison's *An Australian in China*. The publishers sent her a contract for the second book, *Across Asia*. Mary signed it and returned it.

The missionaries helped her to find a servant — a tall, strong man named Mr Wang, who could lift her onto a mule litter and down again. The alternative for getting down from the cart was to slither forward almost to the rump of the mule in front and risk a kick from the mule's back legs. With the mission's help she found an interpreter and a cook — both of very limited ability, she was to discover. She packed some simple medical equipment and — reluctantly — the pistol.

She decided against carrying heavy supplies like tinned foods, which she had taken with her to Africa and given away unused, and to get the cook to buy food along the way. She would take a few basics only — biscuits, coffee, some tinned milk. She packed her clothes and belongings into canvas bags; they would be easier to carry by mule or in a cart or litter, than the boxes and cases she had brought by train. She wrote to mission stations along the way, announcing her arrival; they would be the ones to tell the outside world if she failed to arrive. She culled her equipment to the minimum; folding table and chair, enamel plates, a couple of glasses, minimal kitchen utensils. She had learnt lessons in Africa. And she put in a cushion for her faithful companion, James Buchanan.

She was almost ready to leave when the telegram came from an official in Hsi An:

> Delay journey. White Wolf in Shensi.

Pai Lang (White Wolf) was one of the most notorious of the warlords terrorising the countryside. Not long before, he had been in Anhui, hundreds of miles away near the coast and behind Mary's route across China. Now he had moved inland and was between her and the Silk Road. A telegram to the missionaries in Hsi An confirmed the news. Not only was Pai Lang in the area but the Society of Elder Brethren, an anti-European movement, had joined forces with him. The missionaries suggested that Mary change route and go via T'ai Yuan Fu, capital of Shansi. There was a route across the mountains that would take her in a large circle detour and bring her back onto the road to Lan Chou and her original route, if she got the 'all clear'.

In Mary's mind, all was settled. She said goodbye to her friends at the American mission and with her interpreter and cook, and the faithful James Buchanan, she caught a train to T'ai Yuan Fu on the first leg of her journey.

If Mary could go by the circular detour across the mountains she might have to bypass Hsi An (later to become famous for its terracotta warriors) but she might get further, perhaps to Lan Chou where the 'lady missionaries' spoke the language. From there, Mary argued, she might be able to travel another 300 kilometres north and west to Liang Chou, one of the last major cities of China for travellers heading out along the Silk Road. Then, before long, she would have crossed the border. After Liang Chou, where the Great Wall extended the limits of its protection in the north-west, she would be in what was then known as Chinese Turkestan, and follow the old Silk Road all the way to Kashgar. Then she could head west along the Silk Road to Samarkand and across the Caspian Sea into Georgia, and she would be back in what she saw as civilisation — Georgia, European Russia — across the Baltic and home. It was a journey of thousands of miles in uncomfortable transport over rough roads amongst nomadic peoples, with the first British presence at Kashgar, somewhere about the

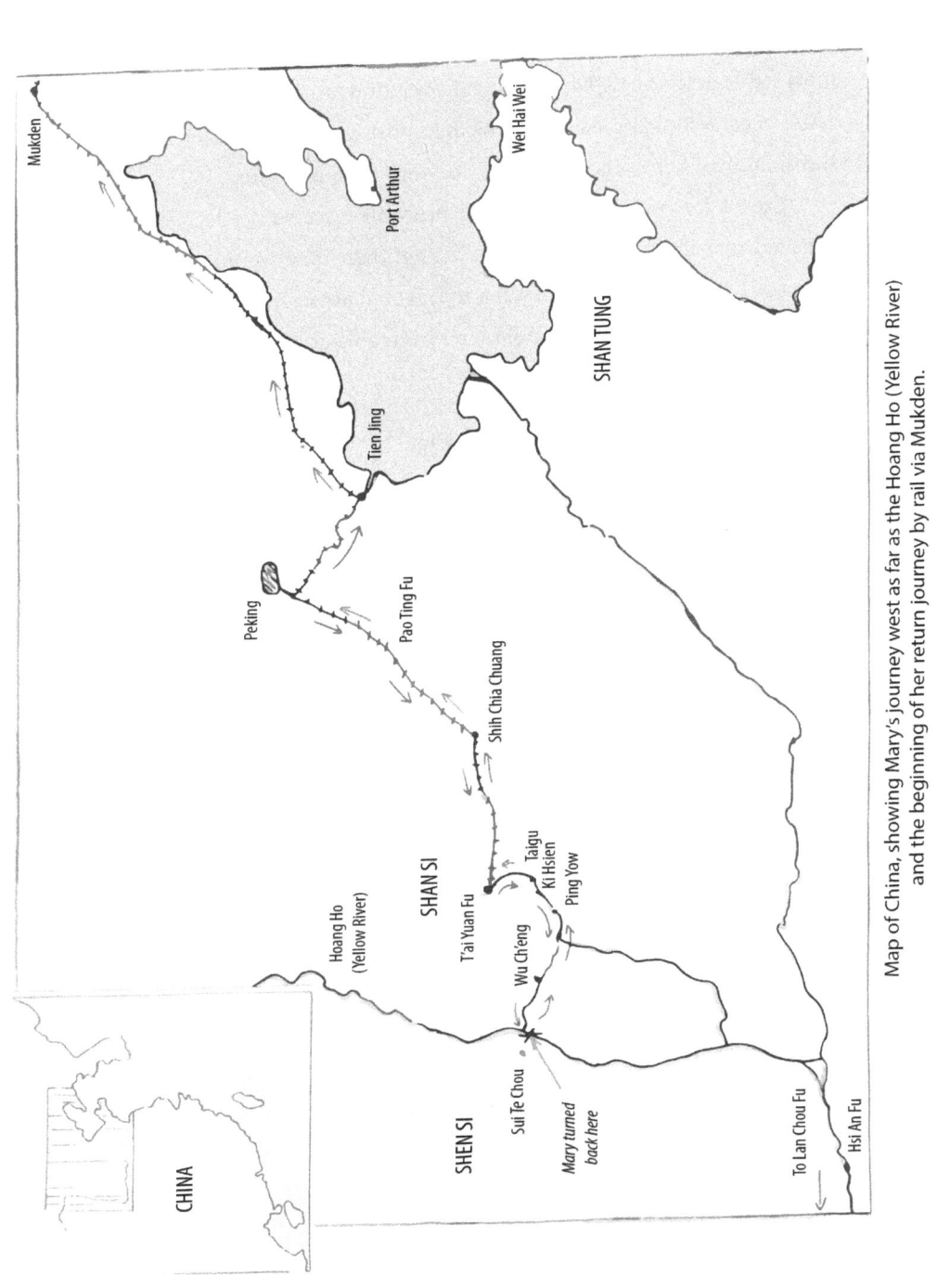

Map of China, showing Mary's journey west as far as the Hoang Ho (Yellow River) and the beginning of her return journey by rail via Mukden.

middle of the vast Europe-Asia landmass she was crossing. Even at the most stable of times, with help along the way, it was a stunning plan. But in 1914, to contemplate crossing China in its post-republic turmoil, was — in the opinion of her friends, at least — beyond comprehension.

Except for one man, she would probably have succeeded. She was satisfied that the Chinese were not violent, that they would not do her harm — but she was well aware that they would not risk their own lives on her behalf, and no Chinese would have been able or willing to defend her from Pai Lang.

…oOo…

The train climbed steadily towards the loess country, past old walled cities, through hills terraced for agriculture. At the English Baptist mission in T'ai Yuan Fu, 4,000 feet up, Mary heard the story of the Boxer rebellion — nuns raped, missionaries killed, children butchered. It was horrifying, fascinating. She wrote notes about it.

Mary started out from the Baptist mission to travel by mule. But after two days riding on a mule with no reins and no stirrups, she was desperately tired and uncomfortable and was having an asthma attack. She could not face another 1,700 kilometres of travel like that, so she turned back to the mission. With the help of the missionaries, she started off again the next day in a litter, a kind of hammock between two poles. The poles were strapped to the harness of one mule in front and one behind.

Melbourne people read later of her progress:

The Argus, 7 May 1914, page 9

Mrs. Mary Gaunt
Journey in Strange Lands

Peking, May 6: Mrs. Mary Gaunt, the well-known author and traveller, who is a daughter of the late Judge Gaunt of Victoria, is undertaking a six months journey through Chinese Turkestan, Tibet and the Gobi Desert. She left this city yesterday, travelling in a specially made wheelbarrow drawn by two coolies.

When Mary had arrived at T'ai Yuan Fu, their senior missionary, Dr Edwards, was away on a trip over the mountains to Hsi An. At her next stop, Ki Hsien, the missionaries got a letter from Edwards. Pai Lang had surrounded Hsi An, he said, and Edwards was turning back. Mary was loath to give up. She decided to push on to Fen Chou Fu, where there was a big American mission; if things got bad, *they* would have to escape to a safe place and Mary could escape with them.

The first sign of trouble came next day — a day of cloudless blue sky — on the road just outside Ping Yow, when they saw ahead a crowd of people at the edge of the road. She asked her servant, Mr Wang, to investigate and tell her what was happening. Mr Wang came back to report:

> 'I do not know the word.'
> 'What word?'
> 'What is a lot of people and a dead man?'
> 'Ah!' I said, 'that is a funeral.'
> 'Would you like to see the funeral?' he said.
> …He lifted me down and the crowded people made a lane for me to pass through, and half of them turned their attention to me, for though there were missionaries in the big towns, a foreigner was a sight to these country people, and, Mr. Wang going first, we arrived at a man with his head cut off.
> 'Who killed him?'
> 'They think an enemy has done this thing.'[5]

Mary meditated on this as she moved on towards Ping Yow, where she planned to stay the night. It seemed that soldiers were moving out through Ki Hsien to guard the crossing of the Yellow River; it was possible the soldiers had done it. Nobody in the crowd knew. They were waiting for the coroner to come.

At Ping Yow, a large walled town, she sought out the former camel inn occupied by the China Inland Mission, and found there a young Australian woman. She was from Ararat, in country Victoria, and she was alone with her five small children. In the evening her Canadian husband came back from his work, as well as two other missionaries from the other side of town. They talked a long time. Perhaps there was nothing sinister about it — a dead body was a dead body, one said, and if he had turned back for every dead body he had seen…Mary felt the same.

> At breakfast the children sang a song of thanks for their food, and when their elders with the same simple fervour went down on their knees and asked their God to guide and help the stranger and set her on her way, though it was against all my received canons of good taste, what could I do but be simply grateful.[6]

In the morning, Mary climbed into her litter and headed out of the gate of Ping Yow, and across the wheat fields towards Fen Chou Fu and the big American mission.

CHAPTER 27

'You Say "Go", Mus' Go!'

There were many caravans of ragged camels, and to these my animals objected with all the spirit a life on the roads had still left in them. When we met a string of them at close quarters in the loess my white mule in the lead nearly had hysterics, and his feelings were shared, so I judged by the behaviour of the litter, by his companion behind, and they both endeavoured to commit suicide by climbing the bank, having no respect whatever for my feelings.[1]

One of the missionaries at Fen Chou Fu insisted that in his tours around the countryside he had seen no sign of unrest. Mary stayed awhile there, walking around the ramparts of the town which had been there for two thousand years, going to see a fair in the Taoist temple, attending a wedding at the mission. It was a friendly town, with narrow dusty streets and, not far off, a tall pagoda — the second tallest in China. The people explained the *feng shui* of the pagoda: its purpose was to balance the phoenixes on the northern wall and protect the southern approach to the city.

The mission at Fen Chou Fu was a medical mission, and Mary watched in the clinic as women with bound feet were treated. The horror of foot-binding itself was bad enough, but they suffered in so many ways: the leg from big toe to knee became thin and as hard as marble; they developed corns and sores — often tuberculous — which ate into the foot; they developed curvatures in the lower spine and, because of the displacement of organs, frequently died in childbirth. Mary felt that, whatever the success of their religious teaching, the missionaries did great work in bringing medical services to the poorest of the poor.

Mary started off again. It was no good to go south to Hsi An and risk meeting Pai Lang. She turned west; she would cross the Yellow River and swing north, away from danger. Her muleteers were not happy. They wanted to go by the regular road, through Hsi An, and seemed not to have heard of Pai Lang. But Mary was adamant. Ahead was a small town with a Scandinavian mission; she would head for that.

'You say "go", said Mr Wang sorrowfully, 'mus' go!'

Now the road went up through stony hills and grew difficult and dangerous. They travelled first through the dry and dangerous loess country, with her men watching the skies anxiously for dust storms that could blot out the sun. Then they climbed into the mountains, up paths that seemed too narrow for a mule litter and only occasionally widened enough for one to pass another. It was then she realised the importance of the bells on the mule harnesses — the vital signal that gave one group the chance to shuffle to one side to allow the other to pass.

The roads were busy. Strings of camels, strings of pack-mules and donkeys, men with loads on bamboo poles across their shoulders, coming and going with goods from Peking and Canton going west, and wheat going back to the coast. But as she travelled further west, she noticed that the pack-saddles of the animals she met — the ones coming back from the west — were empty, and her men noticed it too. Whatever was going on in Shensi with the *tufeis* (robbers) was not good for trade.

The crunch came at the old walled town of Yung Ning Chao, only twenty-five miles from the Yellow River. Her interpreter brought her two muleteers travelling east, with the report that the gates of Sui Te Chou had been closed for the past four days because of Pai Lang. And Sui Te Chou was her first stop across the river. The river had been the goal ahead of her for days of exhausting travel, along all the narrow mule tracks on the side of steep mountains. It was not the finishing post, but it was an important milestone on the way. Now, only twenty-five miles from it, the first town ahead of her across the river was closed to her, and there was no alternative route to get her to Lan Chou and up into Russia.

The bearers assumed they were turning back — what else could be done? But Mary was adamant. All along the way she had been travelling among peaceable people — poor, dirty they might be, but there was no hint of malice or danger from them. She must accept that across the river, around Sui Te Chou, it was dangerous, but here on the peaceful roads of Shansi she felt safe. And she wanted to *at least* see the Yellow River. She was determined: '"We will go on," I said firmly, "to the Yellow river."'

Somewhere past Ping Yow, somewhere along this narrow mule track, 'courageous' grew into 'reckless'. The men grew increasingly anxious. Mary, understanding nothing of the conversations that passed between them and the other travellers, pushed stubbornly on towards a situation of which she understood very little, and that they understood all too well. Tired and worried, she had an asthma attack, and had to be helped to climb to the top of the mountain pass, but she insisted they keep going.

> At last through a cleft in the hills I saw one of the world's great rivers and — was disappointed. The setting was ideal. The hills rose up steep and rugged, real mountains, on either side, pheasants called, rock-doves mourned, magpies chattered, overhead was a clear blue sky just flecked here and there with fleecy clouds, beyond again were the mountains of Shensi, the golden sunlight on their rounded tops, purple shadow in their swelling folds, far away in the distance they melted blue into the blue sky, close at hand they were green with the green of springtime, save where the plough had just turned up patches of rich brown soil, and at their foot rolled a muddy flood that looked neither decent water nor good sound earth, the mighty Hoang Ho, the Yellow River, China's sorrow. China's sorrow indeed; for though here it was hemmed in by mountains, and might not shift its bed, it looked as if it were carrying the soul of the mountains away to the sea.[2]

She could have taken a much better route, along the broad valley of the Yellow River, climbing gently towards the hills from which the river came endlessly down. Many travelled this route; there were roads and she could have ridden on wheels. Instead, she had ridden in a mule litter along breath-stopping tracks, where the mules were at the crumbling edge of the pathway, where the muleteers could not walk beside, and where one instance of bad behaviour by an animal (and she had seen a few) could have sent her hurtling into oblivion in a mountain ravine. And now, after all this, she had to turn back.

She had set off so jauntily, waving airy farewells in the spring sunshine. In West Africa, she had pushed her carriers on through fetish territory where they were terrified to go at night, and she had crossed swollen rivers and difficult terrain; she did not give in too easily.

But in China, she had to admit defeat. She turned back bitterly to the camel inn just before the river and slept in her litter in the courtyard.

'I have failed,' she wrote. But her notebooks recorded an extraordinary journey across China — 800 kilometres as the crow flies, and she could not travel like the crows but took every difficult bend and turn. Her box of glass photographic plates recorded the old world of China — its walled cities, pagodas and primitive inns — and the pitiful state of the poorest of its people, which would not change for many years to come.

Failed, but she had collected stories of real-life adventures and horrors that she could put to good use in the future.

She sent word to the English *Daily Chronicle* that she was turning back. The Melbourne *Argus* picked up the news item and published it, adding its own explanation with a smirk:

The Argus, Monday 18 May, 1914

Mrs. Mary Gaunt. Returning to England.

London, May 16: According to the *Daily Chronicle*, Mrs. Mary Gaunt, the well-known author and traveller, who set out on a trip to Chinese Turkestan, is returning to England by the steamer *Taiyuanfu* owing to the threatened disturbances. 'In consequence of the general unrest,' says Mrs. Gaunt, 'the interior will now be no place for a foreigner, especially a solitary woman.' Mrs. Gaunt is a daughter of the late Judge Gaunt of Victoria; early in the present month it was announced that she was undertaking a six months journey through Chinese Turkestan and Tibet. She left Peking in a specially constructed wheelbarrow drawn by two coolies.

The missionaries at T'ai Yuan Fu welcomed her back, and Dr Edwards was relieved that she had been told of his letter and avoided Hsi An. With time, she conquered her disappointment and turned towards Peking.

She travelled more confidently now, staying at wayside inns. At T'ai Yuan Fu, where their journey had begun, the muleteers left her, and she thankfully paid off Mr Wang and the cook. As they were at the railhead now, she gave them the money for their fares back to Pao Ting Fu, their starting point.

Before Mary herself left T'ai Yuan Fu though, she wanted more time to talk with Mr and Mrs Green at the China Inland Mission. She had heard a little of their experiences during the Boxer Rebellion and wanted more details. They had escaped with their children, but only just. They had hidden in a cave, where Chinese friends brought them supplies, then had hidden in a field and had finally given themselves up. They were slung on poles to be carried to their deaths, imprisoned and finally — unaccountably — freed. Now they were back running the mission again. Mary grew fond of Mrs Green, and the story of their experiences would have been fascinating at any time, but Mary had a novel in mind.[3] When it was time for Mary to leave, they parted as old friends.

Back at her starting point in the Presbyterian mission hospital at Pao Ting Fu, the Lewises, who were sorry they had ever let her go, welcomed her back with open arms. Coming back meant relaxing time with them again.

Mary wrote to Morrison once more about her travel plans. He sent back kindly encouragement, assuring her that a return by train would be more interesting than going via Kashgar and there would be much to write about. There was time for one last pleasant dinner with Mr Long, the young professor from the big Chinese college — the closing meeting of the Travellers' Club, they called it. Then she packed up her belongings and took a leisurely trip down to the coast by river, sharing the houseboats of the missionaries who were going off on their summer holidays.

…oOo…

Mary began the long journey home by train, going north to Mukden in the Japanese zone, then on to Kharbin in the Russian zone, where she dined with the British Consul, who knew her brother Ernest from his time as British Commissioner in Weihaiwei. She bought food supplies at the market, and boarded the train again for the twenty-seven hour stretch to Vladivostok.

In the harbor at Vladivostok, she saw old wooden ships like the ones her grandfather would have known in the East India Company. Guy had sailed from there to guard the busy, seal rookeries north of 53 degrees. The Russian fleet was anchored there, and ships of the British fleet were on a visit.

The old feeling of the adventure of travel was returning. She took a steamer trip on the Amur and Assuri Rivers, north as far as Alexandrovsk, and crossed over to the island of Saghalien where, after invasion by the Japanese, many empty houses looked forlornly out over the Pacific Ocean. On the other side of the continent, an Austrian archduke had been shot in Serbia, but she knew nothing of it. She went back down to Blagoveschensk and to the Trans-Siberian Railway. She had been travelling now for eighteen months.

She wrote of the language problems, the setbacks, the currency difficulties, with the same insight and wry humour that had permeated her book about China. Werner Laurie's instinct was justified — it was going to be an interesting book.

In Blagoveschensk she learned of the incident in Serbia and that it was growing into a major conflict, and that Germany and Russia were involved and, a little later, that Britain had joined the war. She joined Danish and Russian friends for dinner in a restaurant where the band played national anthems and stirring songs. Someone asked for the British national anthem, but the bandmaster refused to play it — it was, after all, a well-known German hymn. Mary began to hum 'Rule, Britannia!' and a Russian friend beside her took it up; all their small party join in singing it and the band followed along until the crowd in the restaurant were all singing 'Rule, Britannia!'[4]

Now she faced a threat of a different kind. Britain, Russia and France were at war with Germany, and her route back to England lay across Russia and Germany. She was advised to get a protection order, written in Russian, from the Governor of Blagoveschensk before she left.

The order was little help in the confusion and uncertainty that followed. Soldiers were on the move, and soldiers had priority on ferries, boats and trains. Civilian passengers were off-loaded or left to wait. There was no shortage of hardship and adventure to write about.

At last, she boarded the train and started off across Siberia, around Lake Baikal — the Holy Sea — Irkutsk, Chelyabinsk, Petrograd, and got a through ticket across Finland, Sweden and Norway and over the North Sea to Newcastle-on-Tyne. Because no dog from Russia would be allowed into Sweden, she bought drugs from a vet and a large basket, and James Buchanan slept his way through one potential crisis. Then he was not allowed on board the steamer, until a kindly crew member intervened and another dose of sulphonal got him through customs. But the events of the steamer journey took her mind off James Buchanan.

When she and the other passengers boarded the ferry in Finland, they were joined by twenty-five young merchant seamen. They were Scots, and were going back home, since their ships were trapped by the fortunes of war in Petrograd and Kronstadt. During the crossing, the ferry was hailed by a German torpedo boat and the captain demanded that the young seamen be handed over. There were four enemy ships around them, their guns trained on the steamer. The steamer captain protested, but that was all he could do. There were murmured questions, mutterings of betrayal and treachery, then the passengers watched in disbelieving silence as the sailors climbed quietly down the ladder, jumped onto the deck of the German warship and disappeared.

…oOo…

By now, Mary was tired of travel. 'I wanted a house of my own; I wanted a seat in a garden; I wanted to see flowers grow, to listen to the birds singing in the trees.'[5] It was not long before she found it all.

Chapter 28

The War Years

She did not cover a great distance, as distances go in those parts. She reached the Hoang Ho at Chun Pu and there turned back, for "White Wolf was out". The activities of this brigand appear to recur in China like railway strikes in England, and with the same effect on communications, also with the same assurances from the authorities that all necessary precautions are being taken.[1]

Along the Foots Cray Road leading south out of London, the red-brick houses stood shoulder to shoulder, hiding the green open spaces that stretched out behind them. Across from the new railway station and past the shops was *Thorndene*, the home of Elsie Lang, Mary's editor and friend, and her husband Lewis. Lewis was curate at All Saints in New Eltham, a country village in Kent, although the coming of the railway not long before Lewis and Elsie was edging New Eltham towards the status of a London suburb.

Mary went to see Elsie and Lewis on her return to London. She had given up her house in Finborough Road when she left for China nearly eighteen months before, and needed somewhere else to live. New Eltham was a quiet, pretty place. The houses along Foots Cray Road were joined in pairs, with pocket-handkerchief patches of green in front and generous gardens behind, and a large open sports area between them and the Eltham High Street a mile north, where London began in earnest.

Thorndene was the last house to be considered part of the City of London. When, late in 1914, the sign *Mary Haven* went up on a house several doors down from *Thorndene*, it was part of Kent. There Mary settled down to write the book about her journey home from China, and her novel. She was close to Elsie Lang, whose help had become indispensable to her. She had easy access to London by train, and a lovely garden. James Buchanan must have been very pleased with his new surroundings. When he died a few years later, Mary's 'faithful companion and friend' was buried in the garden.

The quiet village atmosphere did not last, unfortunately. Not far away was the great sprawling giant of the Royal Arsenal, last roused into action during the Crimean War, and now stirring to life again. The Arsenal, on the south bank of the Thames, had been supplying ammunition to the armies of the Empire since the seventeenth century. When Mary moved into her new home, there were several hundred workers in a mass of buildings that made up the ordnance factory complex; three years later there was a total workforce of 80,000.

Within a few months of her return, areas of London were observing partial blackout because of a fear of hostile airships. Before she had been there a year, a German airship — huge, silent and ominous — had dropped a bomb on a kindergarten in Shoreditch, East London, across the river from Mary — and twenty children were killed. From then on, the peaceful life of the residents was disturbed with rumours and searchlights, and the dread of Zeppelin attack.

It was inevitable that this war would be an industrial war, fought between burgeoning industrial powers. It would require energy, equipment, vehicles, munitions and weapons of mass destruction, on a scale undreamed of in previous wars, and the greed for materials would draw the civilian population into the vast, insatiable machine of war.

From the beginning, the cost of living rose and consumer goods became scarce, as the goods themselves and the labour to produce them were diverted to the war effort. The streets grew dark, the trains were less frequent. But it was to be over by Christmas — anyone could put up with a small amount of hardship for a short time.

Christmas came and went, and the war went on. If there were any doubts about the involvement of civilians in the war, they were dispelled with the sinking of the passenger liner *Lusitania* by a German submarine in May 1915. The loss of 1,200 lives brought the message home — this war would include everyone.

Mary's five brothers were all involved in the war. Cecil came out of retirement at the age of fifty-one, and served with the Dragoon Guards in Mesopotamia and the Middle East. Ernest commanded a squadron at the Battle of Jutland. Guy, exonerated from blame over the loss of the *Derna*, was appointed naval attaché in Washington, served as liaison officer with the USA, then joined Naval Intelligence staff at the Admiralty. Clive served with the volunteer forces in Burma, and Lance was with the Royal Naval Volunteer Reserve. And Lucy's son Atherston (nicknamed Pat), the next generation of the family, was serving with the Australian Army. The Gaunt family, like Britain herself, was fighting on many fronts.

The determination of the German Army to take Verdun, the last French fortress to fall in the Franco-German conflict of 1870, led to a ten-month battle in which 300,000 French and German soldiers died, with no gains in territory. And Gallipoli, when the details finally emerged, introduced the people of Britain and its Empire to the horrors of mass attacks against impossible odds, of pitting humans against machinegun fire, of soldiers sacrificed because of unacknowledged tactical error or inadequate support.

As the nightmare continued, civilian morale suffered. Although there was little personal danger for Mary and others in England — enemy action by sea and air caused fewer than 1,500 civilians casualties throughout the war — there were outbursts of violence against German shops and businesses, particularly after the *Lusitania* sinking. There were murmurings about the King's German ancestry, and anxieties about enlisting the 'slackers' who chose not to volunteer. Families waited for news, learning sometimes that their sons and brothers had died weeks or even months before. There was bitterness about bad organisation at the front, of men without warm clothing in the mud and misery of the trenches in winter, and of men killed by shells from their own side. The lists of killed and wounded in the newspapers grew longer.

Life in London grew spartan, as shortages and restrictions went on. The anxiety about Zeppelin attacks was ever-present. Even by the end of 1915, there was hardly a family that had not lost a father, brother, cousin or friend. Early in 1916, Britain brought in conscription, and thousands of young men were compelled into military service in time for Britain to send its armies to the Somme.

The Battle of the Somme lasted from July to November 1916. In an Allied offensive, bombardment of the German lines was to make the taking of their defences a walkover. The sound of the guns could be heard across the Channel in England. But the shelling was scattered on too long a front, and the Germans had dug in too deep. Sixty thousand men, bayonets fixed, walked towards the German trenches and were cut down in a hail of machinegun fire. More than one million who were wounded and killed achieved nothing; no victory, not even territory gained.

The first ever war documentary was shown in cinemas in London in the summer of 1916. Although it avoided the worst horrors, it was still so realistic a portrayal of modern warfare that some cinemas hesitated to admit women. By the time the season ended in the autumn, twenty million people had seen the film.

The winter of 1916 to 1917 was one of the coldest winters on record. Sowing and harvesting had been abandoned, domestic needs neglected because of the fighting; coal was scarce, cities were dark and cold. In Berlin they called it 'the turnip winter'. Russians, already devastated by the war effort and with two million dead, were growing hungry; in February an International Women's Day rally sparked demonstrations over food shortages and factory workers joined in. As the February revolution gained momentum, the Tsar abdicated, and later that year Russia withdrew from the war in Europe.

In a final attack in March 1918, the Germans advanced fourteen miles into northern France in two days, the greatest gain of the entire war. But their munitions and morale were low, and successive attacks by France, Britain and its Imperial forces forced them back. By August, German troops were surrendering in large numbers; in November sailors at Wilhelmshaven mutinied rather than sail to certain defeat and death at sea. Further south, fresh American troops joined the battle, and by late 1918 it was clear that Germany could not win the war.

..oOo...

Soon after her return to England, Mary visited the Horsfalls in Liverpool again. From the captain of the *Torino*, on which she had gone to Sicily two or three times, and from his colleagues, she heard stories of merchant seamen and the dangers they faced. She wrote up one of the captain's experiences as a short story and began thinking that she could use other stories for propaganda work. She contacted the novelist John Buchan in the War Propaganda Bureau and offered her services and he said he would put her in touch with the right man. Her health after China was not great, but she could do this much to help the war effort. She wanted no payment from the British Government, only permission to publish and the usual payment from the magazines. But her offer was never taken up.

> Try as I would, I could not get permission to publish. The Propaganda Department would not look at my work — and of course no magazine could publish without the censor's permission. I ate my heart out in bitterness. [Much later] I heard from a journalist of standing the reason I was banned. There was a dry-as-dust old Colonel in that particular department who was dead against the employment of women.

In December 1914, the Lyceum Club held a Travellers' Dinner to which Mary was invited, along with Werner Laurie, her publisher. The distinguished foreign correspondent and editor Sir Donald Mackenzie Wallace was also a speaker, as was Stephen Graham, the young author who had published travel books on Russia. Mary recounted her experience of crossing Russia in wartime and her discovery that she was suspected of being a German spy. She admired the Russian people, she said; they were 'a strong, virile race, though somewhat dirty and very averse from fresh air.' She added, though, that 'Russian naval officers were the most charming men in the world.'[2]

Mary planned to go on giving lectures as her contribution to the war effort. It was work she was confident about: 'I knew my subjects and I could always hold my audiences,' she wrote later.[3] But her asthma was giving her trouble, and on a trip north she was ill and had to call a doctor:

> I told him I had to lecture that night and wanted something to buck me up.
> 'I'll give you something'll do the trick,' he said.
> The something did not do the trick...It made me so ill that henceforward to the end of the war it was out of the question to think of taking up any regular employment.[4]

A Woman in China came out in November 1914. 'Vivid and sympathetic,' said the *New York Times*; 'Full of instructive information, fascinating description and appreciative comprehension of the Chinese civilisation,' said the *Literary Digest*; 'Entering the country by the Siberian Railway in mid-winter shortly after the revolution, she spent some weeks in Peking observing and studying and then travelled without companion by cart to Jehol, Inner Mongolia...Her opportunity for forming an independent impression of the Chinese was thus very different from that of the ordinary tourist,' said *Dial*, Chicago.[5]

Late in 1915, Mary's nephew Pat came to stay with her. Pat, who was in his early twenties, had been seriously wounded at Gallipoli and had been in hospital for six months. His casual, almost brutal references to death and dying brought home to her the dehumanising effects of the war, and intensified her concern for her brothers. But for all the diversity and danger of their roles, Pat was the only one of the family injured.

Mary busied herself then with a collection of stories, *The Ends of the Earth*, which came out in October 1915. Most of the stories had appeared earlier in magazines. The settings for the stories stretched — literally — to the ends of the earth; from Tasmania to Siberia, Cape Horn to Canada. Four were inspired by Guy's adventures, two were from China. Writing and collecting these together occupied Mary during her first year back, and Werner Laurie's decision to publish them was vindicated by two English editions and one Colonial edition. Perhaps he felt that, in uncertain times, people would prefer something short and safe to read.

By October 1915, Mary had a picture in her mind of what the China novel would be like, and she signed a contract with Laurie for it. Its title was *The Awakening of Pleasant Conant*. She was to deliver the manuscript in four months.

The story was one of Mary's best — well-constructed, well-plotted, and with an authentic historical flavour such as few writers of the time could have delivered. The heroine, Rosalie, is a doctor at a Brethren mission in Kansu, where Pai Lang is terrifying the countryside. Rosalie holds many of Mary's views: she doubts that many Chinese will be converted; she dislikes being prayed over ('It is such shocking bad form. It makes me wince'); she was influenced by a strictly religious nurse as a child. She is in China to 'indulge that insatiable craving for adventurous travel which a small patrimony rather restricts' and has a black-and-white Japanese pug, MacTavish ('He loves me as no-one in the world loves me, or ever has loved me').[6] She has not learnt much Chinese — only enough to get by on — and she detests the practice of foot-binding. Mary was forced to turn back at the Hoang Ho (Yellow River), but Rosalie, Martin Conant (the missionary she loves) and a few other Westerners go far out into what was then Tibet, are confronted by Pai Lang himself, and dramatically rescued by an Englishman. They return in comfort to Peking by train, and on their way back to England their boat is stopped by a German U-boat. This time, however, Martin (who speaks German) boards the U-boat, drops a grenade down the conning tower, fires on the crew on deck and then, as the passenger ship rams the U-boat, he dives into the sea. He does not come to the surface. He has served his country as he had hoped — and has died for it.

Many details of Mary's experience in China are there, but she has turned defeat into resounding success. What she could not achieve in real life, she has achieved in fiction. It is a triumph of the writer's craft.

Mary's income was mainly from book royalties, which fell with falling sales during the war.[7] In September 1916, she wrote to the publishers Edward Arnold asking for work as a reader, and accepted their offer of occasional work at fifteen shillings per manuscript, plus postage.

Although her social life was generally sober, the area around Mary offered lively diversions, as well-paid munitions workers looked for recreation in their free time. Music halls were popular and the Woolwich Hippodrome, not far from Mary, offered variety in entertainment. There were benefits for the Red Cross, dances, and there was the cinema — by war's end the most popular indoor entertainment.

Late in the war, Mary had a young companion, Eva, staying at *Mary Haven* with her. Even in wartime London, and living near the Arsenal at Woolwich, she was more curious than concerned:

> I remember on one occasion [we] were out in my garden looking up at the anti-aircraft above. There was an exciting battle going on. The summer night was full of sound and up there in the sky we could see the flashes. [Eva] and I and my little dog Bubbles, a very superior Japanese, watched with the deepest interest.
>
> Eva was a very pretty girl and was much beloved by a Corporal in the Army Service Corps. He came over to see his lady love and presently mistress and maid with a small dog at their heels were being rushed into the house by an extremely agitated young soldier.
>
> 'Don't you know that's shrapnel falling - shrapnel? I wonder you're not both dead!'
>
> The next day by his orders the village policeman, a very nice man who in his off time attended to my garden, came in and solemnly led me round the garden, just to show me the damage the shrapnel had done. It was extremely convincing.

...oOo...

At last, the bitter years of the war came to an end. For many, with loved ones dead and missing, there was little to celebrate except the end of exhaustion and despair. Fighting had continued to the last. As the bells rang on 11 November 1918, the parents of the poet Wilfred Owen received the dreaded telegram to say that he had been killed only days before.

In London, the streetlights were turned on again, crowds jammed the streets, dancing and waving flags. Sirens blew, bands played. King George V and Queen Mary went to a Thanksgiving Service in the Albert Hall. It was victory, at a terrible cost, but it was victory, and the Allies began to hammer out the humiliating terms of the armistice to be imposed on the losing side.

As they began their work, a new and fearful menace crossed the Channel into Britain. In October 1918, the first English victim succumbed to influenza, and soon it was making its presence felt all over Britain. It had begun somewhere in the East, and had marched, inexorable as any army, across India and Central Europe, claiming more victims than the war had done. In India alone, sixteen million people died. In England, people were hungry, weary and vulnerable, and by the time the winter of 1918 was over and spring came, 150,000 people had died.

Mary had been ill with the flu in China early in 1914. Because of her asthma she was vulnerable to any illness that affected the lungs, so she spent time away from London — she was in Weymouth in May of 1919, and staying at *Gauntswood* in August. She was unwell; she wanted to get away from England, go somewhere warmer.

A Broken Journey, previously *Across Asia*, came out in February 1919. The review in *The Times Literary Supplement* had its accustomed one-eyebrow-raised, sarcastic tone which said as much about the reviewer's limited vision and self-importance as it did about the book. Mary had commented, about foot-binding, that 'the older women were lined and had a look of querulousness and irritability that was not on the men's faces.' The reviewer asked:

> [B]ut does Miss Gaunt regard that look as an exclusively Chinese characteristic? If she is rested and feels equal to another broken journey, let her continue her studies in comparative sexual expression at Oxford Circus at the hours when matrons storm omnibuses.[8]

Mary must have come to dread the flippant responses of the *The Times Literary Supplement* critics.

The review of her next novel *A Wind from the Wilderness*, formerly *The Awakening of Pleasant Conant*, was little better. There was grudging praise for the adventure of the story, followed by the caustic comment that 'the convention adopted by the authoress of allowing the various chapters to be told by different characters needs a great deal of working up to make it convincing.' It ends by noting the sad end to the story and saying, 'Most of us by now have little taste for tragedy in fiction.' The book had only one edition — perhaps *The Times* critic was right.

Mary had short stories aplenty, and in August 1919, while she was staying with Guy and Margaret at *Gauntswood*, she arranged with Werner Laurie to prepare another collection. She called it *The Surrender and other Happenings*, and dedicated it to 'the best of friends, my sister-in-law Margaret Elizabeth Gaunt'. The collection came out in February 1920.

The *Argus* critic was impressed at the range:

> For many years Mary Gaunt has been a wanderer on the face of the earth, but a most purposeful wanderer. She gleans material in every quarter. In her new volume of short stories…she ranges from West Africa to Alaska, from Yucatan to Northern China. Her fertile imagination and her power of vivid description are abundantly in evidence…[9]

The collection included three stories from China, including one called 'White Wolf'.

Chapter 29

The Other End of the Trade

I found on the shelf an old slave account book from [Jamaica] which meant so little to them that they jotted down on the blank pages the number of eggs their hens laid. How I wished I could see the place…but Jamaica [was] far away in those days.[1]

The *Camito* steamed down the Welsh coast from Liverpool, headed for the West Indies. On board, cabin windows open despite all advice, Mary smelled the salty sea air and pondered the prospect of another adventure, another world, another book.

In Liverpool in 1890, at the home of Guy's friends the Horsfalls, she had seen models of their West African factories and found an old record book from 1817. It was a register of the slaves on 'Prosperity' Estate, the plantation of William Cockburn Esq. in the parish of St Mary, Jamaica — the grim record of the lives of desperate and unwilling immigrants. She was going to see where the slaves who haunted the coastal forts in West Africa lived out their days, and the new world they helped create for their owners in the West Indies.

The ship turned west, leaving behind the approaching winter, the flu epidemic and the dreariness of post-war England. In Accra, Mary's stepping-off point for West Africa, a million were dead — the markets were closed and the streets were empty and silent. Mary was not well herself, and this was the first shipping lane opened since the war ended that would take her to a warmer climate. Once again she had packed up her house. Her dog, Bubbles, successor to the faithful James Buchanan, was boarded with friends. Mary was fifty-eight and she was on the way to better health, adventure and — she hoped — books about Jamaica.

For the first time in all her travels, Mary was not going alone. She was travelling with a companion. Eva Parsons was the young Londoner who had been staying with Mary in New Eltham. Eva was expecting a baby. If her situation in England was difficult, she found the ideal milieu in Jamaica, where marriage conventions were a good deal more relaxed than those of respectable London.

On the ship, Mary met Herbert de Lisser, journalist and writer. He was starting a magazine of Jamaican life, and Mary arranged to write an article on her impressions of Jamaica for him. The first issue of *Planters' Punch* came out a few months later in December 1920, and in it de Lisser wrote about meeting Mary on the ship and about her plans. He reported that she intended trying to settle in Jamaica, to see if she could 'do her literary work' on the island, especially if she could bring her dog Bubbles over with her.

Mary found ways to let people know her needs. Clarence Lopez, also a passenger on the *Camito*, had a house near Falmouth, on the north coast of the island, which he used only one or two days every six weeks, and he offered it to Mary. She was happy to accept. Mary and Eva moved in to The Hyde, and settled comfortably there, and Eva's baby — Samuel Hyde Parsons — was born not long after.

The Hyde was a large, two-storey house of faded grandeur, which stood on a lonely vantage point high up above the coast. The house was unoccupied most of the time; there were bats in the roof and rats scurrying about downstairs, and outside the noises of strange birds and animals. The house had been built with defence in mind; there were loopholes to shelter men with guns. It was an introduction to the life of Jamaica — the history of wealthy landowners in great houses and desperate, rebellious slaves.

Travel in Jamaica was not the challenge of travel in Africa or China. It was civilised and easy, and the climate was pleasant. Mary did most of her travelling by car and Jamaica was, after all, a small island — about 300 kilometres long. 'As an old traveller, no-one can appreciate better than I the comforts of a good hotel.'

When they needed milk for Eva's baby, Mary and Eva made the acquaintance of Charlotte Maxwell Hall, who was developing a property not far away and had dairy cattle on it. She became their regular supplier of milk. In the 1830s, during an uprising, Major Hall and his wife had escaped down the mountains under cover of night to the safety of the coast. Slaves burned their house and destroyed the property; only an avenue of mango trees remained as witness of a hated regime. Years later, Charlotte's father returned and built an observatory on the hill above where the old house had stood, and Charlotte was now Government Meteorologist as well as running a dairy herd and developing the 600-acre property of *Kempshot*.

This was the stuff of the books Mary wanted to write. She wanted to give a readable, visitor's-eye-view of Jamaican history. She wanted to tell all the stories, particularly the story of the African slaves she had come to Jamaica to find. She belonged by race, breeding and education to the class of property owners — she wanted to tell their story too. It was, after all, white property owners, not descendants of slaves, who would buy the books.

From de Lisser and Lopez and Charlotte Maxwell Hall she collected the landowners' stories; from the household servants and other coloured Jamaicans — descendants of those far-off African slaves whose fate had horrified and fascinated her — she found the story of the unwilling settlers of the island. She added their unorthodox lifestyles and philosophies of life to the store for her writing.

Charlotte epitomised for Mary the free and independent young woman, making her own choices, earning her own living. 'I would like to have been her,' Mary wrote. Charlotte, 'the laughing girl with the motor', invited Mary and Eva to stay with her at *Kempshot Pen*, her hilltop house 1800 feet above Montego Bay. Mary celebrated her sixtieth birthday — on 20 February 1921 — while she was at *Kempshot Pen*.

In the clear, clean air of the Jamaican hills, Mary read about Jamaica's past. She sat on the cool verandah and in the shady gardens, and made notes about early landholders and explorers, pirates and desperadoes, sea captains and settlers. She was not a dedicated researcher and could be impatient about details, but she loved the colour and life in the history, and made good use of it. She stayed with Charlotte for three months, and wrote a substantial part of her next book at Charlotte's house above Montego Bay.

...oOo...

In the December 1921 issue of *Planters' Punch*, Mary's impressions of Jamaica appeared. In a long article of around 9,000 words, she began with complaints: 'It is exceedingly difficult to get anywhere comfortable to stay at a reasonable price, the mosquitoes are a nuisance, the ticks run them a very good second, and the post office facilities are the very worst in the world.' Then she went on to describe the beauties of the island, although she pointed out that man's handiwork had spoiled it. She found Kingston houses dusty and untidy: 'Wander through Jamaica, and it looks as if wherever man has come he has done his level best to spoil Nature.' She also wrote that 'the average Jamaican peasant is dishonest', but she had some good things to say as well, and ended with: 'I have much for which to thank Jamaica. Nowhere in the world have I received greater kindness.' She saw Jamaica, as she saw West Africa, as a great untapped storehouse, ripe for exploitation:

> Jamaica is a fertile land, every inch of her crying out for the capable man who shall find out exactly the crop that is suited to the soil... who shall help make his country what it ought to be, one of the great producing territories of the Empire.

In the next issue — the magazine came out once a year — Mary wrote a fanciful story of what might have happened to one of the old houses. In the story, the planters knew no difference between African races, and the new slaves they thought would be docile and work hard were Ashanti warriors, who rose up, killed the son of the house and disappeared into the surrounding hills. It was strong on detail about Africa and African racial features, fortified pioneer houses, island history and Jamaican race relations — the writer, the historian, the observer at her keenest.

When she came to writing the book, she had no particular knowledge of economic affairs, nor any great interest in current politics, but emigration interested her and she saw potential for it in Jamaica.

> There are wild places still in this island…waiting for man to come and turn to good account their wealth. Here is room, and more than room, for the dwellers in the great cities who have never seen a glorious sunset and know not the scent of a pimento grove.'

In the big cities of England — London, Liverpool, Sheffield — she had seen working people she pitied: 'It seemed to me they were slaves in a bitter cold and cheerless country…[with] no hope of bettering their condition.' They could be shipped over from England to live in the great abandoned and crumbling houses of Jamaica. 'The ignorant peasant in Jamaica,' she wrote, 'wastes the timber, he wastes the animals he has under him, he wastes the soil, the earth brings forth not one-tenth of what it might under more enlightened rule.' She thought that someone British should start an agricultural colony there: 'Here is a fertile soil crying out for cultivation, here is a peasant population waiting for employment…'

There had been a push to import labour in the nineteenth century to rescue the big plantations, but it was not a success; the labourers preferred to take up small parcels of land for themselves rather than work for low wages on big plantations. Mary knew of the lesson from history, but she seemed willing to recommend the risky gamble again.

Many of the Jamaicans she met spoke excellent English. '[E]ducated, they are delightful, so long as the speaker does not think about himself and become pompous and bombastic.' She had not forgotten the self-asserting locals in Liberia who refused to accept British superiority and have their photographs taken.

As Jamaica's rainy season approached, Mary began to think about moving on. She found much to enjoy in Jamaica, but there was much she disliked, too. She wanted what she saw as higher moral standards. She wanted her dog Bubbles with her, and was denied that. She wanted British efficiency for the post office; she felt cut off from the publishing world, and from her reading public, when ships took two weeks to make the crossing from England but a letter could take seven weeks to arrive.

With the manuscript of her book close to completion, she took a ship back to England. She stayed for a time in London and undoubtedly went to see Elsie Lang, to whom she was dedicating the book.

> My dear Elsie,
> I wonder if you remember as vividly as I do the very drastic criticism of a book of mine that first introduced us to each other. My publisher showed it to me with some hesitation because it was so scathing, but it went right to the point. Most of the book was scrapped there and then, and my literary education was begun under your care. It was you indeed who taught me that I needed educating in my art. That is twelve years ago, and I have never since let a book go into the world till it has received your approval. I am afraid I have sometimes tried you severely, but it has always been my ambition to be your prize pupil. I owe more than I can say to my sympathetic teacher.
> It is a small thing to offer my latest book to you, but I hope you will accept it with my love and warmest thanks.
>   Affectionately yours,
>   Mary Gaunt.

Where the Twain Meet was published in November 1922. It was part personal travel narrative, part retelling of Jamaican history, with quotes from its own historians and writers. She used some material on the West African forts, which had been sitting unused in her notebooks since the second trip to Africa in 1911. She wrote of the cruel treatment of the slaves at the hands of brutal masters, the savagery of the rebellions and of the punishments that followed them. There was enough murder, torture and inhuman behaviour to titillate the most demanding reader. Yet the 1,260 copies published by John Murray never earned the advance on royalties paid to Mary.

Only two of the photographs in the Jamaica book are Mary's, and these she took in West Africa. She had been determined to visit Annamabu

— a small, British-built fort, well preserved, standing grey, square and forbidding on a rocky outcrop of the coast. As there was no landing place for a boat, Mary had landed further up and got bearers to carry her back ten spray-whipped miles along the surf beach in a hammock, with the lens of her camera safely covered, to see the castle and take the pictures.

Mary stayed eighteen months in Jamaica. It did not provide her with the long-term home she wanted; she needed somewhere not quite so far from family and friends, and from her agent, editor and publishers. She needed a climate suitable for an asthmatic, not too far from England, and a dwelling suitable for a writer of modest means. She knew the southern part of France from her motoring holiday there between Africa trips with Guy's wife Margaret. When she left Jamaica, she was heading for the south of France.

…oOo…

The village of Sainte Agnès is a folk-tale illustration from a children's book — a walled village 671 metres (2,200 feet) up on the peak of a mountain (*un village perché*) in the Alpes Maritime, where the mountains come down almost to the sea. Nearby, the ruins of Augustus Caesar's triumphal monument, at the highest point on the Grand Corniche, look right down to the coast as far as Monaco and across the border to Italy. In the Middle Ages, the Celtic Ligurians built villages like Sainte Agnès high up, and protected them against attacks by warlords, Saracens and the Barbary pirates of the Mediterranean. The road winds up to it over rocky outcrops, through the mediaeval wall, into an old stone village of cobbled streets. It is the highest *village perché* on the coast, and when the late afternoon mist rolls up towards it, it floats like an eagle's nest above the valley. It is the epitome of the village of Adlerstein in the book that fascinated Mary as a girl — *The Dove in the Eagle's Nest*.

In Sainte Agnès, Mary wrote the dedication of her Jamaica book to Elsie. From there she sent a letter to *The Times*: 'I have been reading with great interest [the column] 'The Woman's View', hoping that the writer would touch upon the great question of careers for women.' Since that had not happened, Mary gave her own view on the desirability of women having a career and earning an income for themselves. The letter appeared on 20 September 1921.

Then she was on the move again. Her next letters to *The Times*, on the same subject, were from the Hôtel de Paris in Bordighera, Italy, not far along the coast[2]. When she posted a copy of *Where the Twain Meet* to her sister Lucy in Melbourne, Australia, she was still there. Bordighera was to be her home for the next twenty years.

Chapter 30

To Italy

The Englishman does not go abroad to mingle — or even to meet — with the people of the land he visits. He lives in a colony of Britons. He looks for his own newspaper, his own tennis, bridge, golf and social clubs; he dances only with his own compatriots. He and his wife and daughters come to the Riviera putting up in an hotel that caters for Britons and they spend the greater part of their time in the vitiated atmosphere of overcrowded rooms.[1]

Of the many places where Britons settled in clusters to escape the cold and rain, Bordighera is surely one of the most fascinating. The little fishing town lies in a sheltered bay on the Mediterranean coast, east of the glamour spots of the French Riviera, across the border into Italy. The old rock village, high up out of the reach of Barbary pirates, looks down on the buildings of the new town and out to where Cap Ferrat peers down into the sea. Here, as legend has it, Saint Ampelio once watched from his hermit's cave and collected seeds that washed ashore from Africa, to plant the Bordighera palm trees.

In a small laneway off the Via Romana, a huge old Moreton Bay fig tree shades the gateway to the Bicknell Institute. The low wall of the entrance is gripped in the gnarled roots of the tree; the sinewy fingers of *ficus macrophylla* are slowly crushing the neat rows of brickwork. Visitors to the Bicknell Institute can contemplate for a moment the living sculpture of which Clarence Bicknell would have been proud — the power of the Almighty, and the natural world, triumphing over the works of man.

A few blocks away, the shutters of the English Library open onto the Via Romana. Inside the grey stone walls, there is an Aladdin's cave of books in English. There are novels by J. M. Neale, E. Nesbit, Mrs Molesworth and Mabel Quiller-Couch, the pencilled borrowing dates on the fly-leaves all coming to an abrupt end in 1939. There are books of philosophy and politics — Shaw, Ruskin, Mosley on fascism, *Mein Kampf*. There are Biblical studies and church history, Flinders Petrie on archaeology in Egypt and Israel, essays on duty and discipline, books on gardening, tennis and golf. There are reference books — *The Times History of the War*, Tomlinson's *Encyclopaedia of Useful Arts* in three volumes, Henry Watts' *Dictionary of Chemistry* in nine volumes, and *Whitaker's Almanac* from the 1890s up to 1938.

It was an exiled Sicilian patriot in England, Giovanni Ruffini, who began the British literary connection here by setting his hugely successful novel, *Doctor Antonio* (published 1861) in Bordighera. English visitors came to see the place where the handsome Sicilian doctor rescued pretty young Lucy Davenne. In an early rush of cultural tourism they flocked to the coast, Ruffini's book in hand, to the stunningly blue seas and mild climate of the Mediterranean coast, to the unspoilt fishing village with its palm, lemon and olive trees, and its possibility for romance.

The trend of British writers to settle in Bordighera began with Clarence Bicknell, a clergyman who served the small English community from 1878 to 1879. Bicknell was a Renaissance man — botanist, geologist, theologian, writer. He studied the plants and animals of the region and published a book on them. Then, on his excursion into the Alps, he found early rock carvings, which he sketched and recorded. After some years, he abandoned the clerical life and devoted himself wholly to geology, botany and archaeology. Bicknell's papers, fossils and specimens, along with the building to house them and the all-conquering Moreton Bay fig tree, were endowed to the people of Bordighera.

The English mystic George Macdonald, a charismatic figure, settled in the early 1880s with his wife and family. Frederick Fitzroy Hamilton arrived in 1872; an active journalist, he published a scholarly history and guide to the area in 1883. Anne Thackeray, elder daughter of the novelist, set a part of her fictionalised biography of the artist Angelica Kauffmann in Bordighera, where her cousin Colonel Sir Edward Thackeray, VC, KCB was living. Henry de Burgh Daly settled in Bordighera with his wife in 1882. A journalist and freelance writer, he was appointed British Vice-Consul in 1895. Misses Daly ran the Tennis Club until war brought it to an end, and Muriel Daly became editor of the bilingual *Giornale di Bordighera* in the 1920s. Edward Berry and his wife Margaret arrived in 1892. The couple published *At the Western Gate of Italy* in 1931. Berry, who was Bicknell's nephew, was later to join the remarkable series of writer/administrators who were community leaders, and Berry set up a bank and estate agency, which were there to help new arrivals like Mary Gaunt.

Bordighera provided thinkers and writers with a quiet place to work, separated from the extravagant and expensive attractions of the French Riviera. The *Guida di Bordighera*, published in 1930, recorded proudly if somewhat exaggeratedly that '*I piu illustri scrittori britannici*' ('the most illustrious British writers') had resided in Bordighera, and listed among the famous — along with Mary Gaunt, 'writer of travel books and novels' — Edward Carpenter, who wrote *Towards Democracy; Civilization, its cause and cure; The Healing of Nations*; Charles Doughty, Arabian explorer and travel writer; Alice Meynell, poet; William Sharpe, philosopher; and H. de Vere Stacpoole, novelist.

After the Franco-Prussian War, the railways began to proliferate, linking most of the major cities as far east as Warsaw and Vienna by the end of the 1870s. Milord Anglais no longer lumbered in his heavy travelling coach along Napoleon's coast road from Marseilles; now British workers could spend their two weeks of annual holiday in Italy. Visitors from Britain began to arrive all along the Mediterranean coast in increasing numbers, some for the winter, some for the rest of their lives.

Scattered along the Via Romana and down towards the sea, and climbing up the Via degli Inglesi towards the Alpes Maritimes, the British houses were built for the climate, with long shuttered windows, cool hallways and tiled floors, and in their gardens scarlet bougainvillea spilled over old walls into shady green corners.

New English-speaking arrivals could have their money sent out to the English bank, and they could lease or buy a property through Edward Berry's real estate office. They could stay at hotels like the Astor, the Bristol and the Tennis Windsor. They could attend services at the Presbyterian or Anglican church, do their shopping at the British Stores, consult an English-speaking doctor and English-speaking chemist, read their own English-Italian newspaper, borrow books from the English library, play tennis at the English tennis club, go to concerts and lectures at the Victoria Hall and, at the end, be buried in the English cemetery.

The plaques in the English church and the gravestones in the English cemetery bear witness to retirement in the sunshine after years of service abroad: Major-General H. C. Waterfield, CB, Indian Staff Corps; David Gorton Davies, MA, Canon of Malta; W. Howard Campbell, MA, of Londonderry, Ireland, twenty-five years a missionary in India. In Bordighera, with its long hot summer days and mild winters, they found a 'corner of a foreign field that was forever England' — but with lower taxes and a better climate.

…oOo…

Mary stayed first at the Hotel de Paris, overlooking the sea. With the tall palms all along the Lungomare, and sunny skies over the blue Mediterranean, it reminded her of the Warrnambool she remembered from twenty years before. She grew to love the clear heat of the summers, the mild winter climate, the convenience of enjoying Italy without having to learn Italian. Ernest and his wife Louie had earlier taken a villa there so that Louie, who was asthmatic, could escape the English winter; now Mary was doing the same.

In August 1922, Mary's mother died — restless, adventurous Elizabeth, who had been living in Folkestone on England's south coast. Elizabeth —

cultivated, clever, with many practical skills and a sometimes impractical fidelity to upper-class manners, even in the Australian bush. Elizabeth, who could buy stock, breed laying birds and manage a farm, but cultivated the air of a leisured and genteel lady.

Elizabeth had lived on the income from William's estate since his death in 1905. Upon her death, the estate was divided between her seven children. This inheritance probably allowed Mary to move into a home of her own — modest compared with many of the lavish villas of the British, and simply furnished. She had a housekeeper, Anselma, who lived in, with her husband and child. And she had a dog again, this one brought for her from the Battersea Dogs' Home by Ernest and his family.

She gave her address in a letter to *The Times* in March 1923: 6 via Sant'Ampelio. Later it was Villa Camilla, perhaps because 'Camilla' was the novel whose proceeds enabled the eighteenth century novelist Fanny Burney to have a place of her own.

...oOo...

The *Giornale* recorded something of the social life of the *Inglesi*: tennis tournaments at the Hotel Windsor, musical evenings at Victoria Hall, a lecture on fascism in Britain by Captain Coates, a bridge tournament, a meeting of the British and Foreign Bible Society. Mary was not at any of these (the paper often listed names of people who were there). She was at home, writing.

Mary gathered a circle of friends around her, particularly literary friends. She met up with old acquaintances like George Raymond of Dunedin, New Zealand, now a retired King's Counsel, once a student with her at Grenville College in Ballarat; she played bridge with Dr Colquhoun, the kindly doctor who had helped her in New Zealand when Hubert had been ill and difficult; and met with Sir Robert Roden, late Chief Justice of British Honduras. She had long talks with Harald Swayne, explorer of Abyssinia, who was living in retirement in the Villa Cristina, and Phillip Hall, who had been a civil servant in West Africa. She had coffee regularly with Muriel Daly, editor of the *Giornale di Bordighera*. She walked her dog along the sea front and up to the Via Romana; she did a little sewing and played bridge. She wrote letters about her work and to friends, and did crosswords. She not only read *The Times*, she wrote to *The Times*.

Mary had read *The Times* when possible, wherever she travelled. It becomes an interest — a preoccupation — to make her views public and to see them in print. Of the 26 published letters she wrote to them throughout her career, 22 of them are from Bordighera. She wrote about the need for young women to have careers; surely, she reasoned, the war should have broken down the idea that women must be kept and provided for all their lives. She got letters in response — 'mostly deficient in postage', she observed — questioning the economics of her ideas and the femininity of any young woman who would follow them.

> I would judge men and women by the same standards, and what a waster we should rightly think a man were he to spend his youth as many girls of the middle classes are expected to spend theirs.[2]

She wrote to encourage emigration to Australia and the other British colonies, to have work for women decided by capability, not marital status, to emphasise that life in the warmer colonies could be enjoyed, and that settlement schemes for people on small, fixed incomes should be encouraged. She gave a picture of the community in Bordighera to make this last point:

> In Bordighera alone during six months of the year there are over 3,000 English [on small fixed incomes] and Bordighera is only a small town. In the French and Italian Riviera alone, millions of money must be thus lost to the Empire. But the people who spend this money are not specially wedded to France or Italy; most of them only speak English. They are people seeking a comfortable home within their means, a genial climate and agreeable society. If they could see their way to making a little money as well, they would be very content, for a man cannot put his energies to good use in a foreign land. He fills in time playing golf or bridge, and sighs for the day when he was of some account in the world.[3]

She protested about sunless cities, recommended nursing as a career for women. She promoted the social and financial benefits of living abroad for people on their own in England:

> ...the English man abroad is a friendly animal. Why he requires the stimulus of foreign surroundings I cannot say, but the fact remains that here on the Riviera it is possible to have the kindly social pleasures that at home are only for the very rich.[4]

In 1933, during the Depression, she recommended to *Times* readers that the unemployed of Britain should be resettled in Northern Australia, 'a fertile land with no native question'. The practicability of such a plan, with Australia also suffering the Depression, and the naiveté of the description, seem to have escaped her.

Chapter 31

At Work in the Villa Camilla

The society here is sociable and friendly. There is a saying that Cannes, Nice and Monte Carlo represent the World, the Flesh and the Devil, and there is some truth in it; Bordighera, on the other hand, has been described as 'Oh yes, you know! Intellect,' with a shrug of the shoulders, adding, 'One can hear a pin drop in the streets!'[1]

Mary was in Bordighera in November 1922 when her Jamaica book, *Where the Twain Meet*, was published. The reviews were mixed. Those looking for entertaining reading would find it 'graphic and delightful', said *Boston Transcript*; 'a remarkable volume', said the *Literary Review*. Others like *The New Statesman* were looking for meatier stuff, and concentrated on the historical and political comments: 'Marred though it is by a somewhat flamboyant style as well as by the author's prejudices, it is a suggestive study of the island where Britain is experimenting in negro rule'. The *New York Times* felt it would appeal to 'those who like a great deal of history, even if unpleasant, interwoven with more agreeable reactions to life in the tropics'. *The Spectator* was dismissive of her political analysis: 'She shows no appreciation of the difficulties of the colour-question but, embedded in her expansive moral comments there are interesting extracts from the journals of old slave traders.'[2] Perhaps the greatest surprise came from *The Times Literary Supplement*, which printed a full-column review of 1,100 words. Unfortunately, the reviewer discussed at great length the philosophy of slavery and its demoralising effects on both slave and slave owner, and hardly mentioned the book![3]

With the decision of what to write next to be made, Mary got out the manuscript she had begun back in Warrnambool and put aside when Hubert was ill. She had taken it with her to England in 1900 and worked on it in London. She told an interviewer in 1910 that she had it 'in hand', but she left on her second trip to Africa soon afterwards, and the manuscript was packed away in the house in Finborough Road to await her return. *Mistress Betty Carew* had been awaiting her return for twenty years.

It was a story set in the colony of New South Wales in its early days, when Governor Hunter was in charge and Macarthur — later to be famous for sheep-breeding — was building up his landholdings and his flocks. Its hero was George Bass, naval surgeon and explorer, who rescues and marries Betty Carew. It had been published as a newspaper serial (it appeared in the *Tarrangower Times*, a country Victoria newspaper, in 1903) but she felt it was big enough for a book, and began to revise it. She added a chapter at the beginning to flesh out the story of her heroine Mistress Betty Carew who became, in the revision, Mistress Beulah Lord. She added helpful detail, replacing 'summer' with 'the hot season of December, January and February'. She changed and updated the quotes at the chapter headings, put in more detail about the voyages of exploration of Flinders and Bass. With an eye for reader appeal, she added graphic detail about the cruelty and injustice of convict conditions.

By the end of 1922, Elsie Lang was finishing off her manuscript for part two of *Old English Towns*. She was about to start work on two new books — a translation from Italian of *Beatrice and other Stories* and one on cathedrals and churches in Italy. She needed time in Italy to research them, preferably avoiding the long, wet, grey days in England and enjoying the mild Italian winter sunshine. There is a good chance that Elsie went to Italy and spent some time with Mary in Bordighera around Christmas 1922.

This would have been the time for Mary to get out the manuscript of *Mistress Betty Carew* and for Elsie to go over it, or take it back home to work on and return by post. Encouraged by Elsie's support, Mary sent the revised manuscript to her publisher, John Murray, and it was accepted; it came out in October 1923.

The book shows signs of a good editor's handiwork in its metamorphosis from serial story to bound book. The archaic 'thee' and 'thou' in conversations between the lovers are almost gone, and ambiguous phrases and outdated expressions disappear. The ending is tighter, more dramatic. The worst, most convoluted sentence in the early version remains, though — 'Stay there any longer he felt he could not'!

There is careful detail of life in the colony at Sydney Cove that makes both stories feel 'true to life'. But both are a subversion of the historical record. George Bass, naval surgeon and explorer, who served on *The Reliance* with Matthew Flinders, is firmly established as a historical figure in the narrative, but the real-life Bass married back in England in 1800. Mary has him marrying Betty Carew/Beulah Lord in the colony, with Elizabeth Macarthur lending her wedding dress. Since the book had English and Imperial Library editions in 1923, and the latter was reprinted, and there was a cheap edition in 1926, readers clearly did not know, or notice, or care about the perversion of the historical record.

Over the next few years, others of Mary's earlier books were reprinted, which boosted her royalty income. In the United States *The Mummy Moves*, serialised years before, was published in book form in two editions, and a cheaper edition of *As the Whirlwind Passeth* came out three years after the original. A. & C. Black's Novel Library brought out a cheaper edition of *The Uncounted Cost* in 1925. Times and moral attitudes had changed since 1910; only a few years after *The Times* and the book clubs had blackballed Mary's book, D. H. Lawrence published *Sons and Lovers* (1913), with its intense emotions and frank sexuality. The twenties had seen post-war social freedom unimaginable in 1910, and the issue of living together before marriage, treated as dispassionately as Mary had done, made few ripples on the water in 1925.

...oOo...

In 1926 Guy Gaunt was in the news — in the Australian papers as well as the

English ones. Both of her sailor brothers had done well; Ernest was made an Admiral in 1924, and Guy was not far behind him. But now Guy, the larrikin companion of her childhood years, teller of stories, adventurer and friend, member of the House of Commons since 1922, found it necessary to resign after being named for misconduct in a society divorce. In the fallout of the scandal, Guy himself was divorced the following year, in 1927.

In September 1926, *The Forbidden Town* was published and Charlotte Maxwell Hall of Jamaica lived again, but this time in West Africa. In Jamaica, Mary had wanted milk and had written to a neighbouring landholder:

> My letter brought me a visit from a laughing girl in a motor, who said she did sell milk, rather to the horror of some of her relations who felt that the most she ought to do was to 'oblige a few friends'. She had set to work putting that milk-walk upon a business basis. *Kempshot Pen* was run by a woman, a young woman…of an age when many girls are thinking only of their amusement, run not only with the intention of getting every ounce of good out of the soil, but of putting back into that soil all the good that came out of it.[4]

The 'laughing girl', independent and adventurous, is introduced to us in one of the best opening chapters of any of Mary's novels. Two London businessmen are expecting to buy for a song the West African estate left to an English woman. They imagine an elderly spinster:

> But it wasn't an old lady who came out of the gloomy fog laden passage into the richly furnished office…It was a tall, slight young woman with bright, honest blue eyes, a fresh complexion, a straight nose and a strong, firm little chin…She looked first at the young man and then at the old one. Garraway noticed a certain boyish directness in her glance. He was quite sure that she knew exactly what she wanted and for all her youth and inexperience would not lightly be turned from it.[5]

In the three Africa novels that Mary wrote jointly with Tonkin, the heroines rarely dominated as individuals. Even in the next two, that she wrote alone, the lives of the heroines are often dominated by the career choices and decisions of the men. But in *The Forbidden Town* there is again the gutsy, self-reliant heroine of Mary's earliest novels. Fabia Vrooman strides independently onto the page from the very beginning — the young woman who inherits a run-down plantation and is determined to work it herself and revitalise it. 'Freshly and vigorously drawn,' said the *Daily Chronicle*. 'The tale is one of breathless excitement,' said *Woman's Pictorial*.[6] The book had two English editions, a second impression and two US editions.

...oOo...

Among the British living in retirement in Bordighera was Colonel Swayne, who had led the first exploration party into British Somaliland in Ethiopia in 1884 and stayed on as surveyor there. He had then commanded British troops in Somaliland and the Aden hinterland. Born a year before Mary, he shared her love of travel (especially in Africa) and of writing. Swayne told Mary tales of exploration and adventure in Aden and Abyssinia, and evoked memories in her of the bleak and blasted landscape of Aden familiar to P & O passengers, that she had seen on a stopover on her way to England as a hopeful young writer in 1890. Swayne's stories began to work the old magic in Mary. She began plotting stories of her own, set in and around Aden and Abyssinia. The first to come into the world was *Saul's Daughter*.

There was a rather surprising, left-handed acknowledgement of Swayne's help in the dedication of the book. 'But for the public's dislike to two names on a title-page, yours should have been alongside mine as part author. If I wrote the story and thought out the characters, the local colour was certainly yours...' Perhaps Swayne was on a comfortable pension and didn't need a share of the royalties.

Saul's Daughter had a rambling plot and lacklustre characters, and was by no means up to the standard of *The Forbidden Town*. It had much of the biographical feel of earlier books: the heroine has younger brothers and a younger sister, is closer to her father than the mother whose preoccupation with fashion and social problems makes her distant and detached. She is also besotted with a pet dog. But she is flat and unexciting, the hero and the anti-hero — the man she runs away with and marries — are even less engaging. Even the latter, bounder and cad as he turns out to be, is bland to the point of boring. Like *The Forbidden Town*, the book came out with T. Fisher Unwin, but was the last to do so. It had only one edition.

In 1929, Mary wrote a small book on George Washington for A. & C. Black in their series *Peeps at Great Men*. Having brought out *The Uncounted Cost* in their Novel Library series a few years before, A. & C. Black were acquainted with her writing style. The small, eighty-one page book was designed for young readers and for the American market — and for Mary it was a competent, bread-and-butter book.

The second book to be inspired by her talks with Harald Swayne had a much more promising plot than the first, and a much more reasonable dedication: '…I dedicate this book in grateful acknowledgement of the help he has given me…' The heroine of *The Lawless Frontier* is a governess in Abyssinia, and is a typical Mary Gaunt heroine: she does not think of herself as pretty, but she is resourceful and engaging. She has as a foil a much prettier woman who is shallow and impractical. The Mary-heroine believes in independence for women, is not outraged by sex outside of marriage, and has a feet-on-the-ground practical approach to life. When a friend questions her remaining in a well-paid but dull job, she responds:

> I am earning money. Good sound coin of the realm. They pay me for being dull, and I like to earn money. No, don't bring up Dad. You know better than that. Of course he would provide bitter bread [if I went back home]. But if there's one thing I do thoroughly despise, it's the woman who serenely gets up at ten o'clock in the morning wondering how she can put in the hours of the long day…[Her father is] much troubled at the thought of four daughters all over six-and-twenty and all unmarried!

The Gaunt family over again — two daughters, rather than four, unmarried at twenty-six. Mary goes further: when the anti-heroine admits that she lives on a handsome allowance from a married man, thoroughly-modern Rosamund's response is: 'I think you were lucky. Virtue doesn't provide the most of us with anything half so useful!'

The Lawless Frontier came out in April 1929. The publisher Ernest Benn had bought the Fisher Unwin list a few years before, and Mary's books now came out with the Benn imprint.

...oOo...

Early in her time in London, with the cold and dark of the English winter wearing her down, Mary had stayed in a small hotel in Polperro, Cornwall. She had heard stories of men press-ganged onto ships, and of transportation for life for horse-stealing, and had made notes about them. Guy had spent a holiday with her there, and talked to her about his experience of sailing the *Bounty*'s boat across the Pacific, from Tahiti to Australia. Now, after many years, she began blending the ideas together and working them into a book. She had William Bligh and Fletcher Christian in the story, but inserted her fictional characters into recorded events without quite so much distortion as before.

Joan of the Pilchard begins with the cruelty of forcing men into naval service. An experienced sailor, Daniel Reynell, captain of his own boat, is kidnapped to make up the crew for an expedition to the South Seas. When the famous mutiny happens, and Fletcher Christian sets Captain Bligh and his men adrift in a small boat, Reynell volunteers to go with them. Mary describes their voyage — a combination of courage, clever seamanship and remarkable good fortune in fiction and in real life. The heroine, Joan, has worked as a servant at The Pilchard Inn in Polperro. She manages to become, if not one of Mary's most memorable heroines, at least a capable and independent young woman with some control over her destiny, who finds fulfilment in the convict colony of early Sydney and is reunited with Reynell when he arrives in the colony from his voyage with Bligh.

One of Mary's friends was Sir Robert Roden, who had retired from his position as Chief Justice of Honduras to settle in Bordighera. Mary had to arrange legal matters relating to horse theft, transportation and pardoning of convicts, and needed accurate information. Roden supplied it for her, and she thanked him on the frontispiece of the book, along with the faithful Elsie Lang, whose drastic criticism was 'always a godsend'. She drew on Guy's nautical knowledge once again, and dedicated the book to him 'with grateful thanks for the trouble he has taken with it.'

After delivering her manuscript to Ernest Benn, Mary took up an invitation to go back to Jamaica. She wrote about the trip in a letter to another writer, Winifred Holtby, five years later:

> In 1929 I got a general invitation from the Touring Society, I think, though I'm a little vague as to who sponsored me. Anyhow, Elders Fyffe gave me a passage and all the first class hotels put me up and the Touring Society provided me with a car so that I saw the country well and enjoyed myself immensely.[7]

This time she had in mind a book with a more personal tone. The writings of Speke, her childhood hero, were disappointing because they left out things she wanted to know. 'Only the very great writers remember to say what they saw with their own eyes,' she claims. She would put them in: the little details of everyday life, the personal observations, the eyewitness accounts.

She had a second manuscript with her. She had told an interviewer from *Bookman* nearly twenty years earlier that she was writing a novel about slavery in Jamaica. She had expected the book to be finished on her planned trip back to Africa later that year. She had completed the Africa trip, but not the novel. It was, after all, set in Jamaica; now she was in Jamaica she would finish it at last.

In the novel, a plantation owner sees his son and heir, and then his wife, sicken and die. He has fathered a light-skinned boy by one of his slaves, and he sends him abroad with a companion and tutor to be educated in England. When the young man returns and is presented to society as the heir, no-one guesses the truth, but the father faces the nightmare of the revelation that will ruin both of them. The book was to have the name of the plantation — *Harmony*.

Mary was in Jamaica for just over a year. The Jamaican people, from the Governor down, entertained her and helped her with transport and hospitality, and she was treated well there. She visited some of the big old slave-owning estates of the past, and worked on her story of the slave uprisings that she had begun back in West Africa. She travelled all around the island: this was no Peking cart or hammock expedition, but leisurely and self-indulgent touring by car, with much of the cost covered by local people and organisations. She stayed in big hotels and was entertained by the owners of some of the big estates.

Jamaica had a steady stream of holiday-makers from the USA throughout the 1920s, when the federal prohibition of alcohol was in force at home. Mary's book was intended to promote the island as a holiday destination.

While Mary was working on her books, enjoying the sunshine of Jamaica, a huge shadow was cast across the world. The devastating events on Wall Street in October 1929 would affect not just her income and her return home but the lives of millions around her. As the effect of the crash spread, as banks collapsed and savings disappeared, spending reduced — and people who could not afford food and clothing did not spend their money on books.

The trip to Jamaica would be Mary's last major journey. Age (she was now almost seventy), ill-health and the worsening financial situation would keep her in Europe from now on. She wrote of visiting the town of Moneague, and of enjoying her stay: 'I was asked to come again...' but concluded: 'I'm afraid I shall never again visit Moneague, much as I liked it.'

...oOo...

While Mary was in Jamaica, word came of Guy's promotion to Admiral of the Fleet. He had been knighted in 1919. She had grown close to her brothers Guy and Ernest; they had been geographically the closest of her six siblings for most of her forty years in England and Italy. After the grim days that followed the *Derna* disaster in 1913, with the threat of disgrace that followed with the court-martial, his promotion to rear admiral at the end of the war, vice admiral and now admiral, was professional recognition which soothed the wounds of scandal and resignation. The news was sweet indeed.

Chapter 32

The Darkening Skies

It cannot be claimed for her that the people of her own creation will remain in the memory; but she sees to it that they play their parts adequately, and she contrives their exits and their entrances with the skill of an experienced novelist.[1]

The May 1930 *Times Literary Supplement* was guardedly positive about *Joan of the Pilchard*. There was the typical left-handed acknowledgement that she had managed the plot quite well. Details of the plot followed, and a nod to the historical figure of Bligh and Mary's handling of him:

> Miss Gaunt has recognised her responsibilities towards Bligh — the man whose professional qualities were so outstanding that he was put in authority a second time, only to be deprived of it in another mutiny not referred to in this book. She illustrates both his nerve as a leader of men and his fanatical and tactless insistence on discipline for the furtherance of her own ends when she tells us that after the worst of the boat voyage was over he marooned Daniel on the North of Australia for giving a dying man more than his share of the food.[2]

Mary has her hero marooned because she wants him to get to Sydney and meet up with Joan again. This way, readers are left with a pleasantly open and suitably optimistic end to the story.

...oOo...

Mary stopped in England on her way home from Jamaica. It was nearly ten years since she had lived in England. The trauma of the war and the influenza epidemic were gone, but their legacy lived on. The economy had still not recovered from the huge drain of the war, and the ugly signs of economic depression were there. Britain responded to the worsening financial crisis by cutting wages, so that even those who still had work could barely afford to live. There were protest marches and unemployed people drifted towards London in the hope of finding better conditions, and its population grew by fourteen percent between 1931 and 1938. Unemployment benefits, which were barely enough to keep a family fed, were cut from 17s to 15s 3d, and even this was means-tested by local authorities.

While she was in England early in 1930, Mary met up with her old journalist friend Frank Fox. Mary had known him when he had first arrived in London from Adelaide twenty years earlier, as a good-looking larrikin journalist on *The Morning Post*. Now Sir Frank, he was Honorary Secretary for the huge British Empire Exhibition project. He had an impressive twenty-eight books to his name, mainly non-fiction works on military and colonial matters. Fox agreed to use his influence to try to find a better publisher for Mary's Jamaican manuscript, and wrote to Macmillan on her behalf in January 1931:

> Mrs. Mary Gaunt, whom probably you have heard of as the author of several successful books, and who is now living in Italy, has sent to me the manuscript of a book on the West Indies, *Reflection — in Jamaica*.
>
> She has asked me to submit it to you, and in the unfortunate event of it not being suitable to you, to pass on to another publisher. She tells me that she has a good set of photographs for the illustration of the work. May I send the manuscript on to you?
>
> If, as I hope, it proves suitable, I should ask you to deal directly with Mrs Gaunt at the Villa Camilla, Bordighera, Italy. I am not a Literary Agent but am obliging a friend in this matter.[3]

There is no record of Mary ever asking for help before this to get work published. She had the professional services of her agent, Watt, who looked after her writing for over fifty years, with Daniel Jones and later Curtis

Brown for the US market. And she had her long-time editor Elsie Lang. She had no hesitation about using the help of friends and acquaintances to get to difficult places (like Morrison, for Peking), and drawing on their ideas and stories (like Swayne's, for Abyssinia), but the writing, publishing and sending out into the world had always been her own business.

While Fox was interceding for her with Macmillan, Mary was also at work; she was now beginning to actively promote her books. She wrote letters to shipping companies about *Reflection — in Jamaica*, and reported on her efforts in a letter to Macmillan:

> Since the Book Society in their blatant arrogance have decided that they rule the roost in the book world and since I can not even read their masterpieces, it has occurred to me I had better do a thing I have never done before — make an effort to personally influence the sales…
>
> Voyaging…to Jamaica, I was particularly struck with the appalling choice of books offered to the traveller. I therefore wrote to the Harrison Line, Elders Fyffes, and the Royal Mail. I don't think this is a bad beginning so I shall try further. True the Harrison Line suggested I write a book about Guiana and only wanted to know the price of the Jamaica book, but they did answer on the nail and they did declare themselves interested.[4]

But neither Frank Fox's intervention nor Mary's publicising moved Macmillan. Their reader rejected the book. Within a few weeks Macmillan returned the manuscript, along with a reply from Royal Mail, presumably a little more encouraging than the one from the Harrison Line that Mary had sent to them.

Mary went back to Ernest Benn, and *Reflection — in Jamaica* came out in March 1932. With a new book there was always hope for success. But the book fulfilled the gloomy opinion of it that Macmillan's reader had formed.

There was a stunning difference between the world Mary pictured in her Jamaican book and the world that greeted the book when it was published. She had gone to Jamaica early in 1929 — sailing towards the sunshine in a world unaware of approaching disaster. The book appeared in March 1932, into a world sliding into Depression. The reception was not good. Her hosts expected a book that would generate goodwill for the island and boost the flagging tourist trade, but they got a book that was rambling, self-indulgent and critical. People were reminded that she came on invitation to write a book about the island: she'd had free passage on the ship; de Lisser had planned her tour and helped her get around the island; and she had enjoyed hospitality from many people, starting with the governor and his wife.

When copies of the book arrived in September 1932, the Port-of-Spain *Guardian* went through the book and extracted a list of Mary's criticisms and complaints. 'Mrs. Mary Gaunt, the Australian novelist, has just published a book about Jamaica. Mrs. Gaunt was invited to Jamaica to write a book about it, and this is what she says.'[5] There followed the long list, unbroken by any of Mary's positive comments. Herbert de Lisser, now editor of *The Daily Gleaner*, copied the list in the Saturday Magazine section of his paper.

A few days later, a critique appeared in *The Daily Gleaner*. Expressing concern that there would be people reading the book who did not know what Jamaica was really like, the writer — probably de Lisser — went on to say: 'People may take seriously the silly drivelling misrepresentations perpetrated in this book in the endeavour to make a sensation, or satisfy a personal motive; they may take this wretched caricature as a true picture of Island life and conditions.'[6]

It was reasonable comment. In her book, Mary tells anecdote after anecdote in which the people she meets are friendly and an interesting topic of study, but short-sighted, lazy, superstitious and childish. That there is sympathy and humour in the telling is small comfort. Neither is the praise, as it is mostly for the natural beauty and agricultural potential of the island, for which the people get no credit.

Jamaica was feeling the worsening economic conditions. European-grown sugar beet was replacing cane sugar on the European markets, so their export income was suffering. This was no time for negative publicity.

Mary was clearly growing world-weary; she was losing the freshness and excitement of new experience that enlivened her earlier books. 'I have seen so many new things, had so many new sensations, that now everything is — well just so-so,' she said candidly in the book. She thanked Elsie Lang yet again for her help, but there were signs of carelessness in the editing — repetition, things out of sequence, and so on.

Ernest Benn brought out two 7s 6d editions of *The Lawless Frontier* and two cheaper 3s 6d ones in three years. Next came *Joan of the Pilchard* in April 1930, and a second, cheaper edition in 1931. Another cheap edition — this time of *The Lawless Frontier* — came out in July of that year. But sales were not good, royalties on cheap editions were poor, and Mary's income was going down.

Worried about what she would live on in her old age, Mary could no longer afford to reject an offer to publish. She was unhappy with Benn, but she realised that times were hard, and was forced to accept that she was not the success she had been. She signed up again with Benn for the publishing of *Harmony*.

Mary felt that *Harmony* was one of the best books she had written, but it did not have the style of her earlier work. It was published in 1933, twenty-three years after she began it. Only *As the Whirlwind Passeth*, at twenty-five years, had a longer period of gestation.

When Winifred Holtby, a rising young English novelist, wrote to say she had enjoyed *Harmony*, Mary responded:

> The poor book did so badly that I began to fear my right hand had lost its cunning. That and *Reflection — in Jamaica* only brought me in £3 more, taken together, than the first book ever I wrote ages ago when I was a girl in Australia. I was the more disappointed because I heard by a side wind that my publishers said the only books they had published that were paying were Mary Gaunt's. All I can say is that while they had headed me to the workhouse, their other unlucky authors must have been chucked right inside.[7]

By the end of its first year, the income from it was only £30, the lowest of any book she had published. A cheaper edition came out two years later.

...oOo...

By now it was not only her income that concerned her. In sending a copy of *Harmony* to Ernest, she wrote: 'I have been very ill and this is the first time for some weeks that I have attempted a letter.' She was now in her seventies, having passed the milestone in January 1931, and even the blue skies of Bordighera were sometimes bleak.

When she was well, she continued writing. For her next book, she went back to the setting she loved — West Africa. She thanked Phillip Hall, former provincial commissioner in Northern Rhodesia, for his help with the book, and dedicated it to her brother Ernest 'because for the last year I have never seen him without inflicting it upon him.' She called it *Worlds Away*:

> The little more and how much it is,
> The little less and what worlds away.[8]

The book is a remarkable amalgam of characters, places and details from previous books, but woven together skilfully to make a convincing plot and an entertaining story. Her heroine, Audrey Rowan, goes to West Africa and almost marries a man she later finds is dishonest, disloyal and universally disliked. Having inherited a part share in a concession, she is determined to stay and work it with her partner, and becomes involved in the crime of her former fiancé and his dramatic rescue from tribal vengeance by a trader and the district commissioner. The heroine, Audrey, travels with a colonial official along the hard sand of the foreshore to avoid the narrow paths through the trees, just as Mary did in *Alone in West Africa*. She also falls in love with West Africa against all advice and expectations, as Mary did. She even has a dog, Daniel, from the Battersea Dogs' Home, as Mary had. The provincial commissioner dispenses British justice from El Capo d'Oro, the magnificent castle on the coast which is in fact Elmina, and featured in *Every Man's Desire* under the same name, and has the guest chamber which has visitors waking in unaccountable terror in the night. The character of Peter Addie, the trader from *Every Man's Desire*, appears again as a friend and helper.

Mary writes with the sure hand of someone who has been carried through the forest in a hammock, has boarded a coastal steamer by mammy chair, has camped in a rest house overnight and has experienced the onset of the wet season, with its storms and torrential rain. This is Mary on sure ground and at her atmospheric best.

It is also vintage Mary in her views. After Audrey's marriage is cancelled: 'Do you think I could possibly go back to Dad and Beth at High Aveling and entertain all the busy bodies at tea?' and 'Nowadays every school girl looks forward to a career as a matter of course. But in the days before the [First World] War an object in life, unconnected with matrimony, was somewhat uncommon for a girl of Audrey's class.' And an interesting insight into Mary's enjoyment of her visit: 'If a woman wanted to feel herself of real importance in the world all she had to do, twenty years ago, was to land on the much-abused Guinea Coast…'[9]

When the book was finished, her agent tried to place it with Heinemann, Gollancz, Hodder and Stoughton, and at last, successfully, with Hutchinson, passing on Mary's claim that she always got '£40 down' from Ernest Benn. The terms were not great, but by now Mary could only swallow her pride and be grateful. She wrote to Watt:

> 'I am truly humble that I should be worth so little. [The humility does not last long.] I think of course it is Benn's fault. I have seen their authors drop off one by one during the last seven years and was an utter fool not to have gone before.' [But, more reasonably…] Still I must admit they have been bad years for every one.' [And she rallies a bit later in the same letter…] [Still] No-one could have done less advertising than Benn, except for those wretched ninepennies.'[10]

The book came out at last in September 1934. Mary suggested serialisation in a newspaper also. Watt had already tried a few in England; what about *The Age*, *The Australasian*, *The Argus*? Watt suggested that, since Mary had

had dealings with them before, she might like to try them. None of the Australian papers took it up. The book had only one edition.

...oOo...

While in Italy, Mary did not get to England to see her family very often. She wrote to her agent in March 1934: 'I can't come to England as I'd like until the weather cheers up.'[11] And again a few weeks later: 'I am coming to England as soon as I can, but the doctors here doubt if I can live in England even in the summer so I daren't fix any date, which is provoking.'[12] It was the year that Ernest's wife Louise died.

The winters, even in Bordighera, were not good for Mary; over the next winter she was ill with the flu, and she suffered regularly with bronchial asthma. Ernest had, years before, rented a villa in Bordighera and he spent some of his retirement in the 1930s in a villa in Monte Carlo; he at least was sometimes not far away.

...oOo...

For a long time, Mary had been writing her autobiography. She put *Strange Trails* on her list of published books for *Who's Who in Literature* in 1925. By 1936, she was calling it *Strange Roads*. 'The author Mary Gaunt has travelled many strange roads on her travels,' a critic had written after her African travels, and she adopted it as a title. So definite was the entry that in 1939 *The Bulletin* listed it among her published works in answer to a reader's enquiry. She was adding to it over the years, and it suffered from the defects of its long-drawn-out writing process: it was self-indulgent and rambling, and careless as to dates and details, filled with anecdotes that did nothing to amuse and little to instruct. But Mary was to get help and support for it from an unexpected source.

In 1931, Winifred Holtby published *Poor Caroline*. Mary read and enjoyed it, and wrote to the author to express her interest and admiration. It was the beginning of a two-year correspondence that kept Mary in touch with writers and the writing world in England, and was to lead to very practical help. Winifred was an astute and very talented writer, young enough to be Mary's daughter; she had a strong social commitment, which Mary admired. She had published several well-received books; she wrote prolifically for newspapers and magazines and had many demands on her time, but she responded courteously and kindly to letters from many quarters.

The English Library in Bordighera had only one of Winifred's books. In earlier days, Mary would have ordered her books from England at the *libreria* (bookshop) on the Via Vittorio Emanuele, but those days were gone. She was still curious to see how authors were writing and what readers were reading. It was particularly satisfying, therefore, when Winifred Holtby wrote back, enlarging on her characters a little and discussing Mary's comments.

Although most of Winifred's letters to Mary have not survived, Mary's to Winifred were found among her papers after Winifred's death. They are conversation pieces — gossipy, newsy, critical.

> What makes the public rush to buy books? I'm afraid I've turned a deaf ear to praise of late. Dr. Cronin, Vera Britain [sic], Louis Golding etc. I tried *Magnolia Street* [by Golding] inside out and upside down. Which ever way I looked at it I struck a fresh lot of deadly uninteresting people and I could not understand the praise the critics gave it for I never met any one who could read it. Then I read he was dramatizing it. I felt he might just as well try and dramatize a Railway Guide Book!

That the two women continued to correspond regularly suggests a generosity of spirit on Winifred's part, since she and Vera Brittain were working partners and close friends.

Winifred read Mary's *Harmony* and praised it. She was interested in Jamaica and the Jamaican people, she said. 'It is curious to find you are interested in coloured people,' Mary wrote back.

> I have always felt keenly their disadvantages but it is very hard indeed to keep on friendly terms with them. They all seem to me to

suffer from an inferiority complex and to think you are patronizing [sic] them.

In her letters, Mary chatted about her previous books, her name, the ups and downs of publishing, her experiences during the war, and so on.

Then, in January 1935, she asked Winifred's advice about publishing *Strange Roads*. Did Winifred think that Hutchinson might be interested? It was, on the surface, an odd question; Hutchinson had published *World's Away* only months before, and in her contract Hutchinson had an option on her next two novels. But Mary had lost the confidence of earlier years; she was hoping that Winifred, a rising star in England, would help her along.

Winifred replied with a list of likely publishers, with Gollancz at the top, and offered to talk about the book with their reader. Mary was jubilant. 'I know your word will be invaluable,' she wrote.

Mary wrote to her agent, asking him to send the book to Gollancz. She confided her feelings to Winifred Holtby later:

> I've always rather hankered after Gollancz. He used to be in with Ernest Benn and just before I to my deep regret became one of their authors he left them. I was told he differed with them on the question of some policy in publishing. Knowing Benn's methods I came to the conclusion he was probably quite right.

For a while, Mary could do nothing more. A bad attack of influenza, with high temperatures and the listlessness that followed, left her unable to contemplate a planned trip to England. 'I have been down in the depths of woe of late,' she wrote to Winifred. She would have to wait as patiently as possible.

The spring returned, and her spirits lifted as her health improved. Meanwhile, the agent had sent Mary's book to Gollancz and the reader's report was poor, so Gollancz turned it down. When Winifred intervened, Gollancz asked her to read the manuscript herself and give him a second report on it, and this she did. Her three-page report on the book is thorough, detailed and critical; she recommends drastic revision and then publication. After acknowledging its defects and the need for editing, she wrote movingly of the way Mary had talked about the gradual onset of Hubert's madness: 'Anyone who has ever loved a man or woman stricken by nervous disease will find some comfort in the courage and pity of the narrative which follows', she said. 'I don't see it sweeping England, but I do see it selling about 5,000 copies very creditably...This sturdy natural feminist will blow the gaff on a good many illusions about Victorian ladies. She has humour, humanity and a generous spirit.'[13]

Winifred sent a quick note to Mary to let her know. Finally, in May, she sent the manuscript back to Mary. Desperate for time, she had completed her reading and comments on a long train journey. She was astute, but kindly. 'I have never met a kinder critic in my life,'[14] Mary said. With the manuscript came good news. Gollancz had agreed to publish if Winifred would work with Mary.

Mary was grateful, but not confident she could do what Winifred suggested. She offered to pay Winifred, and failing that she asked that Winifred mark a few passages with the sort of changes she felt were needed, and Mary would try to follow them through.

Winifred had mentioned in a letter in January 1935 that she had the mumps, and Mary was sympathetic. What Winifred didn't mention was that this was just one in a series of debilitating setbacks to her health. Even when Winifred was told the news she did not tell her family, or Vera Brittain, and certainly not Mary, the woman she had never met who was more dependent on her help than she would ever know. A specialist had given her two years to live in the spring of 1932; she had already lived beyond that time. Not until May 1935 did she finally confide to Vera Brittain what the specialist had told her, and only then because she believed she had outwitted the doctors. She had only three months left to live.

Unaware of the diagnosis that weighed Winifred down, Mary enthusiastically set to work on the revisions.

Mary felt her biography could perhaps be serialised, too. There is a copy of a letter, with no address and no date, offering it to an Australian newspaper, probably the Melbourne *Age*. Mary's typing, always a little erratic, was now peppered with mistakes and missing letters. 'Gollancz I hope will publish either in the late autumn or early spring,' she wrote to the newspaper late in 1935 or early in 1936. 'Winifred Holtby, one of <u>the</u> modern powers in the literary world, is <u>so</u> great in its praise that I am hoping for a big success.' Winifred might have hesitated at the comment, and the enthusiastic underlining of certain words that went with it. 'My sister Mrs Archer will act as my agent in Australia.'[15]

None of the Melbourne newspapers serialised the biography. But she succeeded in placing the early part of the manuscript with *The Woman's Magazine*, and it was published serially and came out in their annual for 1938. As it was a magazine for girls and young women, the editors had tidied up the account a bit. Mary grumbled later in a letter:

> ...taking out any reference to religion and sex which, considering it was the life of a young girl seemed to me a little like the play of "Hamlet" without Hamlet.

For all the heavy-handed editing — glitches in the text give away where the more obvious cuts were made — the *Woman's Magazine* excerpt is a valuable record. Apart from short notes to introduce her stories, it is the only piece of autobiography published in her lifetime.[16]

There is no record of how Mary heard the news of Winifred's death, of whether she got word before it was noted in *The Times*. She had her manuscript back and Winifred's notations, and was at work on the revisions when Winifred died. It was sad irony that Winifred should lose her battle with Bright's disease just as Mary's chance of publication by Gollancz was so close. She never came so close again.

CHAPTER 33

'I TRUST I SHALL BE ABLE TO LIVE ON HERE'

In 1926 the majority of Italians accepted the Fascist regime as legitimate, and its air of legitimacy convinced a number of its former opponents to work with it. Some liberal intellectuals salved their own consciences by arguing that the king would have acted illegally if he had dismissed Mussolini after the Matteotti murder, while the king salved his by invoking the conservative bogey of anarchy as the only alternative. Once Mussolini reasserted his power in January 1925, both the army and the police became his loyal servants, as did the civil service and the courts.[1]

As the 1930s went on, the dwindling English community in Bordighera grew uneasy. The rise of fascism in Europe was the subject of academic debate. Cut off to a large degree from local gossip and independent sources of information within Italy, they read in the English papers of the establishment of a small new political party in England. It was set up by Oswald Mosley, a wealthy man who had been expelled from the Labor Party, but whose ideas about the economy were seen by his supporters to be positive and sound. After eighteen months, the British Union of Fascists claimed a membership of 40,000.

It was the 1934 Olympia Rally, where Mosley's men ejected and bashed protesters, that sounded the first warning note. The rallies later that year in Hyde Park — 2,500 Blackshirts at one end, 200,000 anti-fascists at the other — opened people's eyes. Then followed the march through predominantly Jewish suburbs in the East End of London, the huge crowds who rallied to stop it, the ignominious retreat and the passing of the Public Order Act — the British working class had made their feelings clear. Mosley had become allied with names that were to become symbols of international menace — Hitler, Mussolini, Franco. But the conviction was less clear-cut among intellectuals and the upper classes, who were being reassured by *The Times* that one more concession to Hitler would mean 'peace in our time'. In sunny Bordighera, Mary was reading *The Times*.

Around Mary, fascism was on the rise in Italy. The March on Rome of 1922 had been planned under the very noses of the English community at the Albergo Parco in Bordighera, and given the blessing of the Italian Queen Mother, Queen Margherita, who lived in the town. The march confirmed the position of Mussolini, who became prime minister that year. In a general strike in August 1922, fascist *squadristi* moved in and kept mail and transport moving, which gained them public support, though there were ugly rumours of violence. Women were banned from wearing slacks, and the old polite form of address — *lei* — was outlawed. From 1937, the fascist salute was required of the general population, although many resented these increasing intrusions into private behaviour. In 1939, the Italian Lawn Tennis Association made rules that players should wear fascist uniform and make the fascist salute. At the English tennis club, they continued to shake hands across the net as befitted gentleman players and Englishmen.

The threat of war blew like a chill wind across Europe. But Neville Chamberlain arrived back from Germany with his 'Peace in our time' reassurance and Mary, like many other British people, hoped that she would be able to stay in Italy. Italy had been an ally of Britain during the First World War; there was the possibility that it would remain so.

The brothers Mary had envied in her youth for their freedom to work and travel were now retiring from their professions, crowned with honours and comfortable pensions. Closest to her were Cecil, now settled in Hampshire, Ernest in Monte Carlo and Guy in Tangier. Mary remained in Bordighera. 'I like Italy,' she had written in 1932. 'I live there as long as the income tax commissioners will allow a poor author to stay out of

England without unduly penalizing [sic] her.' But her brothers made her a small allowance to supplement her income.

In 1936 came the news of Lucy's death. It was hard to lose her only sister when she was so far away. Some months later, Lucy's daughter Ellinor came to Bordighera for three weeks' holiday. Ellinor, far more mature and confident than the gauche teenager who had come to stay in London in 1912, was combining a holiday in Europe with two months' study leave from her work as Librarian of the Council for Scientific and Industrial Research in Melbourne. She visited her uncle Guy in Tangier also.

Two years later Clive, the second youngest of the family, sailed from Australia on the *Orontes* to visit the 'European' members of the family: Mary in Bordighera, Guy in Tangier and Ernest, Cecil and Lance in England. Unfortunately Cecil was already ill, and died before Clive arrived.

...oOo...

Mary spent her days writing at the Villa Camilla. She revised and amended her autobiography, the typescript dotted with XXXX overtyping, and the handwriting less firm now. She had begun writing to *The Times* in 1919, giving opinions on the prospects for migration to Australia and the value of allowing women to have paid employment. She wrote about once a year, through the 1920s and 1930s. She watched Britons settle in Bordighera who were still energetic and capable people, and questioned why Britain didn't encourage them to put their skills to use for the Empire. She wrote to say that William Bligh should be honoured for taking breadfruit trees to Jamaica, thereby providing food in hard times. Then there was a long pause; from 1933 to 1938 no letters of hers appeared in *The Times*.

Then they began again. She wrote to praise Jamaican coffee; she sent her anecdote about her 'Rule, Britannia!' episode in Blagoveschensk in 1914. She defended Governor Maclean of Cape Coast, West Africa, whose poet-wife had suffered through marrying 'a man of coarse mind, selfish and cynical', and reminded readers that he had helped save the West African colonies for Britain. Her last published letter urged against a rise in the price of novels. 'Why not [...] issue a volume with paper covers, say at 2/6d?' she asked. She wrote it in January 1940, with war in Europe already a reality.

Daily life grew difficult. When she wrote to her agent, Watt, she sent letters for him to post in England, because it was cheaper than posting them from Italy. She walked her dog along the *passegiata*, down the alley where Lucy walked in *Dr Antonio*, and where many an English tourist had walked since then. As time went on, the walks became shorter and less frequent; the years in a sedentary occupation were taking their toll and by 1939 she found walking difficult. She wrote letters, did some crochet, sewing and mending, and played bridge with an ever-decreasing circle of friends.

As war loomed, coffee was growing scarce. This threatened one of Mary's pleasant rituals — having coffee with Muriel Daly. Mary did not have a radio, and Muriel would come for coffee and bring Mary up to date with the BBC news from the night before. She could still get *The Times*, although it was taking four days to get to her, and she passed her copies on to Muriel. The accounts of the rise of fascism in Britain were disturbing; it was still good to be in Italy in the sun. Travel became more difficult; crossing borders — like the one nearby, into France — was now 'the very devil', Mary said in a letter in January 1938. The English community was dwindling; there were fewer dates pencilled into the books in the English Library. On the graves in the English cemetery, the flowers withered and died.

…oOo…

In nearly nineteen years in Bordighera, Mary had published ten books and completed at least two more. She was still working steadily. She was also still hoping to publish her autobiography, now called *Strange Roads*. She was more realistic about it now; instead of listing it among her published works, as she had done in the past, she listed 'My Victorian Youth', the extract published in *The Woman's Magazine Annual* in 1938, among her publications in *Who's Who in Australia* for 1941.

In November 1937, she had almost completed a novel she called *The Grey Wolf*. Years before she had learned the old Breton saying, 'God keep thee from the grey wolf and thy heart's deep desire'. Now it provided the title for her book. It was a story set on the West African coast — in the Mandated Territory of the Cameroons, the old familiar territory. She wrote to Arthur Sullivant Hoffman, an American agent, to ask if he could place her newest novel. She hadn't quite finished writing it, but expected to by the time he replied. Would Mr Hoffman read it for her, and give her his opinion as to whether it would be suitable to enter for the Atlantic Monthly novel prize?

Hoffman sent a politely encouraging reply and a request for a US$15 reading fee. Mary wrote back, sending the manuscript and promising the fee:

> Don't be afraid if those dollars take time in arriving. For — for some unknown reason I bank in a little Staffordshire town where my father was born 107 years ago, and the manager I often think has some of the methods of past ages. I shall try and explain that there are such things as dollars, and you'll get them in time.
>
> Why I don't change I can't imagine. I'll have to.

She also sent him a copy of *Harmony*:

> I want badly to sell *Harmony* in the United States. Of course I know the colour question is against it. But in spite of the mess those unspeakable wretches Benn Bros. made of it, I think it must have some merit.

She offered an anecdote to highlight the merits of the book:

> The other day there came to my apartment, which is modest, no less a person than Sir John Simon and his wife and he is the Chancellor of the Exchequer of Great Britain, which I at least consider a very important position indeed. He was very interesting, very good-looking and I found him very charming. I didn't know him, but he came because he admired *Harmony* so much.
>
> As he was only in Monte Carlo for ten days and crossing the frontier is now the very devil, I was immensely uplifted. I told him

I'd never seen a Chancellor of the Exchequer before and now I had entertained him.[2]

It was an odd letter — chatty, coy, self-important. And unsuccessful.

A few months later she had finished writing *The Grey Wolf* and, with no positive response from Hoffman, sent it to Watt. He sent the manuscript by hand to Hutchinson in Paternoster Row, with a hopeful note. He knew the prospects were not good; three other publishers had rejected her last novel, *Worlds Away*, before it went to Hutchinson.

The letter that went in the parcel is the last one in Watt's file of correspondence with Mary. There is no record of a reply. The book was never published, and the manuscript disappeared.

...oOo...

The growing power of Germany began to dominate the politics of Europe and the conversations in Bordighera, and the situation was debated with increasing urgency. The library acquired books on fascism, including *My Struggle* by Adolf Hitler. Captain Coates, of the Villa Primavera, gave lectures on fascism in Britain, praising the role of Oswald Mosley and offering further information on the British Union of Fascists. Meanwhile in France, the line of defence down the eastern border that had been started when Maginot was Minister of War and finished in 1934, was extended and strengthened. A vast underground fortress at its southern end was cut into the hillside above Menton, just across the border from Bordighera.

Bordighera had benefited from the presence of the English community for over sixty years. The young *Bordighotti* who played tennis in the English Tennis Club, the small army of cooks, chauffeurs and gardeners who took care of the *Inglesi*, the hotel proprietors and town business people, saw no reason for conflict with Britain and hoped that Italy would remain neutral. Propaganda images of the British as unwelcome foreigners found little acceptance in a town where Louisa Boyce's children's home had cared for Italian orphans for half a century, and where people had more confidence in the English bank than the Italian one. But as the days grew darker, many of the lovely villas along the Via dei Colli and the Via Romana were sold and their owners went back to England.

Others stayed on. Those who, like Mary, read *l'Eclaireur*, were comforted by France's confidence that it could withstand a German attack. Many had spent all their lives in the friendly Italian community. While some had a family property in Britain to which they could return others, like Mary, had no other home. As the uneasy weeks went by, they waited.

Then events moved swiftly. On 1 September, German troops marched into Poland.

On the night of 3 September, the British gathered around radios to listen to the crackle of the BBC and the Prime Minister's broadcast: 'I have to tell you now that no such undertaking has been received, and that consequently this country is at war with Germany.'

All across Europe, small pockets of British communities disappeared. Italy, as yet uncommitted, stationed troops along its borders. With the help of Muriel Daly, Mary hurriedly packed a few belongings and, with other British residents, crossed the border to Menton in southern France. Her servant, Anselma, packed up the household linen and silver and went home with her family to Reggio Emilia. With very little happening and the threat of war seeming far away, Mary — again with Muriel's help — went back, and Anselma and her family also returned. Mary wrote to Lucy:

> How quickly things change. On a Friday I bought some silk to make a little jacket to use up an old evening dress and ordered the dressmaker Monday. By Monday I had refugeed in France and stayed there for thirteen days, spending evenings in rooms lighted by lamps wrapped up in dark purple paper so that darkness was just visible. And now that I've come home it would be ridiculous to spend money on anything I do not absolutely have to.

In the strange silence that fell on Europe in the weeks that followed — the 'phoney war' — there was a great deal of uncertainty. Along the Mediterranean coast, nothing seemed to be happening. At Cap Ferrat, Somerset Maugham ordered 20,000 bulbs for planting at his villa in the spring.

Italy's allegiances were uncertain. The conquest of Ethiopia had restored national pride to Italy and enhanced Mussolini's leadership, but it had alienated Britain and France. The alienation grew worse when Mussolini joined Hitler in supplying arms and troops to help Franco fight against the republicans in Spain. Still, when Hitler marched on Poland and Britain declared war on Germany, Italy remained neutral.

Daily life in Bordighera was more difficult. Mary's nephew Pat sent newspapers from Australia; they were sent via England, and took nineteen days to get to Bordighera from there. Letters from England were taking ten days to reach her. Ernest was ill, and she was anxious to have news of him. Banking was disrupted and her income, already depleted, was under threat. Ellinor and Pat Archer sent money from Australia. She wrote to Ellinor, telling her of her hasty trip to France and her return, and of how difficult things were:

> I hope and trust that Italy is going to be neutral and I shall be able to live on here. Anselma says she will be ruined if I go away now — and as she has been with me and served me faithfully for eighteen years I'll do my best to stay on. I'm fond of her too, and I love Dar [the dog] and I, who cannot walk out at all now, would feel a brute to take him away with no chance of giving him any exercise.[3]

For all the difficulties, though, she could still be optimistic, however briefly. She asked Ellinor to thank Pat for sending the *Heralds*, and said:

> I shall hope to write articles later on, but I doubt their getting through now, and anyhow I'm an awful old crock not fit to do anything but crochet, and not much of that. It's a nuisance being old.[4]

...oOo...

After the invasion of Poland, Belgium, Luxembourg and Holland fell to the German armies in May 1940. In a swift manoeuvre, the German armies passed north-east of the expensive concrete bunkers and defences on which Maginot — and France — had relied, and headed towards Paris. All along the Mediterranean coast, the English population packed up, turned out the lights in their villas and started for home.

Mary and the others in the tiny remnant of Bordighera's British population could wait no longer. Every day the signs grew stronger that Mussolini would take Italy into the war on what was then clearly the victorious side — that of Germany. Early in June the ultimatum came: if they did not leave now, they faced internment as enemy aliens in a camp at Abruzzo. Mary packed her belongings, found a home for her dog and, for the second time, went across the border into the south of France.

By 5 June, Mary and the other refugees were safely settled in Vence, an old walled village in the mountains inland from Nice at the end of a narrow road that wound up through the rocky hills. In Vence, they were well away from the railway line and the main roads along the coast.

On 10 June, Italy joined the war as an ally of Germany. Italian soldiers moved into position along the border of France. Civilians in the villages near the border were evacuated, and many of the townspeople in Bordighera also left. The young Italian tennis players who had played at the English tennis club were drafted into the Italian army and sent off to fight — against the English.

On 14 June, German soldiers marched into Paris. While Hitler hesitated about a date for talks, his troops pushed on; the strategic port of St Malo was taken on 20 June, and Vichy the same day. Two days later, the French Government signed the Armistice.

France was no longer a safe place for British nationals. Those who had clung on longest were now in real danger. With the British Embassy now evacuated to Bordeaux, along with the French Government, the consulate in Nice waited anxiously for instructions. Word came that all the remaining British subjects were to be evacuated from Nice.

The English hospital closed down and the patients were moved to Cannes, further away from the Italian border. The Vice-Consul, realising that the way north across France would be cut off by a German advance on Paris, managed to acquire two coal carriers that had put into Marseilles to unload. They would come to Cannes and take passengers. They normally carried a crew of thirty-eight, and had one toilet, three cabins and an inch of coal dust over everything. As news about these two boats spread, there were anxious phone calls from residents: could they book a first-class passage back to England? At the Sunny Bank Hospital in Cannes, patients who were fit enough to travel (including those from Cannes) were given a blanket, a pillow and a small parcel of food and taken to the port. A nurse from Sunnybank wrote:

> Frequent reports came to us of people angrily clutching British passports, bottles of Evian water and dogs. I doubt if a sandwich, a biscuit, or a bottle of water was left in any shop in the port area. Cars and heavy luggage were abandoned on the quayside. Many people grumbled and criticised the Consul. [We] had no patience with them. Everyone was advised earlier to leave the country and return to England. Those who had preferred to stay in the sunshine on the coast, were lucky to have the opportunity of travelling on these two boats. Every other form of transport was being used for troops and essentials.[5]

At last, five hundred people — among them Somerset Maugham[6] — were crammed into the two colliers. After twenty days, in a trip that should have taken four, the exhausted and hungry passengers stepped ashore in England. They were covered in coal dust; many had not even had the chance to change their clothes during the voyage.

Mary and some of the other refugees from Bordighera remained in Vence.

Chapter 34

The Darkness Closes In

> I remember attending the funeral of one of my patients, a youngish woman who had one son — a prisoner of war in Germany — and a daughter in England. She had died without seeing them, or hearing from them. I found myself crying and I found I was really upset because I thought if it was I who had died I should have been in the same predicament. My family would be entirely unaware of my death, and the sense of loneliness at this thought was too much for my frayed emotions.[1]

A friend of Mary's, Mrs Graham, was among the British refugees in Vence. She managed to get safely back to England. From there, she cabled to Mary's niece Ellinor in Australia to let her know that Mary was safely out of Italy, but that she had to leave her behind in Vence and could not get in touch with her there. Ellinor began a long and expensive process of sending letters, telegrams and cables to government departments in Australia and Britain to try to get help to her aunt.[2]

Late in June, Mary got a message through to Guy in Tangier, saying that she was well. The British Government had arranged for the US Vice-Consul in Cannes to look after the needs of the handful of British subjects trapped in France. By mid-August, the Department of External Affairs in Canberra let Ellinor know that Mary was 'receiving the usual financial assistance accorded to British subjects'. About the same time, Mary got word to Mrs Graham in Farnham, Buckinghamshire, that she was now well, that there was plenty of food available, and that she and the forty other British people in Vence were getting financial help through the US Vice-Consul.

As was the case for most of the others, Mary's income came via an English bank. Banking transactions became at first difficult and eventually impossible under wartime conditions, but the refugees needed money to pay for their keep at the little *pension* of La Roseraie, where they had settled. The allowance via the US Vice-Consul kept them alive.[3]

The Alpes Maritimes area was rocky hill country with little arable land and relied on food brought in from the more productive agricultural areas of France. As the war progressed, transport was disrupted and food supplies began to dwindle.

Towards the middle of 1941, Mary grew ill. She was taken down to the coast and admitted to Sunny Bank, the British hospital in Cannes that had served the British population there since the Prince of Wales (later Edward VII) had laid its memorial stone in 1897. Its continued existence, in enemy-occupied territory, and in the face of severe food shortages, was a marvel for which its matron, Margaret Williams, was awarded the Member in The Most Excellent Order of the British Empire (MBE) at the end of the war.

The hospital patients were given £5 a month as relief money by the US Vice-Consul. If they had funds in England, or anywhere else, and were likely to be able to repay it, they were given a further £5 a month. The hospital put two beds into each single room to cut its costs so that patients got a bill for just under £5 a month, far less than the actual cost of their keep; the pre-war charge per single room had been between £1 and £2 a day.

There was an ingenious and complex system to keep patients and hospital alive. John Taylor, banker and estate agent, who had been British Vice-Consul at Cannes for twenty years, had gone to England in 1940 and could get access to the English bank accounts of the hospital patients. The patients signed promissory notes for the amount of their bill and the notes were sent to John Taylor in London. Taylor collected the money from the patients' accounts and paid it into the Foreign Office, who sent it to the US

Vice-Consul, who paid the patients' bills at Sunny Bank.

Conditions grew worse as the German occupation spread southward and Italian troops spread across the south also. Food grew scarce. Local people, knowing the desperate situation of the hospital patients, would bring a gift of a few eggs or some produce from their gardens. A section of the hospital grounds was ploughed up and planted with vegetables, but these were confiscated by the Germans as they ripened. In spite of the difficulties, no-one in need was turned away.

Patients could not be sent home, even if they got better. Since some of the nurses had gone back to England, the nurses' home was turned into a convalescent wing-cum-hostel. Staff members who remained took it in turns to go down into the hospital cellar to listen to the news from the BBC on a radio, while someone kept watch at the head of the stairs.

With the town hall under German control, nurses were fingerprinted and taken away for identity checks, and patients were questioned. Mail from England was stopped completely, but letters could be directed via Switzerland. Mary, increasingly frail and with her eyesight now failing, received a conspicuous amount of mail, and was questioned several times because of it and because she had high-ranking brothers who had served in the British armed forces and intelligence during the Great War. But, as one of the nurses later attested, she was elderly and infirm but fully aware, and provided no information that could help the enemy.

Because most of the patients were elderly, deaths at the hospital were not uncommon. The staff did what they could, but families and friends could not come to visit. In the early part of the war, they had a man who was both patient and honorary handyman, who made small wooden crosses for each grave; this came to an end when he was taken away to a concentration camp.

Because they did not want their patients to go alone 'to their long home', as Mary called it, one of the nurses walked behind the coffin at each funeral. Clothing in general was difficult to get at first and then impossible, and the nurses had only one black coat and one black hat between them.

They shared not only the sad duty of funeral attendance, but the clothing as well.

The winter of 1942 was bitterly cold. The hospital had no fuel, and the only way they could keep patients warm on cold days was to keep them in bed. Food was rationed, but there was less and less to be had. Patients and staff grew thinner as time went on. The sweets that Mary had always enjoyed were now a distant memory.

Mary was almost 81 when she died on 19 January 1942. Her burial service was conducted by the English chaplain, and she was laid to rest in the English section of the cemetery in Cannes, France, with one nurse in a black hat and black coat standing beside the grave. Her burial was recorded in the register at the Cimitière de Grand Jas.

…oOo…

Guy, who had been on the staff of the British Embassy in Washington during the Great War, had asked the US Consul to keep him informed about Mary. So it was that Mary's death was announced by telegram from the US Consulate in Nice to the US Ambassador in London, relayed to Mr (later Sir) Anthony Eden, Secretary of State for Foreign Affairs, and passed on to Guy via the United Services Club in London, and to Australia House for the Department of External Affairs in Canberra.

Ellinor and Pat read about Mary's death in the Melbourne papers on 31 January, four days before the official notification arrived.

Chapter 35

Finale

In northern Victoria, on the fringe of the small township of Chiltern, is an empty paddock beside the pioneer cemetery where a few early graves bear witness to the bustle of goldfields life. It was one of William Gaunt's first tasks to set out this burial ground. It was not exactly a Gold Warden's duty, but as the only representative of civil government there, he put his stamp on town life in many ways. In an empty field near the graves stands a gnarled pear tree, claimed by local people to be the remainder of the *Woodlands* orchard; the tree certainly looks old enough. If this was indeed the site of *Woodlands*, it is the most tangible remaining link with Mary's earliest years — the garden where she played as a child. As her childhood homes were on the frontiers of the gold rush and in government residences in bush towns, little evidence of them remains.

In 1971, a fire destroyed the lovely Gothic-style Wilson Hall at The University of Melbourne, where the student records were stored. There is little evidence remaining of Mary's one and only year at the university, and of Lydia Harris and her studies. But their achievement as the first two women at The University of Melbourne, and therefore the first two women at any university in Australia, remains unchallenged.

In Malvern, once on the genteel fringe of Melbourne, now an old-established suburb, is the house that was Mary's home for four years. The Gaunt family moved to Malvern from Ballarat in 1890 and from this house — *Koonda* — Mary drove with her father to their parish church — St George's, Malvern — to marry Hubert Lindsay Miller. It was here, in her upstairs bedroom, that she wrote her first novel. The land around the house, the stables, the big garden, are gone now, swallowed up in suburban development, but the gracious house with its Victorian-era wrought ironwork and bay windows still remains.

The house-and-practice where Mary lived with Hubert in Warrnambool was demolished to make way for a new police station.

In Garran, Canberra, in an area dedicated to writers, there is a street named for Mary. Coincidentally, the street crossed by Gaunt Place is named for Vance Palmer, so that the names of Mary's father and mother are on the same street sign post.

In London, her house in Finborough Road still stands in its 'dull and stony street'. Instead of the cabs of Mary's day, red London buses go up and down, from busy Kensington High Street towards the river. The small hotel in Brompton Square still exists. So does the lovely Frinsted Rectory, where Mary spent many happy hours with Elsie and Lewis Lang, and *Mary Haven* in New Eltham.

The Villa Camilla in Bordighera, in its breathlessly beautiful setting near the sea, is no more. Ten years or so after Mary's death, a second railway line was built, and the house was demolished to make room for it. The huge old Moreton Bay fig tree still holds the shattered brick wall of the Bicknell Institute in its gnarled grip, and the English library makes its books available to a new generation of readers — students of English from Genoa University. The English Church was given to the people of Bordighera and is now a gallery; above the exhibition stands, around the walls, can be seen the plaques: 'Sacred to the memory of Dora Mary Daly'. The graves in the English Cemetery are carefully tended, although very few of the British population remain. In Bordighera they still play tennis, which was introduced into Italy there.

The hospital above the old port in the Avenue du Petit Juas in Cannes has been demolished. Founded in 1893, it cared for all but the wealthiest of British residents (the really wealthy were nursed at home), and stayed open right through the occupation in of the Second World War. The foyer of Sunny Bank proudly displayed, for many years, the MBE presented to the Matron for her services in keeping the hospital open during the war.

In the cemetery in Cannes, an area of wartime graves in the English section has been re-landscaped. There is a grassy open space, about equivalent to eight or ten graves, but there are no gravestones or markers on it. Wildflowers grow on it and a large pine tree stands beside it. Nearby is the grave of a Russian princess and that of Prosper Mérimée. Here somewhere, between a Russian aristocrat and a French writer, Mary Gaunt lies in her long home.

...oOo...

Mary regretted not having had children, but Lucy and the boys had ten children between them, so the family name and traditions live on, and Mary is remembered among them. Her best memorial, however, is her books.

On the shelves of the Baillieu Library at The University of Melbourne are the books Mary sent home to her sister Lucy, inscribed in the moment of exaltation that comes with the arrival of a new book into the world, like the moment of birth: 'To Lucy, with love from the author'. Other libraries have copies — notably the State Library of Victoria — but none has a complete set.

She published twenty-six books — novels, history and travel books. She peopled them with strong heroines unlike the ideal woman Mary was supposed to become — accomplished in French, music and embroidery, docile, obedient to father and husband, and content with domestic life.

Her books were out of print for a long time. But in the Australian Bicentenary year, 1988, her novel *Kirkham's Find* (1897) was reprinted for a new generation of readers.[1] Her stories of the goldfields were collected and reprinted in 2001.[2]

In her seventies she insisted that she only began writing to make money — a modest and comfortable position that makes no claim to literary talent but suggests a down-to-earth approach. With the hard labour and workmanlike approach that Payn recommended at the beginning of her career, she achieved practical success. Despite the death of her husband, the setbacks in her travels, the loneliness and hardships, she continued to write. Her heroines are determined, resourceful, and we see in them a reflection of Mary herself.

The Victorian Honour Roll of Women was launched in 2001, the Centenary of Federation. It acknowledges the achievements of women who have made a major contribution to the community, and names are added each year. In 2002 on International Woman's Day, new names were announced, and Mary's name was added to the Roll.

Acknowledgements

Researching for a book like this is a long and slow and ultimately very rewarding process. The work began as a Master of Arts thesis at Victoria University; during my studies, I was awarded a Travelling Scholarship by Victoria University to do research overseas, and I acknowledge with thanks the enormous help this was.

I was in England for six weeks of research, from November to December 1996. I was grateful for the help of the staff in the British Library Manuscripts Section, the Guildhall Library and the India Office Library, London, and the William Salt Library, the Staffordshire Record Office in Stafford, the West Sussex County Archives Office in Chichester, and the Local History Library in Liverpool. The late Paul Berry gave his permission for my access to the Winifred Holtby archive at the Hull Central Library; the staff there were most helpful, especially Jill Crowther, who earned a gold star for getting copies of the Winifred Holtby letters to me before I left England. Thank you also to Miss J. A. Wilkinson, who helped me with further access to the papers after I left. Michael Bott also earned a gold star for sending me copies of papers in the Macmillan Archives and saving me a trip to Reading. I record my thanks to Miss Elsie Gladman, who nursed Mary Gaunt in her final illness and shared her story with me, and Mr Howard Rigney, who disregarded the pouring rain to help me find the last resting place of Elsie Lang and her family at Sittingbourne in Kent. On a later visit to England I met Robert Taunton, who not only knew where Yapton was, but took me there.

In France I received kindness and help from Pamela and Neville Flower, who took me to the English Hospital and English Cemetery in Cannes. In Bordighera, Italy, I found many kind and courteous people: the staff at the International Library; Signora Igina Bini at the Hotel Windsor Tennis; Avvocato Moreno, who recalled for me the days of the English in

Bordighera; and Sergio Biancheri, who found ways to open many doors, and whose introduction of me to the rest of Bordighera as 'our guest' I treasure.

My thanks also to Penn State University Library for access to the Hoffman letters; to the Wilson Library at the University of North Carolina for access to the A. P. Watt archive, and, for the Century Company records, the Manuscripts and Archives Division of the New York Public Library, Astor, Lenox and Tilden Foundations.

In Australia, I spent many hours in the Public Records Office (then in Laverton) to trace the career of William Gaunt, and in the State Library of Victoria. I am indebted to the staff for their patience and help, and particularly to Mr Des Cowley, of Rare Printed Collections, for his advice on the handling of the fragile manuscript of Mary's unpublished autobiography. I have also been glad to gain access to the archives of the University of Melbourne, The Burke Museum in Beechworth, and the Mitchell Library in Sydney, where I read the Morrison papers. I thank the staff at Deakin University, Warrnambool — Jan Critchett, Jeanette Rhedding-Jones and Jennifer Bantow — for their welcome and their help. People and organisations have made their records available to me: Brian Woodyatt of the Ballarat Club; the Warrnambool Hospital; the Royal Melbourne Hospital; the Flagstaff Museum, Warrnambool; Craig's Hotel, Ballarat. I am grateful to the late Ian McLaren, whose trail-blazing bibliography of Mary Gaunt now lies battered and near disintegration on my desk, and to Mary Lugton, the Baillieu Australiana Librarian who gathered the first information on Mary Gaunt that I found. I was grateful to Dr Chris Buckley and Dr Robert Hare, and to the late Professor Harold Attwood, for medical advice, and to the late Harold Love for the tip-off that led me to the records of Hubert Miller's death. Rex Fuge helped enormously with Chiltern records at the Athenaeum there, and thank you to the kindly people of Chiltern, who are proud of Mary and the Gaunt family's origins there and who have been a great encouragement.

I owe a great debt to members of the Gaunt, Palmer and Morrison families, who have been courteous, helpful and hospitable during my long quest. I remember with pleasure my meetings with Yvonne and Dick Fox, Michael Hemery, Jean Bowyer and her daughter Carol, the late Desmond Gaunt and Kay, and Jill Marshall, who gave me permission to read and quote from Ellinor Archer's diary. I am also grateful to Libby Thomson and Geoff Palmer, whom I hope to meet one day, and to Don Webb, Janice Hilton and the late Alastair Morrison. My thanks also to Wilma Davies and Helen McCallum who, although not members of these families, have been helpful sources of information on them.

Rosaleen Love was a patient and enthusiastic supervisor of the MA thesis which forms the basis of this book, and Kip Chauli, who allowed me to be a 'writer-in-residence' in his empty house during working hours, provided me with hours of quiet working time. I thank them both.

Not least of all the many kinds of satisfaction that writing a biography can bring is the memory of so many kindnesses, so many fascinating people and experiences, that I have known in the researching and writing of this book. For all of them, I am deeply grateful.

Bronwen Hickman,
Melbourne, 2014.

ENDNOTES

CHAPTER 1: THE LETTER
1. Letter from William Gaunt, Melbourne University Archives, archived 20 August 1969.
2. *Australasian Sketcher*, 10 April 1880.
3. Katrine Kelly, *Grenville College: a brief history*, in *Ballarat Historian*, December 1986.
4. 'My Victorian Youth', in *Woman's Magazine Annual*, UK, 1938, p. 12–13.
5. ibid, p. 259.

CHAPTER 2: LIFE ON THE GOLDFIELDS
1. Public Record Office, Letter 7890, Box No. 86, Series VPRS No. 1189.
2. Details from *Chiltern Federal Standard*, especially issues 27 February and 13 July 1861.
3. Public Record Office, Letter 7890, Box No. 86, Series VPRS 1189, to the Colonial Secretary recommending Gaunt's appointment, 9 August 1853.
4. 'Notice of auction of *Woodlands*', *Chiltern Federal Standard*, 20 March 1865, p. 3.
5. Barnard, the Beechworth Warden, had fallen out with Judge Cope over a woman. 'In the heat of a discussion concerning [the matter], some words were dropped which hurried him beyond the bounds of strict propriety', said the *Advertiser*. In fact, Barnard had set on the judge at a race meeting and tried to throttle him. Barnard was being transferred to a minor goldfield in disgrace. With a number of candidates on offer, William got the job.

CHAPTER 3: COLONIAL CHILDHOOD
1. 'My Victorian Youth', *Woman's Magazine Annual*, UK, 1938, p. 70.
2. *Ovens and Murray, Advertiser*, 11 March 1865.
3. Mary Gaunt, *Strange Roads*, p. 14.
4. ibid, p. 23.
5. Mary Gaunt, 'My Victorian Youth', in *Woman's Magazine Annual*, 1938, p. 430.
6. J. H. Kellogg, MD, *Ladies' Guide in Health and Disease*, Echo Publishing Company, Melbourne, undated, estimated 1894, pp. 207–208.
7. *The Ovens and Murray Advertiser*, 25 February 1865, listed prizes for W. H. Gaunt: Best Dorking cock and pair of hens, prize £1; Best turkey cock and pair of hens; Best gander and pair of geese; best collection of poultry; best table bouquet 5/-; best hand bouquet 5/-.
8. Guy Gaunt, *The Yield of the Years*, Hutchinson & Co., London 1940.
9. Winston Churchill, 'Preface', *My Early Life*, Odhams Press edition, 1930.
10. Joan Gillison, 'Two Invincible Ladies: Louisa Anne Meredith and Mary Gaunt', *Victorian Historical Journal*, vol. 51, no. 2, May 1980.

CHAPTER 4: STUDENT LIFE
1. Quoted in Ernest Scott, *A History of the University of Melbourne*, Melbourne University Press, 1936, p. 100. [Comment made in Parliament by Professor Hearn. His daughter Henrietta began lectures in the Arts Faculty soon after Mary.]
2. Mary Gaunt, *Strange Roads*, pp. 84–85.
3. ibid, p. 85.
4. ibid, p. 84.
5. ibid. pp. 85–86.
6. Mary Gaunt, *Kirkham's Find*, p. 10.
7. Gaunt, *Strange Roads*, pp. 7a–8.
8. *The Times*, 31 October 1921.
9. Mary Gaunt, 'Woman in Australia', *Empire Review*, vol. 1, no. 1, 1901, p. 212.

CHAPTER 5: DILEMMA
1. Phoebe, the heroine, speaking to her long-suffering mother in *Kirkham's Find*.

2   James Payn, 'The Literary Calling and its Future', *Some Private Views*, London 1881, pp. 83–85.

3   'My Victorian Youth', *Woman's Magazine Annual*, UK, 1938, p. 428.

CHAPTER 6: RESCUE

1   'Proclaiming a Protectorate', *Picturesque Australasia*, 1887–1889, vol. 3, p. 116.

2   *The Argus*, 19 May 1888.

3   ibid, 28 July 1888.

4   Letter from Price to Melbourne, VPRS 1189, Box 487, and Warden's Report 21 January 1858 in same box.

5   Mary Gaunt, *Deadman's*, p. 2.

CHAPTER 7: BUILDING A WRITING CAREER

1   Mary Gaunt, *Kirkham's Find*, p. 94.

2   Mary Gaunt, *Strange Roads*, p. 115.

3   ibid, p. 117.

4   At 28 Lucy married youngest in the family. Figures quoted in *Families in colonial Australia*. Patricia Grimshaw, Chris McConville, Ellen McEwen (eds.), Sydney: Allen & Unwin, 1985.

5   Interview with Katherine Helen Weston, who was also a novelist, also widowed young, also from Ballarat, and a contemporary of Mary's.

CHAPTER 8: A VOYAGE 'HOME'

1   Mary Gaunt, *Strange Roads*, p. 114.

2   ibid, p. 137.

3   ibid, p. 139.

4   'Across the North Atlantic in a Torpedo Boat' by An Officer on Board, *English Illustrated Magazine*, vol. 8, February 1891, pp. 391–396.

5   Gaunt, *Strange Roads*, p. 146.

6   ibid, pp. 109–110.

7   ibid, p. 151.

CHAPTER 9: CONSOLIDATING

1   Mary Gaunt, 'The Yanyilla Steeplechase', *The Leader*, Melbourne, 31 October 1891, reprinted in Bronwen Hickman (ed.), *Life at Deadman's*, 2001, p. 115–6.

2   Vance Palmer, *The Legend of the Nineties*, Currey O'Neil, Melbourne, 1954.

CHAPTER 10: WARRNAMBOOL

1. Mary Gaunt, *Strange Roads*, p. 153.

2. Letter, from Gabriele Haveaux, Royal Melbourne Hospital Committee of Management Minutes, no.10, p. 262.

3   *Australian Medical Journal*, 15 February 1882.

4   Telegram, Sgt. Hamilton to Chief Commissioner of Police, 20 March 1883, Public Record Office, Melbourne, Series 641, Box 30.

5   *Australian Dictionary of Biography*, 1851–1890, p. 394.

6   *The Argus*, Melbourne, 27 January 1894.

7   *The Argus*, Melbourne, 3 February 1894.

8   Gaunt, *Strange Roads*, p. 158.

9   ibid, pp. 175–176.

10 ibid, p. 176.

11 ibid, p. 96.

CHAPTER 11: PUBLISHING AND PRAISE

1   'Gentle Dan', *The Australasian*, 21 June 1902.

2   *The Australasian*, 5 May 1894, p. 790.

3   Ian F. McLaren, *Mary Gaunt, a Cosmopolitan Australian: an annotated Bibliography*, University of Melbourne Library, 1986, p. 2.

4   'How they broke into print', *The Strand Magazine*, New York, August 1915, p. 93.

5   Letter, to publisher Edward Arnold, 29 December 1893, copy (incomplete) McLaren Collection, Baillieu Library.

6   *The Tatler*, 27 August 1893, p. 3.

7   Mary Gaunt, *Kirkham's Find*, Penguin, 1988, p. 100.

8   *The Argus*, 20 November 1897.

9   ibid.

10 *The Bookman*, vol. 9, October 1895, p. 18.

11 Ian F. McLaren, *Mary Gaunt, a Cosmopolitan Australian: an annotated Bibliography*, University of Melbourne Library, 1986

12 *The Bulletin*, Red Page, 20 November 1897, p. 2.

13. *The Argus*, 18 December 1897, pp. 13–14.
14. Mary Gaunt reprinted in Bronwen Hickman (ed.), *Life at Deadman's — Stories of Colonial Victoria*, 2001.

CHAPTER 12: DISASTER

1. Admission papers, Kew Lunatic Asylum, VPRS.7456/1, Box 45, Public Record Office, Melbourne.
2. Patient Casebook, VPRS 7398 P.1, Unit 15, Public Record Office, Melbourne.
3. *Sydney Mail*, 9 September 1899.
4. Mary Gaunt, *The Australasian*, 21 July 1900, reprinted in Bronwen Hickman (ed.), *Life at Deadman's — Stories of Colonial Victoria*, 2001.
5. 'The Light on Goat Island', *Childhood in Bud and Blossom*, Atlas Press, Melbourne 1900.
6. Proceedings of Inquest, VPRS 1920, Unit 2 (m/film index), no. in Register 1287; Unit 725).
7. Mary Gaunt, *Alone in West Africa*, p. 5.

CHAPTER 13: DAYS OF TURMOIL

1. Henry Lawson, 'Pursuing Literature in Australia', *The Bulletin*, Red Page, 21 January 1899.
2. *Empire Review*, vol.1, no.1, 1901, p. 49.
3. ibid, p. 417.
4. ibid, p. 214.
5. ibid, p. 215.
6. ibid, p. 216.
7. Steele to Turner ML MSS 667/5, Mitchell Library, quoted in A.T. Yarwood, *Chair in the Sun* (biography of Ethel Turner), Viking, Australia 1994, p. 112.

CHAPTER 14: A 'DULL AND STONY STREET'

1. Mary Gaunt, *Alone in West Africa*, pp. 5–6.
2. I am indebted to the late Prof. Harold Attwood, pathologist, for his diagnosis, based on the medical reports. 'Disease of the brain' was shown as the cause of death in official documents.
3. *The Girl's Own Paper and Woman's Magazine*, vol. 30, 1908.
4. Gaunt, *Alone in West Africa*, p. 4.
5. *The British Australasian*, Anglo-Australian column, 13 June 1901.
6. 'A Little Letter from London', from Gouli-Gouli (Louise Mack), *The Bulletin*, 28 June 1902, p. 36.
7. *Independent Review*, London, vol. 3, June–September 1904, p. 448.

CHAPTER 15: THE END OF THE BLEAK YEARS

1. Mary Gaunt, *Alone in West Africa*, p. 7.
2. Royal Colonial Institute Year Book, 1913, p. 30.
3. Mary Gaunt, 'My Victorian Youth' *Woman's Magazine Annual* 1938, p. 430.
4. T.J. Tonkin, 'The Slave Trade in Northern Nigeria', *The Empire Review*, vol.1, no.5, June 1901, p. 513.
5. *The Empire Review*, vol. 4, no. 24, pp. 619–625.
6. *The Empire Review*, 'Susan Pennicuick: a story of Country Life in Victoria' vol.5, no. 25.
7. Gaunt, *Strange Roads*, p. 273.
8. *The Otago Times*, date unknown.
9. Mary's unpublished autobiography in the possession of her family; a photocopy is held by the State Library of Victoria.

CHAPTER 16: COLLABORATION

1. T. J. Tonkin, 'Customs of the Hausa People', *The Empire Review*, vol. 4, 1902–1903, p. 507.
2. *Punch*, 2 November 1904, p. 324.
3. Mary Gaunt, *Strange Roads*, p. 275.
4. Mary Gaunt and T.J. Tonkin, *The Silent Ones*, Chapter 1.
5. ibid, p. 117.
6. William Gaunt's will, Series 7591/P2, Box 383, Public Record Office, Melbourne.
7. Mary Gaunt and T.J. Tonkin, *Fools Rush In*, p. 277.

CHAPTER 17: THE ADVENTURE BEGINS

1. Mary Gaunt, *Strange Roads*, p. 283.
2. *Book Review Digest*, 1925, p. 247.
3. Interview with *Bookman*, London February 1910.

4   *Bookman*, February 1910.
5   Quoted in Hyam, Ronald, *Empire and Sexuality: the British Experience*, Manchester University Press, Manchester 1991. The letter, dated 3 December 1908, was written by three neighbours of the offending official, Silberrad.
6   ibid, p. 157.
7   London *Morning Post*, 16 March, 1911.
8   Gaunt, *Strange Roads*, p. 305.
9   ibid, p. 306.
10 Mary Gaunt, *Alone in West Africa*, p. 355.

CHAPTER 18: WRITING ABOUT AFRICA
1   Mary Kingsley, *Travels in West Africa*, Virago Travellers, p. 89.
2   Mary Gaunt, *The Uncounted Cost*, pp. 9–10.
3   *Bookman*, February 1910, p. 242.
4   Gaunt, *The Uncounted Cost*, p 166.
5   Mary Gaunt, *Alone in West Africa*, p. 7
6   Ian F. McLaren, *Mary Gaunt, a Cosmopolitan Australian: an annotated Bibliography*, p. 9.

CHAPTER 19: LONDON 1909–10
1   Mary Gaunt, 'Married Immigrants in Australia', letter to *The Times*, 29 March 1910.
2   *Royal Colonial Institute Year Book*, 1913.
3   'The Coming Australian Citizen Army', *United Empire*, vol. 1, no. 1.
4   *The Times*, 29 March 1910.
5   Mary Gaunt to Century Publishing, 15 July 1910.
6   Mary Gaunt to Century Publishing, 13 August, 1910.

CHAPTER 20: THE STORM BREAKS
1   Mary Gaunt, letter to *The British Australasian*, 24 February 1910.
2   ibid.
3   *Times Literary Supplement*, 3 February 1910.
4   *The Australasian*, 7 May 1910, p. 1176.

5   Mary Gaunt, *Strange Roads*, p. 316.

CHAPTER 21: BACK TO AFRICA
1   Mary Gaunt, *Alone in West Africa*, p. 64–66.
2   ibid, p. 9.
3   ibid, p. 2.
4   ibid, p. 17.
5   ibid, pp. 25, 26.
6   ibid, p. 28.
7   ibid, p. 29.
8   ibid, p. 47.
9   *Morning Post* (London), 16 March 1911.
10 Gaunt, *Alone in West Africa*, p. 63.
11 ibid, pp. 64–65.
12 ibid, p. 87.
13 Mary Gaunt, *Strange Roads*, p. 335.
14 ibid, p. 344.
15 Gaunt, *Alone in West Africa*, p. 176.
16 ibid, p. 181.
17 ibid, p. 205.
18 ibid, pp. 212–214.
19 ibid, p. 214.
20 ibid, p. 268.
21 ibid, p. 298.
22 ibid, p. 327.
23 ibid, p. 349.
24 ibid, pp. 346–347.

CHAPTER 22: AFTER AFRICA
1   Mary Gaunt interviewed by Alice Grant Rosman, 'An Australian in West Africa' *Everylady's Journal*, 6 June 1912.
2   Ian F. McLaren, *Mary Gaunt, a Cosmopolitan Australian: an annotated Bibliography*, University of Melbourne Library, 1986, p. 18.
3   *The Spectator*, 4 May 1912, p. 716.
4   *Book Review Digest*, 1912, p. 168.
5   *Times Literary Supplement*, 8 February 1912, p. 50.
6   *Alone in West Africa*, p. 16.
7   Mary Kingsley, *Travels in West Africa*, Virago Travellers, 1983.

8   *Strange Roads*, p. 346.
9   *The Scottish Geographical Magazine*, vol. XXIX, p. 113.
10 Ellinor Archer, unpublished diary, entry for 3 January 1912.
11 ibid, 26 February 2012.
12 ibid, 23 March 2012.
13 *A Woman in China*, p 3.

CHAPTER 23: 'WHY NOT A BOOK ABOUT CHINA?'

1   Mary Gaunt, *A Woman in China*, p. 129.
2   Mary to Morrison, Morrison Papers ML.MSS.312, Mitchell Library, Sydney, 31 August 1912.
3   Mary to Morrison, 20 September 1912.
4   Mary to Morrison, vol. 70, pp. 109–116, 17 October 1912.
5   *The Times*, 20 and 21 May 1913, report of court martial.

CHAPTER 24: CHINA OF THE AGES

1   Mary Gaunt, *A Woman in China*, p. 19.
2   Mary to Morrison, Morrison Papers ML MSS 312/72, p. 631.
3   Mary to Century, 25 March 1913.
4   The 'films' are glass plate negatives.
5   Letter, Century Collection, 25 March 1913.
6   Gaunt, *A Woman in China*, pp. 121–122.

CHAPTER 25: THE SUMMER PALACE

1   Mary Gaunt, *A Woman in China*, p. 154.
2   ibid, p. 168.
3   ibid, p. 253.
4   G. E. Morrison, *An Australian in China*, Angus & Robertson, Sydney, 1972, p. 5.
5   Gaunt, *A Woman in China*, pp. 389–390.
6   ibid, pp. 175–178.

CHAPTER 26: 'A SUNDAY WALK IN HYDE PARK'

1   Advice from an unnamed friend in Mary Gaunt, *A Broken Journey*, pp. 4–5.
2   Morrison to Mary, ML MSS 312 vol. 78, 5 January 1914, p. 27.
3   Mary to Morrison, vol. 78, 11 January 1914, pp. 101–103.
4   Mary to Morrison, ML MSS 312/78, 19 February 1914, pp. 423–425.
5   Gaunt, *A Broken Journey*, p. 43.
6   ibid, p. 47.

CHAPTER 27: 'YOU SAY "GO", MUS' GO!'

1   Mary Gaunt, *A Broken Journey*, p. 98.
2   ibid, pp. 122–123
3   Much of the detail appeared in Mary Gaunt's *A Wind from the Wilderness*, 1919.
4   Letter to *The Times*, 25 August 1938.
5   Gaunt, *A Broken Journey*, p. 294.

CHAPTER 28: THE WAR YEARS

1   Review of *A Broken Journey*, by Mary Gaunt. *Times Literary Supplement*, 20 February 1919.
2   *The Times*, 15 Dec 1914, p. 5.
3   Mary Gaunt, *Strange Roads*, p. 477.
4   She was given iodid of potassium, a harmless ingredient of anti-congestants and cough mixtures, which is still used today. It seems most likely that, as an asthma sufferer, she was forced to stop lecturing because of other health issues — Mary's account is unclear.
5   *Book Review Digest*, 1914, p. 204.
6   Mary Gaunt, *A Wind from the Wilderness*, p. 11.
7   Remaining publishers' records do not show how many books were printed and/or sold. Only initial contracts remain, and the standard contract speaks only of minimum runs of 1,000 copies. Since her income depended on the number of copies sold, lower book sales meant lower income.
8   Review of *A Broken Journey*, by Mary Gaunt. *Times Literary Supplement*, 20 February 1919.
9   *The Argus*, 7 May 1920, p. 10.

CHAPTER 29: THE OTHER END OF THE TRADE

1   Mary Gaunt, *Where the Twain Meet*, pp. 1–2.
2   'Idle Mouths or Good Citizens', *The Times*, 7 October 1921, and 'Waste of Girlhood', 31 October 1921.

Chapter 30: To Italy

1. Mary Gaunt, 'An Englishman's Choice', letter to *The Times*, 26 May 1926.
2. 'Idle Mouths or Good Citizens', *The Times*, 7 October 1921.
3. 'Peopling the Empire', letter to *The Times*, 23 July 1924, p. 15.
4. 'Englishmen Abroad', *The Times*, 10 June 1926, p. 12.

Chapter 31: At Work in the Villa Camilla

1. James L Bogle, *Meanderings of a Medico*,, published privately in 1928. Dr Bogle was a long-time resident of Bordighera.
2. *Book Review Digest*, 1923, p. 188.
3. *Times Literary Supplement*, 16 November 1922.
4. Mary Gaunt, *Where the Twain Meet*, pp. 289–290.
5. Mary Gaunt, *The Forbidden Town*, pp. 9–10.
6. Ian F. McLaren, *Mary Gaunt, a Cosmopolitan Australian: an annotated Bibliography*, University of Melbourne Library, 1986, p. 34.
7. Mary to Winifred Holtby, 6 May 1934.

Chapter 32: The Darkening Skies

1. *Times Literary Supplement*, 15 May 1930.
2. ibid.
3. Letter, from Frank Fox to Macmillan, 26 January 1931.
4. Mary to Macmillan, 27 February 1931.
5. Port-of-Spain *Guardian* reprinted in *The Daily Gleaner*, 24 September 1932.
6. *The Daily Gleaner*, 27 September 1932.
7. Mary to Winifred Holtby, 6 May 1934.
8. Quote at start of book; author unknown.
9. *Worlds Away*, pp. 55–56.
10. Mary to A. P. Watt, 19 March 1934.
11. Mary to A. P. Watt, 13 March 1934.
12. Mary to A. P. Watt, 19 March 1934.
13. Reader's report by Winifred Holtby on Mary's autobiography, *Strange Roads*.
14. Mary to Winifred Holtby, 5 May 1935.
15. Mary to unidentified recipient, via her sister Lucy, about mid-1935.
16. Mary's letter to Macmillan, 21 September 1938.

Chapter 33: 'I Trust I Shall Be Able to Live On Here'

1. Edward R. Tannenbaum, *Fascism in Italy*, Allen Lane, 1972, Chapter 2.
2. Mary to Hoffman, 14 January 1938.
3. Mary to Ellinor, 22 September 1939.
4. ibid.
5. *Uncertain Tomorrows*, Elsie Gladman, Excalibur Press, London, 1993, pp. 26–27.
6. W. Somerset Maugham, *Strictly Personal*, Heinemann, UK, 1942.

Chapter 34: The Darkness Closes In

1. Elsie Gladman, *Uncertain Tomorrows*, p. 37.
2. Letters, Ellinor Archer to Department of External Affairs, Canberra, 15 July, 31 July, 1940, CSIRO Series A981.
3. From the archives of Sunnybank, courtesy of Pamela and Neville Flower, interviewed October 1996.

Chapter 35: Finale

1. Mary Gaunt, *Kirkham's Find*, Penguin, 1988.
2. Bronwen Hickman, *Life at Deadman's*, (ed.), 2001.

List of Mary Gaunt's Publications

Novels and nonfiction

Dave's Sweetheart, 1894, Edward Arnold, London (5 editions, 1 Colonial edition).

The Moving Finger, Methuen, London, 1895 (2 editions).

Kirkham's Find, Methuen, London, 1897 (6 editions), also Penguin, Melbourne, 1988.

Deadman's, Methuen, London, 1898 (4 editions).

The Uncounted Cost, T. Werner Laurie, London, 1910 (7 editions).

The Mummy Moves, T. Werner Laurie, London 1910 (6 editions; US: E. Grosset, Edward J. Clode).

Alone in West Africa, T. Werner Laurie, London, 1912 (5 editions; US: C. Scribner Sons).

Every Man's Desire, T. Werner Laurie, London, 1913 (2 editions).

A Woman in China, T. Werner Laurie, London, 1914 (4 editions; US: J.B.Lippincott Co.).

The Ends of the Earth, T. Werner Laurie, London, 1915 (3 editions).

A Broken Journey, T. Werner Laurie, London, 1919 (2 editions; US: Lippincott).

A Wind from the Wilderness, T. Werner Laurie, London, 1919 (1 edition).

The Surrender and other Happenings, T. Werner Laurie, 1920.

Where the Twain Meet, John Murray, 1922 (2 editions; US: — E.P. Dutton & Co.).

As the Whirlwind Passeth, John Murray, London, 1923 (4 editions).

The Forbidden Town, T Fisher Unwin, 1926 (5 editions; US Edward J. Clode Inc.).

Saul's Daughter, T. Fisher Unwin Ltd., London, 1927 (1 edition).

George Washington and the Makers of the American Revolution, A. & C. Black Ltd., London, 1929.

The Lawless Frontier, 1929 Ernest Benn Ltd., London (4 editions).

Joan of the Pilchard, Ernest Benn Ltd., London 1930 (2 editions).

Reflection — in Jamaica, 1932 (1 edition).

Harmony, Ernest Benn Ltd., London, 1933 (2 editions).

World's Away, Hutchinson & Co. Ltd., London, 1934.

Joint works with John Ridgwell Essex

The Arm of the Leopard, Grant Richards, London 1904 (1 edition).

Fools Rush In, William Heinemann, London, 1906 (1 English, 1 Colonial edition).

The Silent Ones, T. Werner Laurie, London, 1909 (1 English, 1 Colonial edition).

Commissioned work in other publications

Morris, Edward Ellis (ed.), *Cassell's Picturesque Australasia*, Cassell & Co. Ltd., London, 1887.

Perceval, Sir W. B., K.C.M.G., *Pictorial New Zealand*, Cassell & Co. Ltd., London 1895.

Serial fiction/novel or novella length works in newspapers and journals

'Bingley's Gap', *The Leader*, 8 September to 3 November 1888.

'Miles Dunlop's Mistake', *The Australasian*, 21 December 1889, Supplement pp.1–12.

'The Riot at the Packhorse', *The Australasian*, 4 January to 22 March 1890.

'The Other Man', *The Argus*, 13 October 1894 to 12 January 1895.

'Mistress Betty Carew', *Tarrangower Times* (Maldon) (Supplement), 9 May to 4 July, 1903 (and other publications); it was revised, altered and published in book form as *As the Whirlwind Passeth*, Murray, 1923.

'Susan Pennicuick: a story of country life in Victoria', *Empire Review,* London, February 1903 to January 1904.

'The Love that was better than gold', *Girls' Own Paper*, London, March 1906.

Autobiography

'My Victorian Youth', *Woman's Magazine Annual*, London, 1938 (part of her autobiography).

Strange Roads, unpublished autobiography (privately owned; a photocopy is held in the State Library of Victoria).

Short stories and articles

'Life on board the training ship Worcester', *The Argus*, 19 May 1888, p. 5.

'Leaves from the log book of a Merchant Apprentice', *The Argus*, 2 June 1888, p. 6.

'Shakings', *The Argus*, 28 July 1888, p. 4.

'A Man's Sacrifice', supplement to *Illustrated Australian News*, 22 December 1888.

'Some Australian Paupers', *The Centennial Magazine*, 10 May 1890.

'Across the North Atlantic in a Torpedo Boat (by An Officer on Board)', *English Illustrated Magazine*, vol. 8, February 1891, p. 391.

Review — 'The Three Miss Kings' (Ada Cambridge), *The Australasian Critic*, 1 September 1891, pp. 276–277.

'The Yanyilla Steeplechase', *The Leader*, Melbourne, 31 October 1891.

'Christmas Eve at Warwingie', *English Illustrated Magazine*, 1891.

'Gentleman Jim — a Story (Trotting Cob)', *English Illustrated Magazine*, 1891.

'Lost — A story of the Australian bush', *English Illustrated Magazine*, 1892.

'The Loss of the "Vanity"', *English Illustrated Magazine*, 1893, p. 843.

'A Picnic at the Austin Hospital', *The Argus*, 28 January 1893.

'Dick Stanesby's Hutkeeper', *English Illustrated Magazine*, February to March 1893.

'The Deaf and Dumb Institution', *The Argus*, 25 March 1893.

'"The Land of Darkness". The Institute for the Blind', *The Argus*, 29 April 1893.

'The Women's Hospital', *The Argus*, 12 August 1893.

'The Other Half: in the slums with the District Nurses', *The Argus*, 23 September 1893.

'The Kindergarten', *The Argus*, 28 October 1893.

'The Little Sisters of the Poor', *The Argus*, 11 November 1893.

'The Old Colonists' Home', *The Argus*, 18 November 1893.

'The Nuns of the Good Shepherd', *The Argus*, 27 January 1894.

'A Butter Factory', *The Argus*, 3 February 1894.

'A Bit of Ancient History', *The Argus*, 11 August 1894.

'The Vintage', *The Argus*, 6 April 1895.

'A Brave Little Lass', *English Illustrated Magazine*, vol. XIII, April to September 1895, p. 459.

'The Tribulations of a Charitable Society', *The Argus*, 17 July 1897.

'By the Niger to the Western Soudan' (review), *The Argus*, 18 December 1897 pp. 13–14.

From the series 'Little Industries for Women':

[Keeping fowls], *The Argus*, 2 October 1897, p. 13.

'The silk industry', *The Argus*, 23 October 1897, p. 13.

'The growing of asparagus, 27 November 1897, p. 13.

'The growing of mushrooms', *The Argus*, 19 February 1898, p. 14.

'Scent-farming', *The Argus*, 19 March 1898, pp. 13–14.

'Poultry farming', *The Tatler*, 30 July 1898, pp. 4–5, 6 August 1898 p. 3.

'Bee-Keeping', *The Tatler*, 20 August 1898 p. 3, 27 August 1898 p. 3.

'Quits', *Windsor Magazine*, vol. 9, 9 December 1898, pp. 61–69.

'And Three is Trumpery', *Sydney Mail*, 9 September 1899.

'Along the Shore', *The Leader*, Christmas Supplement, 16 December 1899.

'The Dire Peril of Sergeant Sells', *Cornhill Magazine*, London, January 1900.

'A Missing Trustee', *The Australasian*, 21 July 1900, p. 163.

'A. P. and O. Flirtation', *The Australasian*, 8 September 1900.

'The Light on Goat Island', in *Childhood in Bud and Blossom*, ed. Lake, Joshua, Atlas Press, Melbourne 1900.

'Melbourne's Welcome to the returning troops', *The Empire Review*, vol. 1, no. 1, January 1901, p. 49.

'Woman in Australia', *The Empire Review*, vol. 1, no. 1, January 1901, p. 211.

'Melbourne', *The Empire Review*, vol. 1, no. 1, January 1901, p. 415.

'When the Cattle Broke', *Pearson's Magazine* (London), vol. XI, January to June 1901, p. 293.

'A Sailor's Darling', Newnes Novelette, 1901.

'Pioneers?', *The Empire Review*, vol. III, 1902, p. 332.

'Fidem Servo', *The Australasian,* 25 January 1902, p. 224.

'He that will not when he may', *The Australasian*, 8 February 1902, p. 317.

'A hardened criminal', *The Australasian*, 1 March 1902, p. 514.

'Annals of a Country Town: Her Limerick Lace', *The Australasian*, 8 March 1902, p. 553.

'For old sake's sake', *The Australasian*, 15 March 1902, p. 636.

'Gentle Dan', *The Australasian*, 21 June 1902, p. 1450.

'Peace Night in London', *The Empire Review*, 3 July 1902, pp. 642–644.

'When the Colt Jammed', *Pearson's Magazine*, London 1902.

'The Humbling of Sergeant Mahone', *The Sphere*, 1902.

'The Unfaithfulness of Jasper Browning', Harmsworth Publications, about 1902.

'The Peril of Lucy Capel', *The Empire Review*, 4 January 1903, pp. 619–625.

'An old record book of slavery', *Independent Review* (London), vol. 3, June to September 1904, p. 448.

'The easiest way', *The Australasian,* 11 June 1904, p. 1362.

'The breaking of the engagement', *The Australasian*, 12 November 1904, p. 1194.

'Twixt cup and lip', *The Australasian*, 31 December 1904, p. 1616.

'Knowledge comes', *Pearson's Magazine* (London), vol. 28, p. 633, 1909.

'Sweet Bells Jangled', *The Western Mail* (NSW), 4 December 1909.

'One small thing: a story of sacrifice', *Pearson's Magazine* (London), vol. 27, p. 1148, 1909.

'Along the Gold Coast: Ring of ancient forts; Ghost-haunted castles', *The Morning Post* (London), 25 April 1911.

'On the Gambia', *The Morning Post* (London), 16 March 1911.

'The Woman Slave Driver', *Literary Digest* (London), 44, 2 March 1912, p. 456.

'A New View of West Africa', *The Scottish Geographical Magazine*, March 1913, p. 113.

'North of 53°', *The Graphic* (prior to 1914).

'A Good Samaritan', *The Graphic* (date unknown, prior to 1914) and *The Ends of the Earth*.

'Roger Blake, Scallawag', in *Pearson's Magazine*, London, 1914.

'The Lost White Woman', in *The Ends of the Earth* 1915.

'Buckley's Chance', *The Australasian*, June and in *Buckley's Chance and other Stories of Australasia*, W. R. Chambers Ltd., London, 1937.

'Zeppelin Nights', *Forum* (London), 57, January 1917, p. 45.

'Cyclone', *Forum*, March to April, 1917, pp. 289, 451.

'Impressions of Jamaica', *Planter's Punch* (Kingston, Jamaica), 1 December 1921, p. 1.

'One of the First Families', *Planter's Punch*, 1922–1923 (date uncertain).

'The Doctor's Drive', *Masterpiece Library of Short Stories*, Hammerton, J. A. (ed.), London 1923.

'A Ceremonial Feast in Abyssinia', *Kalgoorlie Miner,* 18 December 1928.

'On an Australian Farm', in *The Golden Story Book for Girls*, (ed.) Mrs Herbert Strang, London 1933.

Letters to *The Times*

Married immigrants in Australia, 29 March 1910, p. 6.

White men in the tropics [from a Lady Correspondent], 24 May 1913, p. 14.

Disease in North Queensland, 6 May 1919, p. 8.

Jamaican Mail Service, 26 January 1920, p. 8.

The Woman's View — Idle mouths or good citizens, 20 September 1921, p. 13.

Idle mouths or good citizens, 7 October 1921, p. 13.

Waste of girlhood: Discontent or useful service?, 31 October 1921, p. 13.

Youth's opportunity: an inheritance oversea, 22 April 1922, p. 8.

Posts for unmarried women, 15 March 1923, p. 10.

Homesick to a man, 31 March 1924, p. 13.

Peopling the Empire, 23 July 1924, p. 15.

Sunless Cities, 12 September 1924, p. 12.

The art of memorials, 14 November 1925, p. 8.
Better conditions for nurses, 1 December 1925, p. 10.
An Englishman's choice, 26 May 1926, p. 10.
Living on the Riviera, 6 June 1926, p. 10.
Englishmen abroad, 10 June 1926, p. 12.
The old and new worlds, 7 January 1927, p. 8.
A Lady's Plaint, 22 May 1930, p. 17.
West Indian Sugar, 5 May 1931, p. 10.
The bread-fruit tree, 8 January 1932, p. 6.
Empty lands, 26 April 1933, p. 12.
Labour in Jamaica, 15 June 1938, p. 10.
God save the King, 25 August 1938, p. 15.
Governor Maclean, 21 October 1938, p. 10.
Propaganda from Danzig, 8 August 1939, p. 6.
The price of novels, 19 January 1940, p. 9.

Story collection

Bronwen Hickman (ed.), *Life at Deadman's: stories of Colonial Victoria by Mary Gaunt*, Hat Box Press, 2001.

Mary Gaunt's work in some recent anthologies

Gaunt, Mary. 'The Humbling of Sergeant Mahone' in C Burns (ed.), *Eclipsed: Two Centuries of Women's Fiction*, Collins, Sydney, 1988.

Gaunt, Mary. 'Excerpt from *A Woman in China*' in Robin Gerster (ed.), *Hotel Asia: an Anthology of Australian Literary Travelling to the 'East'*, Penguin, Melbourne, 1995.

Gaunt, Mary. 'The Yanyilla Steeplechase' in Fiona Giles (ed.), *From the Verandah: Stories of Love and Landscape by Nineteenth Century Australian Women*, McPhee Gribble/Penguin Melbourne, 1988.

Gaunt, Mary. 'The Lost White Woman' in Ken Gelder and Rachel Weaver (ed.), *The Anthology of Colonial Australian Gothic Fiction,* Melbourne University Press, July 2007 ('The Lost White Woman').

Gaunt, Mary. 'Dick Stanesby's Hutkeeper' in Dale Spender (ed.), *The Penguin Anthology of Australian Women's Writing* Penguin, Melbourne, 1988.

Gaunt, Mary. 'Excerpt from The Uncounted Cost' in Lynne Spender, *Her Selection: Writings by nineteenth-century Australian Women* Penguin, Melbourne, 1988.

Gaunt, Mary. '"Riverina" from *Picturesque Australasia*' in Elizabeth Webby (ed.), *Colonial Voices: letters, diaries, journalism and other accounts of nineteenth-century Australia*, UQP, St.Lucia, 1989.

Bibliography of Mary Gaunt's works

McLaren, Ian F. *Mary Gaunt, a Cosmopolitan Australian: an Annotated Bibliography*. University of Melbourne Library, Parkville, 1986.

INDEX

Stories and articles by Mary Gaunt

'A Butter Factory' 71
'A Dilemma' 50, 66
'A Man's Sacrifice', novella 50
'An old record book of slavery' 110
'A Missing Trustee' 92
'And Three is Trumpery' 92
'A Sailor's Darling' 107
'Bingley's Gap' 49
'Christmas Eve at Warwingie' 60
'Dick Stanesby's Hutkeeper 79
'Gentle Dan' 85
'Gentleman Jim — a Story' 60
'Gold', *Picturesque Australasia* 85
'Little Industries for Women', series 81
'Miles Dunlop's Mistake' 53, 55
'Mistress Betty Carew' 108
'My Victorian Youth' 268
'Peace Night in London' 116

'Proclaiming a Protectorate' 46
'Quits' 85
'Riverina' 46
'Shakings' 48
'Susan Pennicuick' 116–7
'Sweet Briar in the Desert' 151
'The Humbling of Sgt. Mahone' 85
'The Light on Goat Island' 92
'The Loss of the Vanity' 53
'The Love that was better than Gold' 128, 156
'The Other Man' 80
'The Perils of Lucy Capel' 116
'The Riot at the Packhorse' 50, 55, 86
'The Yanyilla Steeplechase' 66, 79
'When the Colt Jammed' 111
'White Wolf' 228
'Woman in Australia' 97, 115, 132, 150, 152

…oOo…

A

A. & C. Black, publishers 246, 249
A Broken Journey 227
A Wind from the Wilderness 228
A Woman in China 205, 224
A'Beckett, registrar, University of Melbourne 9
Abbotsford Convent (Good Shepherd Nuns) 70–1
Abbott, Mrs 23
Abeokuta 135
Aberdeen 177
Aboriginal people 22, 29
Abyssinia 248, 249
Academy 140
Accra 132, 137,166, 167, 229
Across Asia, proposed title 205
Adam Bede 155
Addah 169
Aden 248
Adlerstein (the eagle's nest) 26
Afghan labourers 16
Africa 29, 85, 113, 114, 232
Age, The, Melbourne 42, 43, 44, 49, 82, 259, 264
airships, Zeppelin 220, 222

Akusa 167
Alone in China, tentative title 186, 205
Alone in West Africa 174, 180, 182, 185, 205, 258
American Civil War 15
Amur River 216
An Australian in China 205
Annamabu 166, 234
Anselma, housekeeper 241, 271
Archer cousins 24, 93
Archer, Eliza (nee Palmer) 15, 24, 37, 92, 93
Archer, Ellinor 30, 150, 178, 179, 267, 272, 275, 278
Archer, John Kinder 24, 93
Archer, Atherston (Pat) 221,272, 278
Archer, Lucy, *see Gaunt*
Archibald, J. F. 65
Argus, The 42, 43, 47, 48, 54, 68, 70, 71, 76, 78, 80, 81, 83, 85, 94, 98, 214
Arsenal 220
As the Whirlwind Passeth 246, 257
Ashanti 151, 174, 232
Ashanti queen 137, 170,171
Ashton, Julian 64

Assuri River 216
Athenaeum, The 140, 144
Austin Hospital 70
Austral Club 149, 155
Australasian Critic, The 62
Australasian Sketcher, The 11
Australasian, The, Melbourne 50, 55, 56, 78, 86, 92, 94, 106, 111, 116, 140, 259
Australian Medical Journal 68
Australian, The 52, 54
Austrian Archduke 216
Axim 164, 165, 166

B
Baillieu Library, University of Melbourne 281
Bakewell, 10, 39–40, 76
Bale chieftain, Mary's visit to 135
Ballaarat 57, 58
Ballarat 10, 11, 12, 19, 22, 23, 26, 27, 28, 30, 32,35, 36, 40, 41, 46, 49, 51, 67, 76, 80, 82, 96, 97, 279
Baltic Sea 206
Barnard, Edward 17
Barry, Redmond 32, 33
Barton, Edmund 102
Basel Mission Station, Dodowah 167, 169
Bass, George 92, 108, 246
Bathurst, West Africa 132
Battersea Dogs' Home 258
Baxter, Margaret 149, 150, 155
Baynton, Barbara 64
Beauchamp, Earl of 93
Bechem 172
Beechworth 19, 20, 21, 44, 183
bees, bee-keeping 72, 81
Belgians in Africa 113
Bendigo 32, 40
Berry, Edward 240
Beyin, smallest castle 166
Bicknell Institute, Bordighera 237, 280
Bicknell, Clarence 238
bicycles 76
Bird, Isabella, Geographic Society 203
Bishopscourt 30
Black Dave's Girl, tentative book title 67
blackbirding 43
Blagoveschensk 216-7, 267
Bligh, Captain William, *The Bounty* 250, 253, 267
Bloomsbury 111
Boake, Barcroft 65
Boer War 92, 96, 115
Boldrewood, Rolfe, *Robbery under Arms* 17
Bombay 60-1
book trade, London 120
Bookman, The, London 84, 141, 155, 156, 251
Boots' Library 157
Bordeaux 273

Boston Transcript 128-9, 244,
Botany Bay 44
Bounty, Bligh's ship 250
Boxer rebellion, China 92, 106, 208, 215
Boyce, Louisa, children's home in Bordighera 270
Boyd, Arthur 93
Brassey, Lady, wife of governor 82
Brassey, Lord, Governor 82
Bremen Mission Sisters 169
Brethren mission, Ch'eng-te 195
Britain (in New Guinea) 42
Britannia, HMS 37
Britannia, shipwreck, Ninety Mile Beach 22
Britanny 111
British American Tobacco Company 195
British and Foreign Bible Society 14
British Australasian 103, 105, 106, 107, 129, 135, 136, 140, 149, 151, 156,
British colonial administration 145, 162
British Consul, Liberia 163
British Empire 29, 61
British Empire Exhibition 254
British Library catalogue 143
British Union of Fascists 265, 270
Brittain, Vera 261, 263
Brompton Square 125, 280
Buchan, John 223
Buckland Valley 27, 46, 50, 51, 85
Bulletin, The, Sydney 49, 65, 66, 84, 85, 98, 99, 107, 260
bullock wagons 20
Bungaree 33
Bunny, Rupert 64, 103
bunyip 22, 23, 46
Burma 144
Burney, Fanny 241
bushfire, Mannerim 24
bushrangers 28

C
Calabar 135, 136
Cambridge, Ada 58, 62, 82, 93, 115
camels and elephants 181
Cameroon 113, 135, 136, 269
Camito, ship 229
Campbell, W. Howard 240
Cape Coast Castle 136, 166, 177
Cape Town 132
Captain of the Maintop Starboard, pen-name 47
Carandini, Major, wife, daughter Estelle 150
Carlo, boy in West Africa story 109
Carlton 32
Carpenter, Edward 239
Carrick, Ethel 65
Carter family 97-8
Caspian Railway 202
Caspian Sea 206

Cassell's Magazine 14
Cassell's Picturesque Australasia 19, 45, 46, 85, 93
Cassell's Picturesque New Zealand 81
Cassell's, publisher 45, 47, 108
Castles, Amy 150
Central China Post 189
Centurion, HMS 186
Century Magazine
Century Magazine, New York 151–2, 162, 184, 185, 191–2
Chamberlain, Neville 266
Charles, Lallie, photographer 174
Chelsea 104
Chicago Daily News 127, 128
Chien Men gate 191
Chien Men railway station, Peking 187
Childers, H. C. E., auditor-general 51
Children's Hospital, Melbourne 93
Chiltern 14, 16, 19, 20, 27, 279
China 29, 44, 46,105, 107,147,180, 181, Chs.23–28
China Inland Mission, Ping Yow 209
China station 92
Chinese miners 21, 29, 46, 50, 85, 86, 118, 180
Chomley, Mrs 68, 69, 72, 73
Christ Church, Beechworth 20
Christian missions, faith missions 195
Christian, Fletcher, *Bounty* 250
Christiansborg Castle 132, 167
Church of England 10, 29, 30
Churchill, Winston 29
Civil Service exam 9
Clarke, Sir George Sydenham 106
Clunes 21
Coates, George 103
Cobb & Co. coach 40
Cockburn, William, slave owner 229
Cogdon, John 17
Collins, Captain Robert Muirhead 127, 129, 149
Colombo 57
Colonial Library edition 83, 86, 125, 128, 151, 155,156
Colonial Office 102, 130
Colquhoun, Archibald 147
Colquhoun, Dr 241
Conder, Charles 65, 103
Conference on emigration 148
Congo River 113, 168
Cook, Captain 81
Cooper, James Fenimore 26
Cordner, Edward, Bendigo admirer 39–40
Cornhill Magazine 121
Cornwall 173
Council for Scientific and Industrial Research 267
Court House, Beechworth 20
Craven, Dr, in Africa novels 119–124
Crocodiles 161
Cronin, A. J. 261

Crossley, Ada 103
Curtis Brown 254–5
Customs House, Melbourne 31
Cuthbert, Sir Henry 28

D

Daily Chronicle 185, 214, 248
Daily Gleaner, The 256
Daily Graphic, The 155
Daily Telegraph, London 78, 174
Daley, Victor 64
Daly, Dora Mary 280
Daly, Muriel 239, 242, 268, 271
Daly, the Misses 239
Daniel, Mary's dog 258
Dave's Sweetheart 19, 67, 78, 79, 84
Davies, David Gorton 240
de la Mare, Walter 58
De Lisser, Herbert 230, 231, 256
Deadman's (the Woolshed area) 50, 51
Deadman's, fictional world 19, 51, 67
Deaf and Dumb Institution 70
Deakin, Alfred 102, 179
Dederang 16, 48
Dell, Ethel M. 58
Deniliquin, NSW 40, 46
Denton, Sir George, Governor of Gambia 159
Depression, economic 52, 66, 70, 80, 81, 243, 254, 256
Derna, Italian ship 186, 221, 252
Detroit 105
Dial, Chicago 224
Dickson, James 102
Ditchling village 181
Dixcove, castles 170
Doctor Antonio 238, 268
dogs, Miller's 76, 87
Doughty, Charles 239
Doyle, Sir Arthur Conan 58
Drummond, William Henry 17
Duke and Duchess of York 96
Dunedin, New Zealand 90

E

Earl's Court, London 103, 104, 110
East India Company 180, 216
Echo, The, Warrnambool 80
Echuca, on Murray River 40
Eden, Anthony 278
Edgbaston, Birmingham 105
Edward Arnold, publisher 67,78, 79, 80, 86, 226
Edwards, Dr, missionary 209, 215
Egerton, Lady 135
Elder Dempster shipping line 130, 159
Elders Fyffe, shipping company 251, 255
Eliot, E. C. and Mrs Eliot 150
Eliot, George 155
Elmina 136, 166, 177, 258

emigration to colonies, Australia 148, 242
Empire Review, The 97, 109, 115,116
Empress' death, funeral 188, 190
English Baptist Mission, T'ai Yan Fu 208
English Church, Bordighera 280
English Illustrated Magazine 59, 60, 79, 96, 109
English Library, Bordighera 238, 280
Ernest Benn, publisher 250,251, 255,257, 259, 262
Essex, John Ridgwell 117
Essex, pen-name 143
Ethiopia 272
Eureka Stockade 46
Euston Station, London 159
Every Man's Desire 137, 177, 180, 184, 186, 258–9
Everylady's Journal 173
Experimental cotton farm 168–9

F
Farrer, Reginald, botanist 204–5
Federal Parliament, opening of first 96
Federal Standard, Chiltern 20
Federation 282
Fen Chou Fu 211
feng shui, pagoda, 211
finishing school 36
Fitzgerald, Sir Thomas 89
Flinders, Matthew 92, 246
Florence 111
Folkestone 240
Fools Rush In 125, 126, 140
foot-binding 195, 211, 225, 227
Forbidden City 190, 198
Forestry Officer, West Africa 164
Fort St James, Gambia River 160–1
Fowler, Gaunt & Co. bank 16
Fox, Emanuel Phillips 65, 103
Fox, Frank 147, 254, 255
France, south of 105
Franco, Francisco, General 266, 272
French Colonial administration 145
French Equatorial Africa 136
French in Africa 113

G
Gambia River 160, 168
Gaunt family children 23, 26
Gaunt, Alice Maud Victoria 27, 28, 37
Gaunt, Cecil 12, 23, 27, 34, 37, 58, 92, 132, 150, 152, 159, 179, 221, 266, 267.
Gaunt, Clive 27, 28, 37, 67, 74, 89, 144, 221,267
Gaunt, Elizabeth (nee Palmer) 15, 16, 24, 25, 27, 28, 30, 47, 49, 61–2, 73, 78, 89, 90, 94, 96, 99, 105, 106, (voice) 113, 144, 179, 240–1
Gaunt, Ernest 12, 23, 27, 34, 37, 42, 43, 46, 54, 57, 58, 92, 105, 106,107,144, 159, 179, 181, 216, 221, 240, 241, 247, 252, 258, 260, 266, 267, 272
Gaunt, Guy 23, 27, 28, 34, 37, 47, 48, 53, 54, 57, 58, 59, 74, 105, 106, 107, 109, 110–11, 112, 144, 149, 150, 173, 186, 216, 221, 225, 228, 229, 235, 246–7, 250, 251, 252, 266, 267, 275, 278
Gaunt, infant Vere Arnold 27, 37
Gaunt, infant William Henry 37
Gaunt, Lance 27, 28, 29, 37, 67, 89, 90, 144, 150, 221, 267
Gaunt, Louise (Louie) 107, 240, 260
Gaunt, Lucy 12, 13, 22, 23, 24, 27, 30, 35, 36, 37, 40, 46, 53, 56, 67, 73, 80, 90, 126, 144, 178, 179, 185, 221, 236, 267, 281
Gaunt, Margaret 144,149,150,228,235
Gaunt, Mary, William's sister 58, 185
Gauntswood, Leek 186, 227, 228
Gaunt, Mary
  appearance 10, 58
  Associate Fellow, RCI 146
  Brompton Square 179
  Bubbles, dog 226, 229–30, 233
  careers for women 242
  children 75, 102, 281
  clerical work 96
  Daniel, dog 258
  Dar, Bordighera dog 241, 242, 272
  dogs, in her fiction 225
  education 35, 36
  failure at University 37
  Finborough Road, London 105, 108, 111, 125, 139, 144, 150, 173, 179, 219, 245, 280
  furniture 104, 108, 110, 173
  illness and death 276–8
  James Buchanan, dog 198, 205, 206, 217, 220, 229
  landing in mammy-chair 162–3
  letters 91
  luggage problems in China 198–200
  marriage prospects 34, 39, 40–1, 55, 72
  music lessons 25, 33, 34, 36, 114–5
  photography 175
  pistol for travels 189, 205
  planning to go to China 181,183
  questioned by officials 277
  return to Australia 203
  signature 10, 47, 59, 61
  sings 'Rule Britannia' 217, 267
  street named for her 280
  travel exuberance 193
  travel style, preparations 184–5
  typewriter purchase 61
  uncomfortable with prayers 54, 197, 210, 225
  Villa Camilla 241
Gaunt, Matthew 17
Gaunt, Violet 150, 189
Gaunt, William 9, 10, 12, 14, 16, 17, 19, 20, 21, 22, 24, 27, 28, 29, 32, 35, 36–7, 45, 47, 48–9, 50, 66–7, 69, 72, 88, 89, 90, 94, 95, 96, 99, 105, 106, 107–8, 113, 123,279

Genoa 111, 280
German influence in Africa 85, 113, 145
German torpedo boat, sailors arrested 217–8
German vegetable seller, story 19
Germany (in New Guinea) 43
Gibraltar 57
Gill, S. T. 19
Gilmore, Mary 64
Giornale di Bordighera 241, 242
Girl's Own Paper and Woman's Magazine 101, 128, 156
Glasgow Herald 140
Gold Coast 104, 177
gold escort 20, 47
Golden Horseshoes legend 45
Golden Story Book for Girl, The 98
Golding, Louis 261
Gollancz, publishers, 259, 262
Goodsir, Agnes 64
governesses 12, 23
Government House, Melbourne 31, 97
Graham, Mrs, Vence 275
Graham, Stephen, author 224
Grainger, Percy 103, 106
Grampians 98
Grand (later Windsor) Hotel, Melbourne 89
Grant Richards, publishers 120
Grant, Ansumanah, servant 160 to 172
Grant, Captain, explorer 25, 114
Grant, gold discovery 21
Great Exhibition, Warrnambool 81
Great Game 202
Great Wall 192–3
Green, Mr and Mrs, China Inland Mission 215
Greenwich 58
Gregory, Miss, finishing school 27, 36
Grenville College, Ballarat 10, 12, 13, 241
Guardian, The, Port of Spain 256
Guida di Bordighera 239
Guinea Coast 117, 130, 259
Gulf of St Vincent, South Australia 38
Gulliver 174

H
Half Assinie 164,165
Hall, Charlotte Maxwell *see* Maxwell Hall
Hall, Phillip 241, 258
Hamilton, Frederick Fitzroy 238
Hanley, Stonke-on-Trent 119, 121
Hargreaves, Mrs Basil 181
Harmattan wind 162
Harmony 184, 251, 257, 261, 269
Harpers Magazine 185
Harris, Lydia 11, 31, 279
Harrison (shipping) Line 255
Harvard University's Arboretum 205
haunted room, Elmina 136

Hausa Association of London 115–6, 119, 122
Hausa language 116
Hawthorne, Nathaniel 155
Hay, NSW 40, 46
Heinemann, publishers 125, 259
Herald, New York 145
Herald, The, Melbourne 272
Hsi An 201, 205–206, 209, 212, 215
Hitler, Adolf 266, 270, 272
Ho, Togo 168, 169
Hoang Ho (Yellow River) 201
Hobart 89
Hodder and Stoughton 259
Hoffman, Arthur Sullivant 269,270
Holtby, Winifred 257, 260–3
Hong Kong 46
Hood, John W. Jacomb 17, 89
Hopkins River 82
Horsfall family, Liverpool 109, 110, 111,116 223, 229
Horsfall's Bazaar, Chiltern 14
Horsham 98
Hôtel de Paris, Bordighera 236, 240
Hunter, Governor 245
Hutchinson 259,262, 270
Hyde Park, London 104

I
Ibadan, rest house 135
Illustrated Australian News, The 14, 50
Imperial Press Conference 150
Independent Review, The 110
India 61
Indigo diggings 14, 19
Influenza epidemic 227
Institute for the Blind 70
International Women's Day 282

J
J. C. Williamson 103
Jamaica 7, 110, 229–36, 251, 253, 255, 256 ,261, 267
James, Winifred 58
Janet Clarke Hall, Melbourne 144
Jehol, hunting lodge 191, 194, 198, 201
Joan of the Pilchard 250, 253
John Murray, publisher 234, 245
John Ridgewell Essex, later pen-name 118
John Ridgwell Essex, pen-name 117–8
Jones, Daniel 254
Jones, Francis, New York agent 192
Jones, Sir Alfred 130

K
Kanaka labour, North Queensland 43
Kano, West Africa 116
Kashgar 202, 206, 216
Kauffmann, Angelica 239
Kellogg, Dr, *Ladies Guide* 25
Kempshot Pen 231

Kensington, London 104, 106
Kenya 130
Keta, old castle 167, 169
Kew Lunatic Asylum 89
Khan, Sirdar, worker at *Tooram* 69
Kharbin 216
Kiewa Valley, Victoria 48
King Edward VII, funeral procession 179
King George V 172, 179
King George V, Queen Mary 227
Kingsley, Mary 145, 176
Kingston, Charles 103
Kingston, William 26
Kinloch Cooke 59, 96, 97, 107, 116, 117
Kipling, Rudyard 58
Kirkham's Find 54, 77, 82–5, 92, 112, 148, 281
Kitchen sink leak 110
Knightsbridge 104
Kommenda, crumbling fort 166
Koonda 279
Krobo Hill 167–8, 185
Kumasi 137, 151, 165, 170

L

l'Eclaireur 271
Lagos 135
Lake Wendouree, Ballarat 22, 30, 46
Lake, Joshua 46, 92
Lambert, George 103
Lan Chou 202, 204, 206, 213
Landon, Letitia 177
Lang, Elsie 141, 178, 219, 220, 234, 235, 245–6, 251, 255, 257, 280
Lang, Lewis 219
Lavender, family friends 40
Lawrence, D. H. 246
Lawson, Henry 63, 64, 65, 99
Lawson, Louisa 99
Leader, The, Melbourne 49, 66
Leek, Staffordshire 119
Leicester Square 104
leprosy 45
Lewis, Dr and family 198
Lewises, Presbyterian Mission, Pao Ting Fu 215
Liberia 162
Library of Australian Authors 79
Libreville 136
Literary Digest 185, 224
Literary Review 244
Little Sisters of the Poor 70
Liverpool 110, 131, 153, 159, 233
Livingstone, David 113, 145
loess country 212
Lome, Togo 169
London 101, 102, 104, 146, 233
Long, Mr, Chinese College 216

Longstaff, John 64, 103
Lopez, Clarence, *The Hyde* 230, 231
Lot's Road Power Station 104
Lucas, Sir Charles 130
Lucky Digger, The, pub 61
Lyceum Club, London 127, 149, 150, 152, 223
Lyons, companion to Morrison 43

M

Macarthur, Elizabeth 246
Macarthur, John 245
Macartney, Lord, embassy to China 194, 195
Macartney, Sir George, Kashgar 204
Macdonald, George 238
Mack, Louise, *Teens* 84, 103, 107
Maclean, Governor, Cape Coast 177, 267
Macmillan, publishers 254, 255
Madden, Sir John, Chief Justice of Victoria 82
Magistrates Courts 17
mahogany forest 171–2, 177
Mail, The, Sydney 80
Malta 110
Manchester Courier 155
Manifold, Walter, Warrnambool grazier 95
Marco Polo 174
Marryat, Frederick 26
Marseilles 273–4
Mary Haven, New Eltham, London 219, 280
Maryborough 21
Massilia, ship 60
Master in Lunacy 95
Matadi 136
Matriculation 9, 10, 11, 12, 33, 36, 37
Maugham, Somerset 271, 274
Maxwell Hall, Charlotte 231–2
McCubbin, Frederick 64
McIvor Times and Rodney Advertiser 108
Medical work of missions 197
Mediterranean 116
Melba, Nellie 103
Melbourne Church of England Grammar School 12, 37, 40, 45, 80
Melbourne District Nursing Society 70
Melbourne Hospital 68
Menton, southern France 271
Methuen, publisher 79, 85, 105, 109
Meynell, Alice 239
Miller, Dr Hubert Lindsay 68, 70, 72, 77, 87–8, 91, 93–4, 95, 99, 100,102,107,263
Miller, Mrs Margaret Catherine 73, 74, 75, 76, 89, 90, 95, 97, 103
Miner's Right, pub at *Woolshed* 27
Ming tombs 193
Mining Boards 17
Mistress Betty Carew 245
Molesworth, Hickman 69

Moneague, Jamaica 252
Monrovia 163
Monte Carlo 260
Morning Post, The 147, 149, 154, 162, 166, 79, 254
Morris, Edward Ellis 41–2, 45, 46, 62, 81, 93
Morrison, George Ernest ('Chinese') 12, 43, 83–4, 92–3, 147,148, 149, 150, 182, 183, 184, 185, 188–9, 192, 197, 202, 203, 204, 205, 215, 255
Morshead Mansions, London 128, 139
Moscow 187
Mosley, Oswald 265–6, 270
Mount Lofty, South Australia 39
Mrs Grundy 163
Mount Wellington, Tasmania 90
Mukden 216
Mungo Park, river steamer 160
Murray Colony, proposed 15
Murray, Virginius 17
Mussolini, Benito 266, 272,273
My Struggle (Mein Kampf) 270

N

National Africa Company 85
Nelson, HMAS 37
New Eltham 219, 230, 280
New Guinea 41, 45, 83
New Holland 116
New Law courts, London 108
New South Wales 40, 92, 110, 245
New Statesman, The 244
New York Times, The 175, 224
New Zealand 45, 81, 90, 117
Newnes, publishers 107, 108
Nice 273
Niger River 85, 113,116, 135
Nile 113
Nisbet, Hume 45
North Staffordshire Railway Company 16
Northumberland Avenue 147

O

Observer, The 154
Ogilvie, Will 103
Old Colonists' Home 70
Old English Towns 249
opium 45
Oram, Miss, nursing sister at Sekondi 152, 165,172
Ormond College 12
Otago Times, The 117
Ovens Hardware Co., Chiltern 15
Owen, Wilfred 227

P

Packhorse (fictional name for Buckland) 49
Pai Lang (White Wolf) 195, 206, 208, 212, 225
Palime, Togo 168
Pall Mall Gazette 140
Pall Mall, London 127
Palmer family 16, 48
Palmer, Claude, wife Marjory 150
Palmer, Edward 16
Palmer, Eliza, *see* Archer
Palmer, Elizabeth, *see* Gaunt 15, 16
Palmer, Emily, wife of Octavius 62–3
Palmer, Frederick, Mary's grandfather 15, 21, 180
Palmer, Mary Eliza, Mary's grandmother 10, 15, 21, 27, 180,183
Palmer, Mary Eliza (Polly) 15, 40
Palmer, Octavius 15, 62, 150
Palmer, Rosina 150
Palmer, Thomas 15, 16, 53 ,69, 71
Palmer, Vance 65
Pao Ting Fu 215
Paris 273
Parsons, Eva, companion 226, 230
Parsons, Samuel Hyde 230
Paterson, Andrew 'Banjo' 64, 65, 93, 99
Payn, James, 'The Literary Calling …' 41, 282
Pearson's Magazine 107, 116, 151, 156
Peking 147, 183, 192, 194
Petticoat Pilgrims on Trek 145
Phoebe, heroine of *Kirkham's Find* 34, 82–3
phoney war, the 271, 272
photographic services 185–6, 191
Piccadilly 104
Picturesque Australasia, see Cassell's
Picturesque New Zealand, see Cassell's
Planters' Punch 230, 232
Plymouth 57
Polperro, Cornwall 110, 250
Poor Caroline 260
Port Fairy, Victoria 116
Port Moresby 43
Port Vincent, Yorke Peninsula, SA 76
Portable bath 159
Praed, Rosa 64
Presbyterian Mission, Pao Ting Fu 198, 203, 215
Price, Matthew 17
Prince's, abandoned fort 165
Punch, London 121
Purdom, William, botanist 204–5

Q

Queen Victoria 93, 102, 106 102
Queenscliff 37

R

Racehorse, *Mary Gaunt* 176
Radio, illicit 277
Railways 239
Ramsay, Hugh 103
Raymond, George 241
Reflection — in Jamaica 254, 255, 257
Reid's Creek 50
Reilly, publican, *Miner's Right* 27

Religion 10
Rhodes' Store, Chiltern 15
Richardson, Henry Handel 64
Ridgwell, village in Essex 117
Roberts, Tom 64, 103
Robin, Jennie 182
Robinson, Rev. Charles 116
Roden, Sir Robert 241, 250
Rodger, Sir John and Lady 132, 135, 150
Rosman, Alice Grant 173
Royal Colonial Institute 114, 145 176, 179
Royal Geographical Society 201, 203
Royal Mail shipping line 255
Ruffini, Giovanni 238
Rule Britannia 267
Runic 100
Russia 206, 222, people 224
Ruthven, Jocelyn, character in story 50, 51, 86

S

Sadler, Miss, governess 23
Saghalien 216
Sainte Agnès, village 235
Sale 20, 21, 22
Samarkand 206
Samoa 106
San Shan An, writing retreat 198
Sandhurst 22
Saul's Daughter 248
Scottish Geographical Society 177
Sekondi 127, 137, 140, 165, 166, 170
Senegal 113, 159
Sharpe, William 239
Shaw, George Bernard 58, 120
Sheffield 123, 233
Shuter, Charles 17
Sierra Leone 132, 144, 162
Silk Road 201, 206
Sinclairs, Haymarket, London, 185
Sittingbourne 142
slave record book 110, 229
slave trade 115, 159
Slessor, Mary 135-6
Smith, Elder & Co., publishers 121,123,125
Smith, of Smith, Elder & Co. 121
Smiths, book company 154
Society of Authors 58, 59
Society of Elder Brethren 206
Sokoto, Nigeria 122
Sons and Lovers 246
South Africa 92, 116
Spanish Guinea 136
Spectator, The 174, 244
Speke, Captain, explorer 25, 114, 251
Sphere, The 110
St George's Church, Malvern 73, 279

St Kilda 12, 31, 32, 33, 94, 95
St Paul de Loando 136
Stacpoole, H. de Vere 239
Staffordshire 105
Standard, The, London 84
Standish, Captain 17
Stanley, Henry Morton 113, 136, 145
Star Theatre, Chiltern 14
Stark, Freya 171
Steele, William, publisher 98-9
Stephens, A. G. 65
Stoke-on-Trent 117
Strand Magazine, New York 78
Strange Roads 260, 262, 268
Strange Trails, tentative title 260
Stratford, gold discovery 21
Streeton, Arthur 64, 65, 103
Sub-Treasury building, Beechworth 20
Sun Yat-sen, revolutionary leader, China 202
Sunny Bank Hospital, Cannes 276-7, 280
Sunyani 172
Sutherland, Alexander 93
Swanzy trading company 168, 170
Swayne, Colonel Harald G. C. 241, 248, 255
sweet briar 76
Sydney Morning Herald 42
syphilis, tertiary 101
Szechuan 191

T

T. Fisher Unwin, publisher 125, 249, 250
T'ai Yuan Fu, Shansi 206, 209, 215
Table Talk 99
Taiyuanfu, steamer 215
Talbot 21
Taormino 111
Tarkwa, mines 137, 165, 170
Tarrengower Times, Maldon 108, 245
Tasmania 90, 93
Tatler, The 81
Taverner Lady 103
Taylor, John, British Vice-Consul, Cannes 276
Telegraph Office, Beechworth 20
telegraph 15
Tennyson, Governor of South Australia 93
Thackeray, Anne 239
Thackeray, Colonel Sir Edward 239
Thames 104
The Arm of the Leopard 120, 126, 140
The Awakening of Pleasant Conant, proposed book title 225, 228
The Dove in the Eagle's Nest 235
The Ends of the Earth 224
The Forbidden Town 247, 248, 249
The Grey Wolf 268
The Lawless Frontier 249, 250, 257

The Moving Finger 79, 84
The Mummy Moves 128, 147, 156, 246
The Other Man 60, 80
The Reliance 246
The Scarlet Letter 155
The Silent Ones 125, 126, 140, 151, 156
The Standard, London 83
The Strand, London 130
The Surrender and other Happenings 228
The Three Miss Kings 62
The Uncounted Cost 129, 143,144, 151, 153–4, 156, 177, 246
The Willows 11, 28, 30, 34, 35
Thomson, Rev. J. B. 85, 116
Thorndene, home of Elsie Lang 219
Times Literary Supplement, The 227, 228, 244, 253
The Times, London 35, 43, 125, 127, 130, 147, 148, 149, 153, 154–5, 175, 182, 235, 236, 241, 242, 246, 243, 246, 264, 266, 267, 268,
Togo 113
Tongshan, near Tientsin 197
Tonkin, Thomas J., 116–126, 128, 132, 135, 140, 143, 151, 155, 173, 247
Tooram 53, 54, 69, 71,
Touring Society, Jamaica 251
Trans-Siberian Railway 187
Treasury building, Melbourne 31
Trinity College, Dublin 13
Trinity Women's Hostel 179
trooper police 20
Truscott, Parry, pen-name 181
Tuan, servant 194
Tung-ling, eastern tombs 194
Turner, Ethel 64, 84, 98, 99, 179
Twopeny, Richard, *Town Life in Australia* 45
Typewriter 159

U
US Ambassador in London 278
Uganda 114
Una Tropical Camera 152, 159
University of Melbourne 9, 11, 12, 31, 32–4, 37, 41, 55, 67, 'The Shop' 82, 83, 144, 179, 279, 281
Unyoro 114

V
Van Diemen's Land (Tasmania) 15
Vandyck, portrait of Mary 100
Vence, southern France 273,274
Victor, John 13, 42
Victoria Station 142
Victorian Honour Roll of Women 282
Vladivostok 216
Volta River 145 167,168

W
Wagons-Lit Hotel Peking 189, 195
Walhalla, gold discovery 21

Wallace, Sir Donald Mackenzie 224
Wang, Mr, servant 205, 209, 215
Wangara women 172
War Propaganda Bureau 223
war, horrors 62, 221–2
Ward, Lock & Co 99
Warrnambool 53, 68–77, 79, 80, 81, 82, 89, 91, 94, 96, 97, 101, 103, 106, 108, 111, 116, 178, 240, 245, 280
Warrnambool *Standard* 74
Washington, George 249
Waterfield, Major-Gen. H. C. 240
Watt, A. P., literary agent 60, 254, 259, 268, 270
Watterston, David, *The Australasian* 56, 59, 106, 107, 111
Werner Laurie, publisher 125, 141, 144, 151, 152, 166, 180, 216, 223, 225, 228
West Africa 24, 109, 129, 140, 141, 214, 252, 258
West African coast 129, 130
Westminster Gazette 154
Weymouth 227
Wheelbarrow travel 208
Where the Twain Meet 234, 236, 244
White Man's Grave 176
Who's Who in Australia, 1941 268
Wilkinson, Mrs Spencer 154
Williams, Margaret, Matron, MBE 276
Willows, The 11, 28, 30, 34, 35
Wilson Hall, University of Melbourne 279
Wimmera 98
Windsor Magazine 151, 156
Winnebah 166
Woman's Magazine Annual, The 264, 268
Woman's Pictorial 248
Women doctors 75
Women Journalists' Club 150
Women's Hospital 70
Woman's Magazine Annual, England 42
Women's vote, rights 55
Woodlands 16, 17, 27, 279
Woolshed diggings 16, 27, 50
Worcester, training ship 46
Workers, immigrant 69
Worlds Away 258
Wright, W. H. Goldfields Commissioner 14

Y
Yackandandah 16, 49, 50
Yanyilla, fictional station 64
Yellow River 212, 213
Yonge, Charlotte, *Dove in the Eagle's Nest* 26
Youl, Dr, Melbourne Coroner 68
Young, Florence 103
Yuan Shih-kai, army leader, China 202

Z
Zaria, coastal steamer 162

www.ingramcontent.com/pod-product-compliance
Lightning Source LLC
Chambersburg PA
CBHW032034150426
43194CB00006B/268